How to
Master Skills for the

Second Edition

TOEFL ® iBT

SPEAKING Intermediate

DARAKWON

How to Master Skills for the TOEFL® iBT SPEAKING Intermediate

Publisher Kyudo Chung
Editor Sangik Cho
Authors Michael A. Putlack, Will Link, Stephen Poirier, E2K
Proofreaders Michael A. Putlack, Brian Stuart
Designers Minji Kim, Yeji Kim

First Published in October 2007 By Darakwon, Inc.
Second edition first published in March 2025 by Darakwon, Inc.
Darakwon Bldg., 211, Munbal-ro, Paju-si, Gyeonggi-do 10881
Republic of Korea
Tel: 02-736-2031 (Ext. 250)
Fax: 02-732-2037

ISBN 978-89-277-8091-5 14740
       978-89-277-8084-7 14740 (set)

www.darakwon.co.kr

Photo Credits
Shutterstock.com

Components Main Book / Answer Key / Free MP3 Downloads
7 6 5 4 3 2 1   25 26 27 28 29

Table of **Contents**

INTRODUCTION

1 Information on the TOEFL® iBT

A The Format of the TOEFL® iBT

Section	Number of Questions or Tasks	Timing	Score

Reading	**20 Questions**
	
	• 2 reading passages
	  – with 10 questions per passage
	  – approximately 700 words long each
		35 Minutes	30 Points

Listening	**28 Questions**
	
	• 2 conversations
	  – 5 questions per conversation
	  – 3 minutes each
	
	• 3 lectures
	  – 6 questions per lecture
	  – 3-5 minutes each
		36 Minutes	30 Points

Speaking	**4 Tasks**
	
	• 1 independent speaking task
	  – 1 personal choice/opinion/experience
	  – preparation: 15 sec. / response: 45 sec.
	
	• 2 integrated speaking tasks: Read-Listen-Speak
	  – 1 campus situation topic
	    reading: 75-100 words (45 sec.)
	    conversation: 150-180 words (60-80 sec.)
	  – 1 academic course topic
	    reading: 75-100 words (50 sec.)
	    lecture: 150-220 words (60-120 sec.)
	  – preparation: 30 sec. / response: 60 sec.
	
	• 1 integrated speaking task: Listen-Speak
	  – 1 academic course topic
	    lecture: 230-280 words (90-120 sec.)
	  – preparation: 20 sec. / response: 60 sec.
		17 Minutes	30 Points

Writing	**2 Tasks**
	
	• 1 integrated writing task: Read-Listen-Write
	  – reading: 230-300 words (3 min.)
	  – lecture: 230-300 words (2 min.)
	  – a summary of 150-225 words (20 min.)
	
	• 1 academic discussion task
	  – a minimum 100-word essay (10 min.)
		30 Minutes	30 Points

B What Is New about the TOEFL® iBT?

- The TOEFL® iBT is delivered through the Internet in secure test centers around the world at the same time.
- It tests all four language skills and is taken in the order of Reading, Listening, Speaking, and Writing.
- The test is about 2 hours long, and all of the four test sections will be completed in one day.
- Note taking is allowed throughout the entire test, including the Reading section. At the end of the test, all notes are collected and destroyed at the test center.
- In the Listening section, one lecture may be spoken with a British or Australian accent.
- There are integrated tasks requiring test takers to combine more than one language skill in the Speaking and Writing sections.
- In the Speaking section, test takers wear headphones and speak into a microphone when they respond. The responses are recorded and transmitted to ETS's Online Scoring Network.
- In the Writing section, test takers must type their responses. Handwriting is not possible.
- Test scores will be reported online. Test takers can see their scores online 4-8 business days after the test and can also receive a copy of their score report by mail.

2 Information on the Speaking Section

The Speaking section of the TOEFL® iBT measures test takers' English speaking proficiency. This section takes approximately 17 minutes and has four questions. The first question is called Independent Speaking Task, and you will be asked to speak about a familiar topic based on your personal preference. The remaining three questions are Integrated Speaking Tasks, and you will be required to integrate different language skills—listening and speaking or listening, reading, and speaking.

A Types of Speaking Tasks

- **Task 1** Independent Speaking Task: Personal Preference
  - This task will ask you to make and defend a personal choice between two possible opinions, actions, or situations. You should justify your choice with reasons and details.
  - You will be given 15 seconds to prepare your answer and 45 seconds to say which of the two options you think is preferable.

- **Task 2** Integrated Speaking Task: Reading & Conversation
  - This task will ask you to respond to a question based on what you have read and heard. You will first read a short passage presenting a campus-related issue and will then listen to a dialogue on the same topic. Then, you will be asked to summarize one speaker's opinion within the context of the reading passage.
  - You will be given 30 seconds to prepare your answer and 60 seconds to speak on the question. You should be careful not to express your own opinion in your response.

- **Task 3** Integrated Speaking Task: Reading & Lecture
  - This task also asks you to respond to a question based on what you have read and heard. You will first read a short passage about an academic subject and will then listen to an excerpt from a lecture

on that subject. Then, you will be asked to combine and convey important information from both the reading passage and the lecture.

– You will be given 30 seconds to prepare your answer and 60 seconds to speak on the question.

- **Task 4** Integrated Speaking Task: Lecture
  – In this task, you will first listen to an excerpt from a lecture that explains a term or concept and gives some examples to illustrate it. Then, you will be asked to summarize the lecture and explain how the examples are connected with the overall topic.
  – You will be given 20 seconds to prepare your answer and 60 seconds to respond to the question.

B Types of Speaking Topics

- Personal Experience and Preference
  – The question in Task 1 will be about everyday issues of general interest to test takers. For example, a question may ask about a preference between studying at home and at the library, a preference between living in a dormitory and an off-campus apartment, or a preference between a class with a lot of discussion and one without discussion.

- Campus Situations
  – The question in Task 2 will be about campus-related issues. For example, a question may ask about a university policy, rule, or procedure, future university plans, campus facilities, or the quality of life on campus.

- Academic Course Content
  – The question in Task 3 will be about academic subjects. For example, a question may ask about a life science, a social science, a physical science, or a topic in the humanities like animal domestication or economics.
  – The question in Task 4 will also be about academic-related topics. For example, a question may ask about a process, a method, a theory, an idea, or a phenomenon of any type in fields like natural science, social science, or psychology.

C Important Features of Evaluation

- Delivery

  Delivery means how clear your speech is. In order to get good grades on the speaking tasks, you should speak smoothly and clearly, have good pronunciation, pace yourself naturally, and have natural-sounding intonation patterns.

- Language Use

  Language use is about the effectiveness of your use of grammar and vocabulary to express your ideas. In order to get good grades on the speaking tasks, you should be able to use both basic and more complex language structures and choose the appropriate words.

- Topic Development

  Topic development is related to how fully you respond to the question and how coherently you give your ideas. In order to get good grades on the speaking test, you should make sure that the relationship between your ideas and your progression from one idea to the next is clear and easy to follow.

HOW TO USE THIS BOOK

How to Master Skills for the TOEFL® iBT Speaking Intermediate is designed to be used either as a textbook for a TOEFL® iBT speaking preparation course or as a tool for individual learners who are preparing for the TOEFL® test on their own. With a total of sixty units, this book is organized to prepare you for the test by providing you with a comprehensive understanding of the test and a thorough analysis of every question type. Each unit provides a step-by-step program that helps develop your test-taking abilities. At the back of the book are two actual tests of the Speaking section of the TOEFL® iBT.

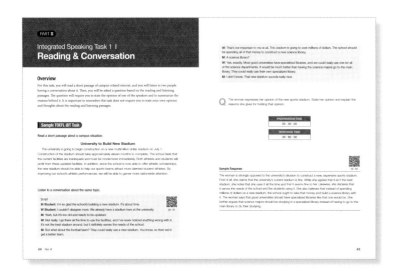

❶ Overview

This section is designed to prepare you for the type of task the part covers. You will be given a full sample question and a model answer in an illustrative structure. You will also be given information on time allotments.

❷ Useful Expressions for the Task

This section offers you a chance to learn various useful expressions before beginning each part. With the expressions listed here, you can make your response more relevant and coherent.

❸ Exercise

In this part of the unit, you will actually do a lot of exercises that the unit covers. The topics in the questions will be various and will reflect actual TOEFL® questions. You will be given an example to refer to and a sample response to compare with yours at the end.

❹ Actual Test

This part will give you a chance to experience an actual TOEFL® iBT test. You will be given two sets of tests that are modeled on the Speaking section of the TOEFL® iBT. The topics are similar to those on the real test, as are the questions. This similarity will allow you to develop a sense of your test-taking ability.

❺ Useful Expressions for the Speaking Tasks

There are a number of expressions and collocations that are typically used in every task and topic. This supplementary part will provide you with a chance to review the expressions and collocations you need to remember while working on each unit.

PART I

Personal Preference

....

The independent speaking section consists of one task. You will be presented with a question or a situation. Then, you will provide a response based upon your own ideas, opinions, and experiences. In this section, you will not read or listen to any other material. You will be given 15 seconds to prepare your answer after the question is presented, and you will have 45 seconds to respond to the question.

Independent Speaking Task **I**
Personal Preference

Overview

This task is about personal preference. It asks you to express your preference from a given pair of choices. In this task, the questions mostly ask you to express an opinion and to support it. Some other questions let you take a position and defend it. When responding to this question, you are to give some details and examples as well as reasons to rationalize your answer.

Sample TOEFL iBT Task

Q Some people prefer to shop for fruit and vegetables at supermarket chains. Others prefer outdoor markets. Which do you think is better and why? Use specific reasons and examples to support your preference.

PREPARATION TIME
00 : 15 : 00

RESPONSE TIME
00 : 45 : 00

01-01

Sample Response

Personally, I prefer to shop for fruits and vegetables at outdoor markets instead of at supermarkets. The first reason is that the produce I purchase at outdoor markets is often fresher than the produce sold at supermarkets. For example, many times, the people selling fruits and vegetables are the farmers who grew the products. Since they came straight from the farm, I know that they're fresh. Another important thing is that you can often negotiate the price at outdoor markets, which is something you can't do when you shop at supermarkets. By negotiating the price, this lets you save money, especially when you buy large amounts of produce.

Useful Expressions for the Task

1 Expressions that can be used to tell one's preference

I prefer to   I prefer to watch movies at home than at the theater.

I believe that   I believe that e-books are better than paper books.

Personally, I prefer   Personally, I prefer to take long trips instead of short ones.

I'm the kind of person who   I'm the kind of person who saves money rather than spending it.

Of the two options, I would   Of the two options, I would prefer the former.

In my opinion   In my opinion, students should work during their summer vacations.

I would rather   I would rather visit a historical building than go to a shopping center.

If presented with these two choices, I would   If presented with these two choices, I would go with the second one.

I think it is better to   I think it is better to have few friends than to have many.

My preference is to   My preference is to cook food at home instead of going out to eat.

2 Expressions that can be used to tell reasons

To begin with   To begin with, I am an outdoor person.

First off   First off, studying hard is very important.

For starters   For starters, everyone needs money in order to live.

In addition   In addition, I want to get the best grades possible.

One reason I prefer this is   One reason I prefer this is that I want to get a good job in the future.

The first reason is   The first reason is that exercise is important.

One of the main reasons   One of the main reasons I support this idea is that pollution can harm people.

Another important thing is   Another important thing is that people should care for their family members.

Additionally   Additionally, I don't like to waste money.

Another good point is   Another good point is that friends can help you in many ways.

3 Expressions that can be used to tell details and supporting ideas

Therefore   Therefore, studying hard will benefit me in many ways.

For example   For example, I always recycle cans and plastic containers.

In other words   In other words, learning a foreign language can help me in the future.

such as   I like healthy foods such as fruits and vegetables.

However, by   However, by staying home, I can become closer to my family.

Thanks to   Thanks to my teachers, I am learning as much as possible.

This would enable me to   This would enable me to have more opportunities.

That way   That way, my skills will improve very much.

On the other hand   On the other hand, some people are not interested in playing sports.

Simply put   Simply put, being kind is the best way people should act.

Exercise Read and answer the question following each step.

Q Some students prefer to study in traditional school classrooms. Others prefer to take classes over the Internet. Which method of study do you think is better and why? Use specific reasons and examples to support your preference.

Before you start

A Listen to the conversation. Then, answer the questions to get some ideas about the subject.

01-02

1 What kind of day did Sue have?

2 What does Sue wish her professor would do?

3 According to Sue, what is the professor probably afraid of?

4 What can you infer about why students still attend the professor's lecture?

B Now, listen to the lecture. Then, answer the questions to get some ideas about the subject.

01-03

1 What are the two areas of education that the Internet has influenced?

2 What is one method of online study the lecturer mentioned?

3 What warning does the professor give the students?

4 What kind of trouble do you think a student caught cheating could get in?

Organization Ask yourself the following questions and organize your ideas.

1 Which of the two choices do you prefer?

2 Why do you find this choice more preferable?

3 Give some supporting details for your choice.

Choice A	Choice B
I prefer To study in a class	I prefer To study online
First reason	First reason
Details	Details
Second reason	Second reason
Details	Details

Responding Make your response by using the above information.

I prefer to

One reason I prefer this is

Another important thing is

Simply put,

Comparing Listen to a sample response and compare it with yours.

Choice A　　Choice B

01-04　　01-05

Exercise Read and answer the question following each step.

Q Some people believe that cities should help their poor by providing them with money. Others believe that the poor should be provided with actual goods such as food. Which method of assistance do you prefer and why? Use specific reasons and examples to support your preference.

Before you start

A Listen to the conversation. Then, answer the questions to get some ideas about the subject.

01-06

1 Why is Catherine sad?

2 What does her friend suggest she do to help?

3 What does Catherine think the city should do to help the poor and the homeless?

4 What can you infer from the dialogue as to why some people are homeless?

B Now, listen to the lecture. Then, answer the questions to get some ideas about the subject.

01-07

1 What is the poverty line?

2 What three things does the professor mention as necessities of life?

3 Why do some people think too much money is spent to help the poor?

4 What can be inferred about the difference in the poverty line for a family of three and a family of seven?

Ask yourself the following questions and organize your ideas.

1 Which of the two choices do you believe is better?

2 Why do you find this choice more preferable?

3 Give some supporting details for your choice.

Choice A	Choice B
I believe Cities should help the poor by giving them money.	I believe Cities should help the poor by giving them actual goods.
First reason	First reason
Details	Details
Second reason	Second reason
Details	Details

Responding Make your response by using the above information.

I think it is better to

First off,

For example,

Another important thing is

Comparing Listen to a sample response and compare it with yours.

Choice A   Choice B

01 - 08   01 - 09

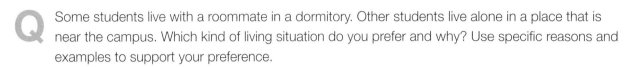

Unit 03 School

Exercise Read and answer the question following each step.

Q Some students live with a roommate in a dormitory. Other students live alone in a place that is near the campus. Which kind of living situation do you prefer and why? Use specific reasons and examples to support your preference.

Before you start

A Listen to the conversation. Then, answer the questions to get some ideas about the subject.

01-10

1 What problem does David have?

2 What is causing David this problem?

3 Why can David not move off campus this year?

4 What can you infer about David's habits from the conversation?

B Now, listen to the lecture. Then, answer the questions to get some ideas about the subject.

01-11

1 What two factors are important for students in deciding where to live?

2 What reason is given for people who want to live alone?

3 What is one problem students have when it comes to living off campus?

4 What can be inferred from the lecture about where most of the university juniors and seniors live?

Ask yourself the following questions and organize your ideas.

1 Which of the two choices do you prefer?

2 Why do you find this choice more preferable?

3 Give some supporting details for your choice.

Choice A	Choice B
I prefer To live in a dorm room with a roommate	**I prefer** To live alone near campus
First reason	**First reason**
Details	**Details**
Second reason	**Second reason**
Details	**Details**

Responding Make your response by using the above information.

I'm the kind of person who

One of the main reasons is

Additionally,

That way,

Comparing Listen to a sample response and compare it with yours.

Choice A Choice B

01-12 01-13

Exercise Read and answer the question following each step.

Q Do you agree or disagree with the following statement?
Music and art should have the same value as other school subjects such as math and science.
Give specific reasons and examples to support your opinion.

Before you start

A Listen to the conversation. Then, answer the questions to get some ideas about the subject.

01-14

1 Why is Betty failing her art class?

2 Why is Betty so concerned about failing her art class?

3 What is Betty's friend's opinion of her drawings and paintings?

4 What can you infer about why Betty's art teacher is failing her?

B Now, listen to the lecture. Then, answer the questions to get some ideas about the subject.

01-15

1 What is the controversy in education the professor examines?

2 What was the problem with the curriculums at some universities in the 1960s and 1970s?

3 What did Harvard do in the 1980s?

4 What can be inferred about Harvard graduates' readiness for the workforce after Harvard made its reforms?

Organization Ask yourself the following questions and organize your ideas.

1 Which of the two positions do you agree with?

2 Why do you agree with this position?

3 Give some supporting details for your position.

Choice A	Choice B
I agree Music and art should have the same value as other courses.	**I disagree** Music and art should not have the same value as other courses.
First reason	**First reason**
Details	**Details**
Second reason	**Second reason**
Details	**Details**

Responding Make your response by using the above information.

Of the two options, I would

The first reason is

Another good point is

In other words,

Comparing Listen to a sample response and compare it with yours.

Choice A   Choice B

01-16   01-17

Exercise Read and answer the question following each step.

Q Some people take trips by themselves. Others take trips with groups of people. Which kind of trip do you prefer and why? Use specific reasons and examples to support your preference.

Before you start

A Listen to the conversation. Then, answer the questions to get some ideas about the subject.

01-18

1 What are they discussing?

2 Where is the group of students planning to go?

3 Why doesn't Henry want to go on the trip?

4 Do you think Henry enjoys skiing?

B Now, listen to the lecture. Then, answer the questions to get some ideas about the subject.

01-19

1 Which two groups of people does the lecturer compare?

2 What is one advantage of traveling in a large group?

3 Why are young people advised to travel with others?

4 What can be inferred about the schedule of a tour group?

Organization Ask yourself the following questions and organize your ideas.

1 Which of the two choices do you prefer?

2 Why do you find this choice more preferable?

3 Give some supporting details for your choice.

Choice A	Choice B
I prefer To take a trip by myself	**I prefer** To take a trip with others
First reason	**First reason**
Details	**Details**
Second reason	**Second reason**
Details	**Details**

Responding Make your response by using the above information.

I would rather

One reason I prefer this is

On the other hand,

Another good point is

Comparing Listen to a sample response and compare it with yours.

Choice A   Choice B

01-20   01-21

Exercise Read and answer the question following each step.

Q Some people save all of their extra money. Others spend their extra money by purchasing various things. Which kind of person are you and why? Use specific reasons and examples to support your preference.

Before you start

A Listen to the conversation. Then, answer the questions to get some ideas about the subject.

01-22

1 Why is Joanne happy?

2 What three warnings does Joanne's friend give her?

3 Why does Joanne spend most of her money?

4 What do you think Joanne will do with her money this payday?

B Now, listen to the lecture. Then, answer the questions to get some ideas about the subject.

01-23

1 What does the professor say a large portion of the national income is?

2 What are two reasons given for why people do not save money?

3 What are some examples of insurance the professor gives?

4 What can be inferred about why young people are less likely to save any money?

Ask yourself the following questions and organize your ideas.

1 Which of the two choices do you prefer?

2 Why do you find this choice more preferable?

3 Give some supporting details for your choice.

Choice A	Choice B
I prefer To save all my extra money	I prefer To spend my extra money on the things I want
First reason	First reason
Details	Details
Second reason	Second reason
Details	Details

Responding Make your response by using the above information.

Personally, I prefer

To begin with,

For example,

Another important thing is

Comparing Listen to a sample response and compare it with yours.

Choice A
01-24

Choice B
01-25

Exercise Read and answer the question following each step.

Q Do you agree or disagree with the following statement?
Computers have made people's lives better.
Give specific reasons and examples to support your opinion.

Before you start

A Listen to the conversation. Then, answer the questions to get some ideas about the subject.

01-26

1 What gift did Alicia get for her birthday?

2 What are some of the details of the new gift?

3 What might Alicia do online?

4 What can be inferred from Jeff's response to Alicia's last question?

B Now, listen to the lecture. Then, answer the questions to get some ideas about the subject.

01-27

1 What are the benefits of computers?

2 What are two problems with computers?

3 How many people in America are believed to be computer addicts?

4 What can be inferred about the amount of money lost to Internet fraud in the future?

Ask yourself the following questions and organize your ideas.

1 Which of the two positions do you agree with?

2 Why do you agree with this position?

3 Give some supporting details for your choice.

Choice A	Choice B
I agree Computers have made our lives better.	I disagree Computers haven't made our lives better.
First reason	First reason
Details	Details
Second reason	Second reason
Details	Details

Responding Make your response by using the above information.

If presented with these two choices, I would

One reason I prefer this is

In addition,

Another good point is

Comparing Listen to a sample response and compare it with yours.

Choice A   Choice B

01 - 28   01 - 29

Exercise Read and answer the question following each step.

Q Do you agree or disagree with the following statement?
When you apply for a job, you should include a photograph.
Give specific reasons and examples to support your opinion.

Before you start

A Listen to the conversation. Then, answer the questions to get some ideas about the subject.

01 - 30

1 What did the man put on his résumé?

2 How does the man feel about that action?

3 Why is the man unable to hide how he looks?

4 What can you infer about some job applicants?

B Now, listen to the lecture. Then, answer the questions to get some ideas about the subject.

01 - 31

1 What is common for job applicants to do in some countries?

2 What is the main reason job applicants in the United States do not put their pictures on their applications?

3 What is a second reason against putting a picture on a job application?

4 What might happen to a person in the United States who puts a picture on a job application?

Organization Ask yourself the following questions and organize your ideas.

1 Which of the two choices do you prefer?

2 Why do you find this choice more preferable?

3 Give some supporting details for your choice.

Choice A	Choice B
I agree Job applicants should put their pictures on their applications.	**I disagree** Job applicants should not put their pictures on their applications.
First reason	First reason
Details	Details
Second reason	Second reason
Details	Details

Responding Make your response by using the above information.

I agree with the statement that

Another thing to consider is

Something to think about is

One more thing to remember is

Comparing Listen to a sample response and compare it with yours.

Choice A

01-32

Choice B

01-33

Exercise Read and answer the question following each step.

Q Some people prefer playing sports in their free time. Others prefer to play computer games. Which do you prefer and why? Use specific reasons and examples to support your preference.

Before you start

A Listen to the conversation. Then, answer the questions to get some ideas about the subject.

01-34

1 What will the man do with his friends this weekend?

2 What does the man say about that activity?

3 What does the man suggest that the woman do?

4 What can you infer about what the woman will do in the future?

B Now, listen to the lecture. Then, answer the questions to get some ideas about the subject.

01-35

1 What are two reasons some people say computers games are bad for young people?

2 How does the professor feel about computer games?

3 According to the professor, how can shooting games help gamers?

4 What benefits can multiplayer games provide for gamers?

Organization Ask yourself the following questions and organize your ideas.

1 Which of the two choices do you prefer?

2 Why do you find this choice more preferable?

3 Give some supporting details for your choice.

Choice A	Choice B
I prefer To play sports	I prefer To play computer games
First reason	First reason
Details	Details
Second reason	Second reason
Details	Details

Responding Make your response by using the above information.

I prefer to

For one thing,

Another reason is that

So I have learned to

Comparing Listen to a sample response and compare it with yours.

Choice A   Choice B

01-36   01-37

Exercise Read and answer the question following each step.

Q Do you agree or disagree with the following statement?
The government should provide free Internet service for everyone.
Give specific reasons and examples to support your opinion.

⌈Before you start⌉

A Listen to the conversation. Then, answer the questions to get some ideas about the subject.

01-38

1   What is the woman's problem?

2   What does the woman say about Internet service providers?

3   What happened to the woman last month?

4   What can you infer about what the woman will do?

B Now, listen to the lecture. Then, answer the questions to get some ideas about the subject.

01-39

1   According to the professor, what can people use to go online?

2   What do some people say that Internet service is?

3   What types of activities do people do online nowadays?

4   Why should the government provide Internet service for free for everyone?

Organization Ask yourself the following questions and organize your ideas.

1 Which of the two choices do you prefer?

2 Why do you find this choice more preferable?

3 Give some supporting details for your choice.

Choice A	Choice B
I agree I agree that the government should provide Internet service for free.	I disagree I disagree that the government should provide Internet service for free.
First reason	First reason
Details	Details
Second reason	Second reason
Details	Details

Responding Make your response by using the above information.

To begin with,

In addition,

For starters,

A second point I would like to make is

Comparing Listen to a sample response and compare it with yours.

Choice A   Choice B

01-40   01-41

Exercise Read and answer the question following each step.

Q Some people believe that the elderly should not take risks or take part in difficult activities like young people do. Others believe that the elderly should be able to do any activities that they want. Which belief do you prefer and why? Use specific reasons and examples to support your preference.

Before you start

A Listen to the conversation. Then, answer the questions to get some ideas about the subject.

01-42

1 What is the man's grandfather doing?

2 How does the man feel about his grandfather's actions?

3 What does the woman think about the man's grandfather?

4 What can you infer about the woman?

B Now, listen to the lecture. Then, answer the questions to get some ideas about the subject.

01-43

1 According to the professor, what are some activities the elderly do nowadays?

2 What do the first group of people think about the elderly doing dangerous activities?

3 What does the professor say about some children and grandchildren?

4 What does the second group of people think about the elderly doing dangerous activities?

Organization Ask yourself the following questions and organize your ideas.

1 Which of the two beliefs do you prefer?

2 Why do you find this belief more preferable?

3 Give some supporting details for your choice.

Choice A	Choice B
Agree The elderly should not take risks or take part in difficult activities like young people do.	**Disagree** The elderly should be able to do any activities that they want.
First reason	First reason
Details	Details
Second reason	Second reason
Details	Details

Responding Make your response by using the above information.

I strongly believe

For instance,

For one thing,

Another thing is that

Comparing Listen to a sample response and compare it with yours.

Choice A Choice B

01- 44　　01- 45

Exercise Read and answer the question following each step.

Q Do you agree or disagree with the following statement?
Robots will never become smarter and more talented than humans.
Give specific reasons and examples to support your opinion.

[**Before you start**]

A Listen to the conversation. Then, answer the questions to get some ideas about the subject.

01-46

  1 What does the woman say about the factory?

  2 What does the woman think about the factory?

  3 What does the man say robots are doing?

  4 What does the man believe robots will do in the future?

B Now, listen to the lecture. Then, answer the questions to get some ideas about the subject.

01-47

  1 According to the professor, what are people concerned about?

  2 What is the first reason the professor thinks robots will never be smarter than humans?

  3 What types of jobs do most robots do nowadays?

  4 What is the second reason the professor thinks robots will never be smarter than humans?

Organization Ask yourself the following questions and organize your ideas.

1 Which of the two positions do you prefer?

2 Why do you find this position more preferable?

3 Give some supporting details for your position.

Choice A	Choice B
Agree Robots will never become smarter and more talented than humans.	**Disagree** Robots will become superior to humans someday.
First reason	First reason
Details	Details
Second reason	Second reason
Details	Details

Responding Make your response by using the above information.

I believe that

Another point I'd like to make is

I disagree with the statement because

Additionally,

Comparing Listen to a sample response and compare it with yours.

Choice A   Choice B

01 - 48   01 - 49

Unit 13　Computer Laboratories

Exercise　Read and answer the question following each step.

Q　Do you agree or disagree with the following statement?
Schools should close down their computer laboratories because all students have computers these days.
Give specific reasons and examples to support your opinion.

Before you start

A　Listen to the conversation. Then, answer the questions to get some ideas about the subject.

01-50

1　What did the woman read about in the student newspaper?

2　How often do the man and the woman visit the computer labs?

3　What will the woman try to do?

4　What can you infer about the man?

B　Now, listen to the lecture. Then, answer the questions to get some ideas about the subject.

01-51

1　According to the professor, what has the school done with its computer labs?

2　What does the professor think of the school's decision?

3　What does the professor say that students who use the computer labs must do?

4　Why is the school's decision a major inconvenience for some students?

Organization Ask yourself the following questions and organize your ideas.

1 Which of the two positions do you prefer?

2 Why do you find this position more preferable?

3 Give some supporting details for your position.

Choice A	Choice B
Agree I believe schools should close their computer labs.	Disagree I don't think that schools should close down their computer labs.
First reason	First reason
Details	Details
Second reason	Second reason
Details	Details

Responding Make your response by using the above information.

The first reason is that

As a result,

First,

Second,

Comparing Listen to a sample response and compare it with yours.

Choice A   Choice B

01-52   01-53

Unit 14 Movie Reviews

Exercise Read and answer the question following each step.

Q Some people like to read reviews before they go to see a movie. Others prefer to watch films without reading reviews. Which method do you prefer and why? Use specific reasons and examples to support your preference.

Before you start

A Listen to the conversation. Then, answer the questions to get some ideas about the subject.

01-54

1 What will the woman do before watching a movie?

2 What does the woman say she reads?

3 What does the woman say movie reviews provide?

4 What can you infer about the man?

B Now, listen to the lecture. Then, answer the questions to get some ideas about the subject.

01-55

1 According to the professor, what do movie reviewers do?

2 What does the professor think of reading movie reviews?

3 What does the professor say about movie reviewers?

4 Why does the professor think movie reviews are worthless?

Organization   Ask yourself the following questions and organize your ideas.

1   Which of the two options do you prefer?

2   Why do you find this option more preferable?

3   Give some supporting details for your option.

Choice A	Choice B
Agree I love to read movie reviews before seeing a movie.	**Disagree** I never read movie reviews before I see movies.
First reason	**First reason**
Details	**Details**
Second reason	**Second reason**
Details	**Details**

Responding   Make your response by using the above information.

I'm the kind of person who

An additional reason I like

In the past, I used to

I have also noticed that

Comparing   Listen to a sample response and compare it with yours.

Choice A   Choice B

01-56   01-57

Exercise Read and answer the question following each step.

Q Do you agree or disagree with the following statement?
Too many young people have become addicted to their electronic devices.
Give specific reasons and examples to support your opinion.

Before you start

A Listen to the conversation. Then, answer the questions to get some ideas about the subject.

01-58

1 What will the woman get for her birthday?

2 What does the man say the woman should do?

3 According to the man, what is the first way people are harmed by their addiction?

4 According to the man, what is the second way people are harmed by their addiction?

B Now, listen to the lecture. Then, answer the questions to get some ideas about the subject.

01-59

1 What does the professor think of addiction to electronic devices?

2 According to the professor, what can some parents do?

3 What does the professor do with his children?

4 How do some young people use their electronic devices?

Organization Ask yourself the following questions and organize your ideas.

1 Which of the two positions do you prefer?

2 Why do you find this position more preferable?

3 Give some supporting details for your position.

Choice A	Choice B
Agree Many young people are addicted to their electronic devices.	Disagree I don't believe many young people are addicted to their electronic devices.
First reason	First reason
Details	Details
Second reason	Second reason
Details	Details

Responding Make your response by using the above information.

It's true that

Another problem is that

For instance, I

In addition,

Comparing Listen to a sample response and compare it with yours.

Choice A

01-60

Choice B

01-61

PART II

Integrated Speaking Task 1
Reading & Conversation

··

The integrated speaking section consists of three tasks. These tasks will present you with a reading passage and a listening conversation or lecture or merely a listening lecture. Topics will come from a variety of fields, but they are normally based on campus situations or are academic topics.

In this task, you will be presented with a short reading passage about a campus situation topic. Next, you will listen to a short conversation between two students about the same topic. Then, you will provide a response based upon what you read and heard. You will be asked to describe one student's opinion about the topic in the reading passage. You will be given 30 seconds to prepare your answer after the question is presented, and you will have 60 seconds to respond to the question.

Integrated Speaking Task 1 |
Reading & Conversation

Overview

For this task, you will read a short passage of campus-related interest, and you will listen to two people having a conversation about it. Then, you will be asked a question based on the reading and listening passages. The question will require you to state the opinion of one of the speakers and to summarize the reasons behind it. It is important to remember this task does not require you to state your own opinion and thoughts about the reading and listening passages.

Sample TOEFL iBT Task

Read a short passage about a campus situation.

University to Build New Stadium

The university is going to begin construction on a new multimillion dollar stadium on July 1. Construction of the stadium should take approximately eleven months to complete. The school feels that the current facilities are inadequate and must be modernized immediately. Both athletes and students will profit from these updated facilities. In addition, since the school is now able to offer athletic scholarships, the new stadium should be able to help our sports teams attract more talented student-athletes. By improving our school's athletic performances, we will be able to garner more nationwide attention.

Listen to a conversation about the same topic.

> **Script**
>
> **M Student**: I'm so glad the school's building a new stadium. It's about time.
>
> **W Student**: I couldn't disagree more. We already have a stadium here at the university.
>
> **M**: Yeah, but it's too old and needs to be updated.
>
> **W**: Not really. I go there all the time to use the facilities, and I've never noticed anything wrong with it. It's not the best stadium around, but it definitely serves the needs of the school.
>
> **M**: But what about the football team? They could really use a new stadium. You know, so then we'd get a better team.

02-01

W: That's not important to me at all. This stadium is going to cost millions of dollars. The school should be spending all of that money to construct a new science library.

M: A science library?

W: Yes, exactly. Most good universities have specialized libraries, and we could really use one for all of the science departments. It would be much better than having the science majors go to the main library. They could really use their own specialized library.

M: I don't know. That new stadium sounds really nice.

Q The woman expresses her opinion of the new sports stadium. State her opinion and explain the reasons she gives for holding that opinion.

PREPARATION TIME
00 : 30 : 00

RESPONSE TIME
00 : 60 : 00

Sample Response

02-02

The woman is strongly opposed to the university's decision to construct a new, expensive sports stadium. First of all, she claims that the university's current stadium is fine. While she agrees that it isn't the best stadium, she notes that she uses it all the time and that it seems fine to her. Likewise, she declares that it serves the needs of the school and the students using it. She also believes that instead of spending millions of dollars on a new stadium, the school ought to take that money and build a science library with it. The woman says that good universities should have specialized libraries like that one would be. She further argues that science majors should be studying in a specialized library instead of having to go to the main library to do their studying.

Useful Expressions for the Task

1 Expressions that can be used to tell about the subject

The notice is about   The notice is about a decision to increase tuition at a school.

The notice describes   The notice describes the opening of a new parking lot.

In the notice, the university   In the notice, the university claims it needs more dormitories.

The subject of the announcement is   The subject of the announcement is the school's annual winter play.

The students talk about   The students talk about the closing of the school's library during summer.

The topic of the notice is   The topic of the notice is the increase in the number of exchange students.

The announcement mentions   The announcement mentions the decision to increase the number of required courses.

The notice covers   The notice covers the closing of a school club.

According to the announcement   According to the announcement, students may not stay in the dormitories during winter break.

The matter the notice discusses is   The matter the notice discusses is an increase in the student activities fee.

2 Expressions that can be used to give the student's opinion in the conversation

The male student opposes   The male student opposes the decision to end the school's baseball team.

The woman thinks   The woman thinks the school is making the wrong decision.

The male student does not believe   The male student does not believe the closing of the dorm is right.

The man agrees that   The man agrees that kitchens should be added to school dormitories.

The male student dislikes   The male student dislikes the new campus shuttle bus.

In the man's mind   In the man's mind, the decision by the school is correct.

The man's opinion is that   The man's opinion is that students should be allowed to take more classes.

The woman supports   The woman supports the right for students to take classes on weekends.

The man fully supports   The man fully supports the decision to create a school newspaper.

In the woman's mind   In the woman's mind, the school should not have acted that way.

3 Expressions that can be used to explain the reasons for holding an opinion

More than anything else, the reason is that   More than anything else, the reason is that students are already too busy.

The man thinks that   The man thinks that the department is making the right decision.

The reason for this is   The reason for this is that tuition is already too expensive.

One reason she gives is that   One reason she gives is that the dorms are too old fashioned.

The first reason is that   The first reason is that the labs need to be upgraded.

The woman says   The woman says the school newspaper should only be available online.

The man claims that   The man claims that students should be allowed to double-major.

The woman believes   The woman believes the campus is too dirty.

The man expresses his opposition by saying   The man expresses his opposition by saying that few people on campus ever recycle.

Another reason is   Another reason is that students enjoy acting in school plays.

4 Expressions that can be used to tell details

According to the woman   According to the woman, there are not enough parking spaces on campus.

One thing the student points out is   One thing the student points out is that many professors don't attend their office hours.

First, the student argues   First, the student argues that there are not enough seminars being taught.

During the conversation   During the conversation, the man says that the school should do more to help sick students.

To begin with   To begin with, many students feel the campus is not safe.

First [Second] of all   First of all, the school is far from the closest subway station.

He claims that   He claims that off-campus housing is too expensive.

Furthermore   Furthermore, the school is not attracting the most talented students.

The woman states that   The woman states that the library does not have enough books.

The male student mentions   The male student mentions that he opposes efforts to ban certain clubs.

5 Expressions that can be used to make comparative remarks

The woman thinks A is superior to B   The woman thinks chemistry is superior to biology.

The man wants to ~ as opposed to   The man wants to have another new dorm as opposed to a new gym.

It is more important to A than to B   It is more important to study than to play sports.

The woman's preference is to   The woman's preference is to repair the laboratory instead of upgrading the dorm.

She believes A is better than B   She believes a new computer lab is better than a bigger parking lot.

It is better to A than to B   It is better to attract quality students than to hire more faculty.

On the contrary   On the contrary, few students are interested in traveling to another campus.

A is more important than B   Taking core classes is more important that taking electives.

A is a better choice than B   Studying abroad is a better choice than transferring to another school.

The school ought to ~ instead of   The school ought to provide more scholarships instead of hiring more administrators.

Exercise Read, listen, and answer the question following each step.

Reading Read the following passage about a campus situation.

University Tutoring System

The new university tutoring system begins on August 22. Students will no longer have face-to-face tutoring sessions. Instead, an online tutoring system will be implemented. The computer-based tutoring system will allow students to receive tutoring help twenty-four hours a day, seven days a week, instead of only during regular school hours. Students will benefit from expanded access to tutors. In addition, the computer-based system will relieve students of stress from the crowded tutoring centers. Students will no longer need to be present on campus for tutoring. They will be able to access the computer-based system from any computer with an Internet connection.

📖 **Words & Phrases**

tutor Ⓥ to teach an individual or small group of people
implement Ⓥ to put into practice; to start

relieve Ⓥ to ease
access Ⓥ to connect; to use

Comprehension Answer the following questions to make sure you understand the reading.

1 What is the notice about?

2 What is the first reason for the new tutoring system?

3 According to the notice, how will it benefit students?

4 What is another reason for the new tutoring system?

5 According to the notice, how will the new tutoring system benefit students?

Listening Listen to a conversation about the same topic and take notes.

✏️ Note Taking

02 - 03

📖 **Words & Phrases**

face to face phr in person; one on one

efficient adj well-organized; not wasting time, effort, or expense

upgrade v to improve; to make better

stick to phr to remain with; to stay with

Q The woman expresses her opinion of the new computer-based tutoring system. State her opinion and explain the reasons she gives for holding that opinion.

Organization Ask yourself the following questions and organize your ideas.

1 What is the woman's opinion of the new tutoring system?

2 What does the woman say about students' typing skills?

3 Why is this important to the new tutoring system?

4 What does the woman say about computers?

5 Why does the woman think it will be difficult for some students to buy new computers?

Responding Make your response by using the above information.

The notice describes

The woman thinks

One reason is

During the conversation, the woman says

Another reason is

The woman states that

Comparing Listen to a sample response and compare it with yours.

02 - 04

Exercise Read, listen, and answer the question following each step.

Reading Read the following passage about a campus situation.

Wall of Art Demolition

University officials have decided to take down the wall separating the art building from the university theater. The demolition will be completed by the end of May. Once the wall is down, access between the buildings will be easier. Students and visitors will no longer have to walk a block to get around the wall. In addition, the wall initially began to feature the work of student artists. Lately, it has merely featured graffiti. This has made it an eyesore on campus, and we wish to beautify our campus. The university apologizes for any inconvenience to students during the removal process.

📖 Words & Phrases

demolition **n** destruction
initially **adv** from the beginning; at first

graffiti **n** writing on walls
eyesore **n** something unpleasant to look at

Comprehension Answer the following questions to make sure you understand the reading.

1 What is the notice about?

2 What is one reason the wall is being taken down?

3 What is another reason the wall is being taken down?

4 What is the way that students will benefit from the demolition?

5 What is the way in which the school will benefit from the demolition?

Listening Listen to a conversation about the same topic and take notes.

✎ Note Taking

02 - 05

📖 **Words & Phrases**

historic adj significant; relating to history

knock something down phr to destroy something; to tear something down

showcase n an exhibit; a display

exposure n coverage; contact

Q The man expresses his opinion of the destruction of the wall of art. State his opinion and explain the reasons he gives for holding that opinion.

Organization Ask yourself the following questions and organize your ideas.

1 What is the man's opinion on the destruction of the wall of art?

2 What does the man say about the wall of art?

3 Why is the wall's age of importance?

4 How has the wall of art benefitted the school's students?

5 What effect will the wall's destruction have on art students?

Responding Make your response by using the above information.

The male student opposes

In the notice, the university

The man thinks that

More than anything else, the reason is that

Secondly,

In the man's mind,

Comparing Listen to a sample response and compare it with yours.

02 - 06

Exercise Read, listen, and answer the question following each step.

Reading Read the following passage about a campus situation.

Dean of Humanities Department Appointment

Dr. William Reynolds has been appointed the new dean of the Humanities Department. Dr. Reynolds has been an associate professor in the department for fifteen years. His reputation as a scholar throughout the country is unparalleled. His appointment will help attract some of the best professors in the field and boost the department's academic reputation. Dr. Reynolds has also won the university distinguished teacher and advisor award for the past five years, which will ensure that students receive excellent advice for their studies and future goals. Let us all welcome Dr. Reynolds and support him in his new position.

Words & Phrases

reputation n a standing; a status
boost v to increase; to raise

academic adj scholarly; educational
distinguished adj renowned; best

Comprehension Answer the following questions to make sure you understand the reading.

1 What is the announcement about?

2 What is the first reason Dr. Reynolds has been appointed dean of the Humanities Department?

3 What is the second reason he has been appointed dean?

4 What is the first way the university will benefit from Dr. Reynolds's appointment?

5 What is the second way the university will benefit from his appointment?

Listening | Listen to a conversation about the same topic and take notes.

> 🖊 **Note Taking**
>
>
> 02 - 07

📖 **Words & Phrases**

appoint ⓥ to hire; to assign
seldom adv rarely; hardly ever

scholar ⓝ an academic; a researcher
attract ⓥ to lure; to draw toward something or someone

Q The man expresses his opinion of the professor's new appointment. State his opinion and explain the reasons he gives for holding that opinion.

Organization | Ask yourself the following questions and organize your ideas.

1 How does the man feel about Dr. Reynolds's appointment to dean?

2 How does the man respond to the woman's claim that Dr. Reynolds is a bad advisor?

3 What does the man say about his roommate's comments?

4 According to the man, what is Dr. Reynolds's academic reputation?

5 How will Dr. Reynold's standing as a scholar improve the school?

Responding | Make your response by using the above information.

The subject of the announcement

The man thinks that

The reason for this is

The man claims that

Another thing the man points out is

According to the man,

Comparing | Listen to a sample response and compare it with yours.

02 - 08

Exercise Read, listen, and answer the question following each step.

Reading Read the following passage about a campus situation.

University Dormitory Policy

Beginning this spring, the university will implement a new dormitory policy. The floors of each dormitory will become major specific, meaning that students with the same majors will live together. This policy will allow students to study more effectively. Because they will live in close proximity to one another, students with the same majors will be able to create study groups more easily. In addition, students will make closer connections with others with the same majors. The school believes students with the same majors should spend more time together outside of class. This will promote both academic and social interaction.

📖 Words & Phrases

implement v to put into practice
proximity n nearness; closeness

promote v to encourage; to support
interaction n contact; relations

Comprehension Answer the following questions to make sure you understand the reading.

1 What is the notice about?

2 What is the first reason the university is implementing the new dormitory policy?

3 What is the second reason for the university's new dormitory policy?

4 What is the first way that students will benefit from the university's new policy?

5 What is the second way that students will benefit from the new policy?

Note Taking

02-09

📖 **Words & Phrases**

definitely adv surely; absolutely

diverse adj different; various

stimulate v to inspire; to motivate

perspective n a view or manner of thinking

Q The woman expresses her opinion of the new dormitory policy. State her opinion and explain the reasons she gives for holding that opinion.

Organization Ask yourself the following questions and organize your ideas.

1 What does the woman think of the new dormitory policy?

2 How does the woman feel the new decision will affect students' grades?

3 Why does the woman believe students need to interact with others who have different majors?

4 What does the woman think about the potential for students living on the same floor to have good discussions together?

5 Why does the woman feel the discussions will not be positive?

Responding Make your response by using the above information.

According to the announcement,

The woman believes

One thing the student points out is

Another reason she gives is that

She claims that

Simply put,

Comparing Listen to a sample response and compare it with yours.

02-10

Exercise Read, listen, and answer the question following each step.

Reading   Read the following passage about a campus situation.

Bus Route Change

The university bus system will begin additional routes and stops at the beginning of the fall semester. The new routes will be in effect between 8:00 AM and 5:00 PM. After 5:00 PM, the old routes will start being followed. The new routes will speed up transportation between major points on campus. Students will no longer have to wait for more than three minutes in between buses. Additionally, having more stops will decrease pedestrian traffic on campus. Students will have more options to get off in previously isolated areas of campus and will not have to walk great distances.

📖 Words & Phrases

additional adj extra
pedestrian n a person who is walking

previously adv before; once
isolated adj remote

Comprehension   Answer the following questions to make sure you understand the reading.

1 What is the notice about?

2 What is the first reason that the bus routes are being changed?

3 What is the second reason that the bus routes are being changed?

4 What is the first way the students will benefit from the new routes?

5 What is the second way the students will benefit from the new routes?

Listening | Listen to a conversation about the same topic and take notes.

02-11

✏ Note Taking

📖 Words & Phrases

look forward to `phr` to anticipate; to expect

considerably `adv` greatly; very much

unlimited `adj` without a limit; infinite

fund `n` money

Q The woman expresses her opinion of the new bus routes on campus. State her opinion and explain the reasons she gives for holding that opinion.

Organization | Ask yourself the following questions and organize your ideas.

1 How does the woman feel about the new bus routes?

2 What does the woman say about the current number of buses on campus?

3 How will the new buses help the woman?

4 What does the woman say about night school students not having access to the new bus routes?

5 Why does the woman feel the day students are more important?

Responding | Make your response by using the above information.

The topic of the notice is

The female student argues

The first reason is that

In the woman's mind,

Secondly,

According to the woman,

Comparing | Listen to a sample response and compare it with yours.

02-12

Exercise Read, listen, and answer the question following each step.

Reading Read the following passage about a campus situation.

New Café at Library

The university is beginning construction on a student café in the library basement. It will be ready for service by October 31. The café will provide students with easy access to snacks and beverages. Students will no longer have to leave campus for food and drinks. Now they can take quick breaks right on the library's premises and then resume studying. The refreshments will also be inexpensive. So long as customers present a valid student ID, all menu items will be discounted. The university looks forward to students taking advantage of the new café once it opens.

📖 Words & Phrases

beverage n a drink
premise n an area; a place

resume v to restart; to start again
valid adj legitimate; legal

Comprehension Answer the following questions to make sure you understand the reading.

1 What is the notice about?

2 What is the first reason the new café is being built?

3 What is the second reason the new café is being built?

4 What is the first way students will benefit from the new café?

5 What is the second way students will benefit from the new café?

✏ Note Taking

02-13

📖 Words & Phrases

junk food 🅝 unhealthy food such as candy, chocolate, and potato chips

alternative 🅝 an option; a choice

procrastinate 🅥 to avoid; to delay

hang out with 🅟🅗🅡 to spend time with others while often doing nothing important

Q The man expresses his opinion of the new café being constructed. State his opinion and explain the reasons he gives for holding that opinion.

Organization Ask yourself the following questions and organize your ideas.

1 What does the man think of the new café in the school's library?

2 What does the man say about the food the café will be selling?

3 Why does the man think these foods are not good options?

4 How does the man think students will act when the café opens?

5 Why does the man feel that students' behavior will not be helpful?

Responding Make your response by using the above information.

According to the announcement,

The male student opposes

One reason the man gives is that

The man thinks that

The second reason the man gives is that

He claims that

Comparing Listen to a sample response and compare it with yours.

02-14

Exercise Read, listen, and answer the question following each step.

Reading Read the following passage about a campus situation.

Student Election Date to Change

The student activities office is changing the date to elect student representatives to the student council. While elections have traditionally been held in May, the representatives for the new school year will now be elected in September. This will give freshmen the opportunity to help select the student representatives, something they have often complained about not being able to do. Additionally, since elections will not be in May, they will no longer distract students from studying for their final exams, which is a common excuse students give for not voting. This should serve to increase voter turnout for the elections.

📖 Words & Phrases

representative n a leader; a delegate
traditionally adv typically; usually
distract v to bother; to keep a person from doing something

voter turnout n the percentage of voters participating in an election

Comprehension Answer the following questions to make sure you understand the reading.

1 What is the notice about?

2 Why has the student activities office changed the date of the election?

3 How will this change benefit freshmen at the school?

4 Why did students often not vote in the past?

5 How will the change in the date of the election change the voter turnout?

Listening Listen to a conversation about the same topic and take notes.

✎ Note Taking

02 - 15

📖 **Words & Phrases**

spectacular adj excellent

be occupied with phr to be busy doing something

have a point phr to make a good observation

candidate n a person running for an elected office

Q The man expresses his opinion on the change in the date for the election of student representatives. State his opinion and explain the reasons he gives for holding that opinion.

Organization Ask yourself the following questions and organize your ideas.

1 What is the man's opinion of the decision to move the election date?

2 What does the man say about students' schedules in September?

3 How does the man feel this will affect students with regard to voting?

4 What does the man think about freshmen getting to vote?

5 How does the man feel that students' knowledge of school issues will affect their voting?

Responding Make your response by using the above information.

The man feels negatively toward

The announcement mentions

The man expresses his opposition by saying

In the man's mind,

The man's second reason is

He claims that

Comparing Listen to a sample response and compare it with yours.

02 - 16

Exercise Read, listen, and answer the question following each step.

Reading Read the following passage about a campus situation.

Student Activity Fees

The school administration has decided to increase the student activity fee. Currently, students pay 100 dollars a semester; however, the new fee will increase to 125 dollars. Previously, payment was optional; however, it has now become mandatory. All full-time students are obligated to pay the fee before they begin classes. The student activity fee is used for various purposes. Among them are securing guest speakers on campus, paying for student clubs, and covering the costs of various other student activities. The fee has increased due to the recent national rise in prices.

📖 Words & Phrases

fee (n) money paid for a service
previously (adv) before; prior to

various (adj) of differing kinds
cover (v) to pay for

Comprehension Answer the following questions to make sure you understand the reading.

1 What is the announcement about?

2 How is the fee changing?

3 According to the announcement, who must pay the fee?

4 How is the fee used?

5 According to the announcement, why is the fee increasing?

Listening   Listen to a conversation about the same topic and take notes.

🖊 Note Taking

02-17

📖 Words & Phrases

disappointed `adj` failing to meet one's hopes or expectations

take part in `phr` to be involved in something

tuition `n` money paid to attend school

afford `v` to have enough money to pay for something

Q   The man expresses his opinion of the increase in the student activity fee. State his opinion and explain the reasons he gives for holding that opinion.

Organization   Ask yourself the following questions and organize your ideas.

1   What is the man's opinion of the increase in the student activity fee?

2   Why did the man not pay the student activity fee in the past?

3   What does the man say about school tuition?

4   What is difficult for the man to do?

5   What does the man say about the school?

Responding   Make your response by using the above information.

The announcement mentions

The man is strongly

First, he points out that

So now he needs to

He also claims that

He states that

Comparing   Listen to a sample response and compare it with yours.

02-18

Exercise Read, listen, and answer the question following each step.

Reading Read the following passage about a campus situation.

New Park to Be Built

The university is pleased to announce it has acquired a new tract of land alongside the northern end of campus. This land, which covers more than thirty acres, will be used to construct a park for students. The park will consist of a large grassy area as well as a pond, tennis courts, and two outdoor basketball courts. Jogging and cycling trails will also be constructed there. Part of the area is wooded. The trees will not be cut down but will remain. The total price of everything, including land acquisition, is estimated at 1.2 million dollars.

📖 Words & Phrases

tract **n** an area of land
pond **n** a small body of water completely surrounded by land

construct **v** to build; to make
wooded **adj** having trees

Comprehension Answer the following questions to make sure you understand the reading.

1 What is the notice about?

2 How large is the land?

3 What will be done with the land?

4 What will be included in the park?

5 According to the notice, what is the price of the project?

Listening Listen to a conversation about the same topic and take notes.

✏ Note Taking

02-19

📖 Words & Phrases

excited adj very pleased or happy

avoid v to refrain from; to keep something from happening

intact adj untouched; in one piece

suppose v to guess; to believe

Q The woman expresses her opinion of the plans for the new park. State her opinion and explain the reasons she gives for holding that opinion.

Organization Ask yourself the following questions and organize your ideas.

1 What is the woman's opinion of the plans for the new park?

2 What does the woman want to do at the park?

3 What does the woman expect the man can do at the park?

4 What does the woman say about the forested area?

5 What does the woman hope will happen soon?

Responding Make your response by using the above information.

The notice discusses

The woman supports

For starters,

Another benefit of the park is

The woman is pleased that

She remarks that

Comparing Listen to a sample response and compare it with yours.

02-20

Exercise Read, listen, and answer the question following each step.

Reading Read the following passage about a campus situation.

New Teaching Assistant Policy

Seniors may now apply to be teaching assistants for professors. Previously, only graduate students have been permitted to be teaching assistants. However, thanks to a generous donation from an anonymous benefactor, there is enough funding to pay for undergraduate teaching assistants. A list of classes requiring teaching assistants will be posted in each departmental office. Only seniors are eligible. A qualified student must have an overall GPA of 3.40 or higher. The student's major GPA must be 3.60 or higher. The student must also have taken the class to be a teaching assistant for it.

Words & Phrases

generous adj being large in size or nature
donation n a gift, often of money

anonymous adj not named
eligible adj qualified to participate in something

Comprehension Answer the following questions to make sure you understand the reading.

1 What is the announcement about?

2 Why can undergraduate students now become teaching assistants?

3 Where will the lists of classes needing teaching assistants be posted?

4 Who is eligible to be an undergraduate teaching assistant?

5 What kinds of grades must eligible students have?

Listening Listen to a conversation about the same topic and take notes.

✎ Note Taking

02-21

📖 Words & Phrases

displeased adj unhappy with
knowledgeable adj knowing a lot

time-consuming adj requiring or taking up a lot of time
coursework n the work a student does at school

Q The woman expresses her opinion of the new policy on teaching assistants. State her opinion and explain the reasons she gives for holding that opinion.

Organization Ask yourself the following questions and organize your ideas.

1 What is the woman's opinion of the new policy on teaching assistants?

2 What is the first reason the woman provides?

3 What does the woman say about the man?

4 According to the woman, what did one of her TAs tell her?

5 What is the second reason the woman provides?

Responding Make your response by using the above information.

The notice points out

The woman opposes

For one thing,

She thinks, however, that

The second reason the woman mentions is

The student believes that

Comparing Listen to a sample response and compare it with yours.

02-22

Unit 26 Graduation Requirements

Exercise Read, listen, and answer the question following each step.

Reading Read the following passage about a campus situation.

Western Civilization Class to Be Required

Starting in the fall semester, Western Civilization 1 will be a required class for all freshmen and sophomores. Juniors and seniors will be exempt from this graduation requirement but may take the course as an elective. The course will focus on the achievements of the West starting with the ancient Greeks and going all the way to modern times. Students will learn important aspects of Western culture through this course. The course will be co-taught by professors in the History, Art History, Literature, and Archaeology departments. For questions about this course, please call 459-9039 extension 42.

📖 Words & Phrases

exempt adj not required to do something
elective n a class not required to graduate

achievement n an accomplishment
aspect n a particular phase or part of something

Comprehension Answer the following questions to make sure you understand the reading.

1 What is the announcement about?

2 Who is exempt from the new requirement?

3 What will the class focus on?

4 Who will teach the class?

5 How can students get answers to their questions?

Listening | Listen to a conversation about the same topic and take notes.

✏ Note Taking

02-23

📖 **Words & Phrases**

look forward to phr to be excited, eager, or happy to do something

courseload n all the classes combined that a student takes in a semester

force v to make a person do something

upsetting adj making a person unhappy or sad

Q The man expresses his opinion of the new required class. State his opinion and explain the reasons he gives for holding that opinion.

Organization | Ask yourself the following questions and organize your ideas.

1 How does the man feel about the new course requirement?

2 How does the woman feel about the new course?

3 What does the man say about his courseload?

4 Why can't the man attend summer school?

5 How do the man's friends feel about the new course?

Responding | Make your response by using the above information.

The announcement notes that

The man is against the decision to

He provides two reasons to

First of all,

The second reason that he discusses

The man points out that

Comparing | Listen to a sample response and compare it with yours.

02-24

Exercise Read, listen, and answer the question following each step.

Reading Read the following passage about a campus situation.

Summer Sports Program

The school will be hosting its first summer sports program in July and August. This will be a summer camp for elementary school students. The students will visit the campus for four weeks and learn to play various sports. Instructors for the camp attendees will be students at the university. This will provide students with work experience and be an exciting summer job. Interested students can apply at the Physical Education Department. All of the profits that are earned from the new program will be spent to improve the school's athletic facilities.

Words & Phrases

host v to hold an event at which people attend
campus n the land and the buildings a school is on

attendee n a person who goes to a certain event
profit n money earned from working

Comprehension Answer the following questions to make sure you understand the reading.

1 What is the announcement about?

2 Who can attend the program?

3 Who will the instructors be?

4 What are two benefits for the instructors?

5 What will the school do with the profits from the event?

Listening Listen to a conversation about the same topic and take notes.

✏ Note Taking

02-25

📖 Words & Phrases

apply v to make a request, such as for a job or school

coach v to instruct and lead players on a team

particularly adj very

get in shape phr to become fit; to become in good condition

Q The woman expresses her opinion of the summer sports program. State her opinion and explain the reasons she gives for holding that opinion.

Organization Ask yourself the following questions and organize your ideas.

1 What is the woman going to do?

2 What does the woman want to do after she graduates?

3 How can the summer sports program help the woman?

4 What will happen if many kids attend the summer sports program?

5 How does the woman want the school to spend the money it earns from the summer sports program?

Responding Make your response by using the above information.

The notice describes

The woman supports

The first reason that she provides

She wants to be

The second reason the woman mentions concerns

She hopes the school

Comparing Listen to a sample response and compare it with yours.

02-26

Unit 28 Student Activities II

Exercise Read, listen, and answer the question following each step.

Reading Read the following passage about a campus situation.

School Clubs to Lose Funding

The school has a large number of approved clubs covering a wide variety of interests. Some have large memberships whereas others have a minimal number of students. The school provides funding for all of these clubs. However, effective immediately, all clubs with a membership of fewer than ten students will lose their funding. They will still be approved clubs and can meet on campus. But they will no longer be able to receive financial support for any activities. This will ensure that the more popular clubs on campus receive the funding they require.

📖 Words & Phrases

membership n the number of people who belong to an organization or group
minimal adj very small

financial adj relating to money
ensure v to guarantee

Comprehension Answer the following questions to make sure you understand the reading.

1 What is the announcement about?

2 What does the school do for approved clubs?

3 Which clubs will lose their funding?

4 What can these clubs still do?

5 What will the change ensure?

Listening Listen to a conversation about the same topic and take notes.

✏ Note Taking

02 - 27

📖 Words & Phrases

defund (v) to remove funding for
tons of (phr) a lot of

lifelong (adj) forever; for as long as a person lives
on the contrary (phr) just the opposite

Q The woman expresses her opinion of the new policy on clubs. State her opinion and explain the reasons she gives for holding that opinion.

Organization Ask yourself the following questions and organize your ideas.

1 What is the woman's opinion about the school's decision?

2 What club does the woman belong to?

3 What has the woman done in the club?

4 How much are the club's supplies?

5 What does the woman say about the club members and the supplies?

Responding Make your response by using the above information.

The notice states that

The woman dislikes

She remarks that

First, she says that

So even though

Next, she comments that

Comparing Listen to a sample response and compare it with yours.

02 - 28

Exercise Read, listen, and answer the question following each step.

Reading   Read the following passage about a campus situation.

Freshmen to Be Allowed in Single Rooms

Starting in the fall semester, incoming freshmen will be permitted to live in single rooms in three of the campus dormitories. This is an outstanding opportunity for freshmen interested in focusing on their studies without having to deal with roommates. Those who are more introverted may wish to take advantage of this opportunity as well. There are 100 single rooms reserved for freshmen. The price of a single room is approximately fifty percent higher than the price of a double room. Single rooms for freshmen are available on a first-come, first-served basis. Contact Kendra Beck at 893-1293 for more information.

📖 Words & Phrases

permit ⓥ to allow; to let someone do something

outstanding adj excellent; very good

introverted adj reserved; quiet

approximately adv around; about

Comprehension   Answer the following questions to make sure you understand the reading.

1 What is the announcement about?

2 Which freshmen might be interested in a single room?

3 How many single rooms for freshmen are there?

4 How much does a single room cost?

5 How are the single rooms available?

Listening Listen to a conversation about the same topic and take notes.

✏ Note Taking

02 - 29

📙 **Words & Phrases**

loneliness [n] a feeling of being all alone

depression [n] extreme sadness

mental [adj] relating to the mind

reconsider [v] to think again about something

Q The man expresses his opinion of the new policy on school dormitories. State his opinion and explain the reasons he gives for holding that opinion.

Organization Ask yourself the following questions and organize your ideas.

1 What is the man's opinion of the school letting freshmen live in single rooms?

2 What does the man say about his roommate during his freshman year?

3 What opportunity will freshmen living in single rooms lose?

4 What do many freshmen suffer from?

5 What does the man say could happen to freshmen without a roommate?

Responding Make your response by using the above information.

The notice states that

It announces that

The man is against

He points out to the woman that

Then, he adds

He also reminds the woman that

Comparing Listen to a sample response and compare it with yours.

02 - 30

Exercise Read, listen, and answer the question following each step.

Reading Read the following passage about a campus situation.

Botanical Garden Off-Limits to Students

Effective immediately, the Harriet Woodrow Botanical Garden is off-limits to all students. The botanical garden is located behind Hamilton Hall and covers approximately ten acres. Many professors conduct important experiments there. Some of these experiments may take three or four years to conclude. Unfortunately, in recent times, some students have damaged these experiments after leaving the paths in the garden. From now on, only authorized individuals may visit the garden. There are several parks and another botanical garden located near the campus. Students are advised to visit them when they wish to spend time in nature.

📖 Words & Phrases

conduct v to lead or direct
conclude v to finish; to end

damage v to cause harm to
authorized adj approved

Comprehension Answer the following questions to make sure you understand the reading.

1 What is the announcement about?

2 What do some professors do at the botanical garden?

3 What did some students do in the botanical garden?

4 Who may now visit the botanical garden?

5 What does the announcement advise students to do?

Listening Listen to a conversation about the same topic and take notes.

 Note Taking

02 - 31

📙 Words & Phrases

mixed feelings `phr` having conflicting emotions about something

ongoing `adj` happening at the present time

ban `v` to prohibit; not to allow something

inconvenient `adj` causing trouble or annoyance

Q The man expresses his opinion of the new policy on the school botanical garden. State his opinion and explain the reasons he gives for holding that opinion.

Organization Ask yourself the following questions and organize your ideas.

1 What is the man's opinion of the announcement?

2 What does the man say he has seen other students do?

3 How does that make the man feel about the announcement?

4 How does the man feel about the botanical garden?

5 What does the man say about the parks located nearby?

Responding Make your response by using the above information.

The announcement informs people that

It points out that

As a result,

The man states that

First, he understands

However, he

Comparing Listen to a sample response and compare it with yours.

02 - 32

PART III

Integrated Speaking Task 2
Reading & Lecture

In this task, you will be presented with a short reading passage about an academic topic. Next, you will listen to a short lecture by a professor about the same topic. Then, you will provide a response based upon what you read and heard. You will be asked to explain how the professor's lecture relates to the reading passage. You will be given 30 seconds to prepare your answer after the question is presented, and you will have 60 seconds to respond to the question.

Integrated Speaking Task 2 **|**
Reading & Lecture

Overview

For this task, you will read a short passage about an academic subject and listen to a professor give a brief excerpt from a lecture on that subject. Then, you will be asked a question based on the passage and the lecture. Although the topics are academic in nature, none of the passages or lectures requires you to have prior knowledge of any academic field in particular. You only need to integrate and convey the key information from both sources.

Sample TOEFL iBT Task

Read a short passage about an academic subject.

Dormancy

Some animals go through periods of their lives where they stop developing for some time. This period of time is called dormancy. When an animal is lying dormant, it has two primary characteristics. First, the animal engages in a very small amount of physical activity. Often, it barely moves, as it tends to stay in one place. In addition, a dormant animal has very little need for nourishment. This is connected to the fact that it is not moving and not being active. For example, when bears hibernate in winter, they are engaging in a period of dormancy.

Listen to a lecture about the same topic.

Script

03-01

M Professor: Now, most of you have probably heard about the lungfish and know that it is a species of fish that is actually capable of breathing air, hence the name lungfish. Well, that capability is integral to the survival of lungfish that live in Africa and South America. Here, let me tell you about what they do.

As you know, various places in Africa and South America have both rainy and dry seasons. During the dry season, the pools of water where the lungfish live often simply evaporate from the heat. So what do lungfish do in order to survive? They dig holes deep in the ground and cover themselves in slime and mud. This helps keep them cool in the heat.

After that, they enter a period of dormancy. This slows down their body functions considerably. For example, their hearts might beat only three times a minute. Incredible, huh? And they might only breathe twice an hour. Simply put, they engage in almost no physical activity. They remain in this state for as long as the dry season lasts. Once the rain starts falling and the water returns, the lungfish can return to their normal existence of living in the water.

 Q The professor describes the behavior of the lungfish. Explain how the lungfish's behavior relates to dormancy.

PREPARATION TIME
00 : 30 : 00

RESPONSE TIME
00 : 60 : 00

03-02

Sample Response

In his lecture, the professor focuses on the lungfish, a species of fish in Africa and South America that can breathe air. When the dry season comes and its pools of water evaporate, the lungfish has to dig a hole deep in the ground to live in. It then covers itself with dirt and slime and promptly enters a period of dormancy. Dormancy is a time when an animal ceases developing and slows down its bodily functions. This is exactly what the lungfish does. It doesn't move, it slows down its heart rate, and it breathes only two times an hour. Because it is lying dormant, it doesn't need any physical nourishment. This allows the lungfish to survive until the rains come back and create more pools of water for it to live in.

Useful Expressions for the Task

1 **Expressions that can be used to tell about the lecture subject**

The lecturer describes   The lecturer describes why some animals look like others.

In the course of the lecture, the professor   In the course of the lecture, the professor talks about an experience he went through.

The subject of the talk is   The subject of the talk is advertising online.

During his lecture, the professor mentions   During his lecture, the professor mentions two reasons why some animals hibernate.

The professor gives a lecture on   The professor gives a lecture on psychological projection.

The professor lectures on   The professor lectures on how animals use camouflage.

The lecture is mostly about   The lecture is mostly about economic recessions.

The topic of the lecture is   The topic of the lecture is different types of dolphins.

In the lecture, the professor focuses on   In the lecture, the professor focuses on why some people prefer advertising on the radio.

The professor's talk mentions   The professor's talk mentions a trip she took to Europe in the past.

2 **Expressions that can be used to tell about the lecture details**

If you look at the details   If you look at the details, you will understand what the professor means.

The professor gives several examples   The professor gives several examples of dangerous animals.

The first was   The first was a problem her friend had.

One thing the professor mentions is   One thing the professor mentions is the importance of marketing.

First, the professor says   First, the professor says that she has direct experience with this.

The reason for this is   The reason for this is that plants require sunlight to survive.

Something else to remember is   Something else to remember is that not everyone agrees.

The first reason is that   The first reason is that not all discoveries happen on purpose.

It is often the case that   It is often the case that patients suffer problems for many years.

The professor states that   The professor states that governments often pass laws against this issue.

3 **Expressions that can be used to refer to and to quote remarks**

The professor says   The professor says, "That's exactly what I mean."

According to the lecturer   According to the lecturer, not all forest animals hibernate.

The professor thinks that   The professor thinks that social responsibility can help the environment.

The lecturer remarks that   The lecturer remarks that the store owner acted improperly.

She mentions   She mentions, "This was very beneficial."

In his opinion   In his opinion, he should have done more to help the injured person.

The professor discusses   The professor discusses a unique type of advertisement.

The reading mentions that   The reading mentions that many stores put profits ahead of customer satisfaction.

In the reading, the author writes   In the reading, the author writes about galaxy formation.

In the professor's words   In the professor's words, "Well-done marketing leads to profits."

4 Expressions that can be used to make relations

This is related to ~ in the reading because   This is related to invasive species in the reading because the animal is not native to that habitat.

This represents the idea of ~ in the reading   This represents the idea of keystone species in the reading.

This relates to the reading passage in that   This relates to the reading passage in that it is an example of impression management.

This is a classic instance of   This is a classic instance of greenwashing.

The professor's example is connected to the reading in that   The professor's example is connected to the reading in that no division of labor was practiced.

The reading passage describes this instance as   The reading passage describes this instance as teaser advertising.

An example of this is found in the reading, which mentions   An example of this is found in the reading, which mentions wind erosion.

The relation between the reading and the lecture is   The relation between the reading and the lecture is that both are about venom.

This fact is strongly related to   This fact is strongly related to coloration warning.

The connection the professor makes to the reading is   The connection the professor makes to the reading is that her company failed to stress profits.

5 Expressions that can be used to tell about the reading passage

According to the reading   According to the reading, animal populations act in a cyclical manner.

The reading states that   The reading states that everyone has different responsibilities.

In the reading   In the reading, marketing methods are covered.

It is considered a fact that   It is considered a fact that the Industrial Revolution happened in the 1700s.

The reading covers   The reading covers aquatic habitats.

The reading passage describes   The reading passages describes why some animals migrate.

As described in the reading   As described in the reading, some people experience buyer's remorse.

The topic covered in the reading is   The topic covered in the reading is the spectrum of light.

This concept is covered in the reading, which states   This concept is covered in the reading, which states how caves are formed.

The reading focuses on   The reading focuses on problems with excessive noise.

6 Expressions that can be used to connect the lecture examples to one another

Both instances   Both instances refer to animals living in tundra.

In both cases   In both cases, the businesses acted as well as possible.

These are two methods   These are two methods of recovering from injuries.

The two examples both   The two examples both show how advertising can be effective.

The lecturer's two examples   The lecturer's two examples refer to Occam's razor.

The professor's two instances   The professor's two instances happened just as described in the reading passage.

Both of the professor's examples   Both of the professor's examples relate to the reading passage.

The two examples mentioned both   The two examples mentioned both prove the professor's point.

This shows how the two instances   This shows how the two instances are similar.

These are both examples of   These are both examples of animal adaptations.

Exercise Read, listen, and answer the question following each step.

Reading Read the following passage about an academic subject.

Keystone Species

Some animals have disproportionate, yet positive, effects upon their environments for a number of reasons. These animals are referred to by scientists as keystone species. They receive this moniker because, just like the keystone is the crucial stone in an arch that keeps it from falling, without the presence of a keystone species, a particular habitat would be changed considerably, often for the worse. Animals can be keystone species for many reasons. The most prominent keystone species are predators, but other animals can positively change their habitats in other ways. For example, some change the environment or spread nutrients through their habitats.

📖 Words & Phrases

disproportionate **adj** unequal; larger than normal
moniker **n** a name

prominent **adj** famous; well-known
spread **v** to pass out; to strew

Comprehension Answer the following questions to make sure you understand the reading.

1 What is a keystone species?

2 What is the importance of the word "keystone"?

3 What would happen to a habitat without the presence of a keystone species?

4 What is the main way in which animals serve as keystone species?

5 What are some other ways in which animals can be keystone species?

Listen to a lecture about the same topic and take notes.

✏ Note Taking

03 - 03

📖 Words & Phrases

environment [n] a specific area or region
prodigious [adj] enormous; very large

vegetation [n] plant life; any kind of plants, but primarily small bushes and grasses
defecate [v] to release solid waste from one's body

Q The professor describes the importance of elephants to their habitats. Explain how the elephant's importance relates to keystone species.

Organization Ask yourself the following questions and organize your ideas.

1 What is the keystone species in Africa?

2 What is the importance of elephants eating so much vegetation daily?

3 What is the importance of elephants defecating in various places?

4 How do keystone species relate to elephants?

Responding Make your response by using the above information.

The professor begins by telling

According to the lecturer,

In the reading,

This represents the idea of

If you look at the details,

Something else to remember is

Comparing Listen to a sample response and compare it with yours.

03 - 04

Exercise Read, listen, and answer the question following each step.

Reading Read the following passage about an academic subject.

Contingency Planning

Unexpected events sometimes happen. They can be natural disasters, such as earthquakes, hurricanes, and fires. They can also be caused by people. For instance, wars, economic problems, and riots can occur at times. These events can all have tremendous effects on businesses. For that reason, many businesses engage in contingency planning. This involves people at the business thinking about potential problems that could affect them. Then, they develop a plan describing how they will react to each problem. By preparing for various contingencies, businesses can be prepared when disaster hits, so they will suffer less harm from various events.

📖 Words & Phrases

unexpected adj not planned or foreseen

tremendous adj being of extreme size, amount, power, etc.

engage in phr to do; to take part in

contingency n an event that may occur but also may not

Comprehension Answer the following questions to make sure you understand the reading.

1 What are some unexpected natural disasters?

2 What are some unexpected events caused by people?

3 Why do many businesses engage in contingency planning?

4 What is contingency planning?

5 What is a result of contingency planning?

Listening Listen to a lecture about the same topic and take notes.

> ✎ Note Taking
>
>
> 03 - 05

📖 **Words & Phrases**

blackout 🅝 a time when the electricity goes out
spoil 🅥 to rot; for food to go bad

financial 🅐🅳🅹 relating to money
generator 🅝 a machine that can produce electricity

Q The professor describes an incident involving his brother. Explain how it relates to contingency planning.

Organization Ask yourself the following questions and organize your ideas.

1   What happened during the summer?

2   What can happen to grocery stores when the power goes out?

3   What was the professor's brother's contingency plan?

4   What was the result of the contingency plan?

Responding Make your response by using the above information.

The professor mentions

He adds that

The professor states

This meant that

Comparing Listen to a sample response and compare it with yours.

03 - 06

Exercise Read, listen, and answer the question following each step.

Reading Read the following passage about an academic subject.

Impression Management

People are often concerned with what others think of them. In many cases, both consciously and unconsciously, they employ impression management to create positive images of themselves. There are many ways to accomplish this, but the most common is to control the flow of information a person reveals about oneself. When people engage in impression management, they typically do not show any of their unflattering or negative characteristics. While this does not necessarily present a person in a completely honest light, it is commonly used, especially when meeting someone for the first time or at an important event.

📖 Words & Phrases

be concerned with `phr` to care about; to be interested in

employ `v` to use

flow `n` a passage

light `n` an appearance

Comprehension Answer the following questions to make sure you understand the reading.

1   In what ways do people use impression management?

2   Why do people use impression management?

3   What is the most common way people use impression management?

4   What does a person not reveal about himself when using impression management?

5   When do people most often use impression management?

Listening | Listen to a lecture about the same topic and take notes.

✏ Note Taking

03 - 07

📖 Words & Phrases

consciously adv on purpose; deliberately
surely adv definitely; certainly

dress the part phr to wear the appropriate clothes for the appropriate situation
organize v to straighten up; to arrange

Q The professor describes two instances in which people must be conscious of how they act. Explain how these instances relate to impression management.

Organization | Ask yourself the following questions and organize your ideas.

1 What kind of role does impression management play for people?

2 When do people use impression management?

3 Why do the students need to wear formal clothes for their presentations?

4 What was the importance of the professor cleaning her office?

Responding | Make your response by using the above information.

In the course of the lecture,

She first mentions

She says

The two examples both

Comparing | Listen to a sample response and compare it with yours.

03 - 08

Exercise Read, listen, and answer the question following each step.

Reading Read the following passage about an academic subject.

Population Growth

In order to increase in numbers, a species must engage in population growth. This is the rate at which a species, be it human or other, increases in numbers. As a general rule, all species increase at consistent rates. However, there are always factors, such as disease, drought, famine, and predators, which help limit a species' population growth. Should a species' population increase or decrease too rapidly, this often has an effect on other species living in the same environment. These effects can be either positive or negative depending upon the species that is involved.

Words & Phrases

engage in phr to practice; to take part in
consistent adj regular; reliable

drought n a long period of time with no rain
famine n a long period of time with no food

Comprehension Answer the following questions to make sure you understand the reading.

1 How can species become more numerous?

2 What is population growth?

3 What factors can cause a species to grow at a slower rate?

4 What happens if a species' population grows or declines too rapidly?

5 What can be the results of a rapid increase or decline in population?

Listening | Listen to a lecture about the same topic and take notes.

✎ Note Taking

03 - 09

📕 Words & Phrases

tremendous adj very large; enormous

take over phr to conquer; to capture

chop v to cut down

rage out of control phr to be unmanageable

Q The professor describes how pine trees and deer can increase their numbers at very high rates. Explain how this is related to population growth.

Organization | Ask yourself the following questions and organize your ideas.

1 What are the effects of rapid rates of increase of various species?

2 What does the professor say about the rate of increase of pine trees?

3 What helps limit the population growth of pine trees?

4 What does the professor say about the rate of increase of deer?

5 What helps limit the population growth of deer?

Responding | Make your response by using the above information.

During his lecture, the professor mentions

The professor states that

The professor's example is connected to the reading in that

The reading states that

The two examples mentioned both

Comparing | Listen to a sample response and compare it with yours.

03 - 10

Exercise Read, listen, and answer the question following each step.

Reading Read the following passage about an academic subject.

Occam's Razor

    William of Occam was a Franciscan monk who lived in the thirteenth and fourteenth centuries. While he was involved in various papal controversies then, he is remembered nowadays for the principle known as Occam's razor. While William himself did not create it, his name has come to be associated with it due to his using it. Occam's razor proposes that when a person is faced with a problem, the person should eliminate everything unnecessary to solve it, thereby "shaving" any unneeded factors. In simplest terms, Occam's razor can be shortened to state that the simplest solution is often the best.

📖 **Words & Phrases**

monk n a holy man in Christianity who lives at a monastery
papal adj relating to the pope

eliminate v to erase; to discount; to do away with
shave v to reduce; to cut

Comprehension Answer the following questions to make sure you understand the reading.

1 Who was William of Occam?

2 Why do people remember William of Occam?

3 Why do people associate William of Occam with Occam's razor?

4 What is Occam's razor?

5 What is the easiest way to state Occam's razor?

Listen to a lecture about the same topic and take notes.

📝 Note Taking

03 - 11

📖 **Words & Phrases**

extinguish v to put out, usually a fire

conclusion n a theory; an idea arrived at after considered thought

run down v to describe; to detail

logical adj reasonable; rational

 The professor describes a fire and two possible conclusions concerning how it started. Describe how Occam's razor is related to these conclusions.

Organization Ask yourself the following questions and organize your ideas.

1 What is the situation that the professor describes?

2 What is the first conclusion the professor arrives at as to how the fire started?

3 What variables does the professor describe concerning the first conclusion?

4 What is the second conclusion the professor arrives at as to how the fire started?

5 Which conclusion does the professor believe is more logical?

Responding Make your response by using the above information.

The professor tells the class about

First, the professor says

The second is that

The professor's example is connected to the reading in that

The reading states that

This shows how the two instances

Comparing Listen to a sample response and compare it with yours.

03 - 12

Exercise Read, listen, and answer the question following each step.

Reading Read the following passage about an academic subject.

Diffusion of Responsibility

Most people have a number of different responsibilities to their families, employers, and other organizations. However, in some cases, particularly ones involving large groups of people, responsibility is not assigned to one particular person. In these situations, this leads to a phenomenon known as diffusion of responsibility. In most cases, the diffusion of responsibility leads to people having a lessened sense of personal responsibility. This is used by some people to excuse themselves from doing tasks that they do not wish to do or to exonerate themselves for having participated in activities that were illegal, improper, or embarrassing.

📖 Words & Phrases

be assigned to phr to be given to someone
phenomenon n an event; an occurrence

diffusion n dispersal; the spreading out of something
lessened adj decreased; smaller

Comprehension Answer the following questions to make sure you understand the reading.

1 To whom or what do people have responsibilities?

2 What is common about responsibilities when there are large groups of people?

3 What is a result of the diffusion of responsibility?

4 How do people use the diffusion of responsibility?

5 In which kinds of situations might people rely upon the diffusion of responsibility?

Listen to a lecture about the same topic and take notes.

🖋 Note Taking

03-13

📖 Words & Phrases

commute (v) to travel from home to work and back
render (v) to provide; to engage in

motorist (n) a person who is driving a vehicle like a car, truck, or motorcycle
likelihood (n) a probability; a chance

Q The author of the passage describes people's reactions to two different traffic accidents. Describe how these two reactions relate to the diffusion of responsibility.

Organization Ask yourself the following questions and organize your ideas.

1 What are the times of the two accidents the professor describes?

2 According to statistics, in which accident is an injured person likely to receive assistance?

3 Why do many people not help those involved in the morning accident?

4 Why is a passing motorist more likely to help in the night accident?

Responding Make your response by using the above information.

The subject of the talk is

According to the professor's statistics,

In the morning accident,

But at night,

This fact is strongly related to

Comparing Listen to a sample response and compare it with yours.

03-14

Exercise Read, listen, and answer the question following each step.

Reading Read the following passage about an academic subject.

Vegetative Propagation

Most plants reproduce through the seeds that they produce. However, there are other ways that new plants can grow. These forms of asexual reproduction are called vegetative propagation. Sometimes a part of a plant, such as a stem or a leaf, may be cut from the parent plant and put in the ground. It will then develop roots and grow into a new plant. In other instances, such as with strawberries, runners develop from stems and become individual plants. Some plants, such as onions and garlic, grow bulbs underground that can develop into mature plants.

📖 Words & Phrases

reproduce 🅥 to make something new
stem 🅝 the main branch or trunk of a plant
runner 🅝 a long horizontal stem coming from the lower part of a plant

bulb 🅝 a part of a plant that develops underground and is capable of creating a new plant

Comprehension Answer the following questions to make sure you understand the reading.

1 How do plants usually reproduce?

2 What is another name for asexual reproduction?

3 What is the first way that plants may reproduce through vegetative propagation?

4 How can strawberries reproduce?

5 How can onions and garlic reproduce?

Listening Listen to a lecture about the same topic and take notes.

✏ Note Taking

03 - 15

📖 **Words & Phrases**

acquire v to get
shoot n the immature stem of a plant
surely adv definitely; positively

transplant v to dig up a plant and to move it to another location

Q The professor describes two different ways that raspberry plants reproduce. Describe how these two ways relate to vegetative propagation.

Organization Ask yourself the following questions and organize your ideas.

1 What does the professor say about raspberry reproduction?

2 What is a sucker?

3 What is the raspberry reproduction method that involves suckers?

4 What is the second way that raspberries can reproduce?

5 What can a person do with the brand-new raspberry plant?

Responding Make your response by using the above information.

The professor tells the class that

The first method is

The second method is

This refers to

Comparing Listen to a sample response and compare it with yours.

03 - 16

Exercise Read, listen, and answer the question following each step.

Reading Read the following passage about an academic subject.

Market Share

An industry may have a large number of companies that work in it. Each company produces a certain percentage of sales in that industry. The percentage of the whole that one company produces is called its market share. Market share can be used to determine the size of a business. In addition, a large market share indicates that a company is dominant in its industry. As a general rule, companies look to increase their market share in their industry to make gains over their competition. This, in turn, helps the companies grow larger and increase their revenues.

📖 Words & Phrases

indicate v to show; to be a sign of
dominant adj powerful; successful
competition n the act of striving for a goal or objective between two or more people or groups

revenue n the total amount of income produced from something

Comprehension Answer the following questions to make sure you understand the reading.

1 What is market share?

2 How can market share be used?

3 What does a large market share indicate about a company?

4 What do companies try to do with their market share?

5 How does this help companies?

Note Taking

03 - 17

📖 **Words & Phrases**

firm 🅝 a business; a company

high-end 🄰🄳🄹 upscale; superior in quality

particular 🄰🄳🄹 relating to one single thing

conglomerate 🅝 a diverse corporation

Q The professor describes her experience owning a firm. Explain how it is related to market share.

Organization Ask yourself the following questions and organize your ideas.

1 What kind of company did the professor use to own?

2 How were the company's sales?

3 Why was the professor's company not very influential?

4 What happened to the professor's company?

Responding Make your response by using the above information.

The professor starts her lecture by telling

The professor notes that

In fact,

As a result,

The professor wound up

This relates to

Comparing Listen to a sample response and compare it with yours.

03 - 18

Exercise Read, listen, and answer the question following each step.

Reading Read the following passage about an academic subject.

Desertification

Desertification refers to the decline in quality of fertile land. Land that could once sustain plants and crops becomes dried out. As a result, it transforms into infertile desert. This can happen for a number of reasons. The primary natural cause is an extended period of drought. There are also human causes. Excessive industrialization can destroy the quality of land. So too can extensive farming and deforestation, which is the removal of trees from an area. Finally, humans can also deplete groundwater supplies in an area, which then causes it to become desert.

📖 **Words & Phrases**

sustain v to support

infertile adj not productive; unable to reproduce anything

drought n a period of time with little or no precipitation

deplete v to use up

Comprehension Answer the following questions to make sure you understand the reading.

1 What is desertification?

2 What happens when land becomes dried out?

3 What is the main cause of desertification?

4 What is the first human cause of desertification?

5 What are some other human causes of desertification?

Listen to a lecture about the same topic and take notes.

✎ Note Taking

03 - 19

📖 **Words & Phrases**

border 🄝 a boundary; a line between two countries, states, etc.

divert 🅅 to change from one course to another

irrigate 🅅 to provide water to grow crops

livelihood 🄝 a means of support

Q The professor describes the shrinking of the Aral Sea. Explain how it relates to desertification.

Organization　Ask yourself the following questions and organize your ideas.

1 Where is the Aral Sea?

2 What made less water flow into the Aral Sea?

3 What happened to the Aral Sea starting around 1960?

4 What is the area around the Aral Sea like today?

Responding　Make your response by using the above information.

The professor lectures to the class about

The professor states that

Starting around

In addition,

This refers to the

One reason for this is

Comparing　Listen to a sample response and compare it with yours.

03 - 20

Exercise Read, listen, and answer the question following each step.

Reading Read the following passage about an academic subject.

Internal Competition

Many businesses promote competition between their employees. They believe it can result in employees being more efficient and productive. They may encourage internal competition for their workers to receive awards, bonuses, and promotions. Some large companies may even have two or more teams working on the same project in an attempt to get each team to work harder and faster. However, this method is not always effective. Some employees may suffer from anxiety and fear for their jobs due to internal competition. And others even engage in improper or illegal behavior to compete against their colleagues.

📖 Words & Phrases

promotion 🄝 the act of being raised to a higher rank or position

suffer 🅥 to endure; to undergo; to experience, often in a bad way

anxiety 🄝 nervousness; a feeling of apprehension

illegal adj against the law

Comprehension Answer the following questions to make sure you understand the reading.

1 Why do businesses promote competition between employees?

2 What can employees receive as a result of competition against others?

3 What do some large companies do?

4 What can some employees suffer from as a result of internal competition?

5 What kinds of behavior can some employees engage in because of internal competition?

Listening   Listen to a lecture about the same topic and take notes.

📙 Words & Phrases

athlete [n] a person who plays sports, often well

get fired [phr] to be dismissed from a job

unauthorized [adj] without permission

unrequested [adj] not asked for

 Q   The professor discusses an event a local bank. Explain how it relates to internal competition.

Organization   Ask yourself the following questions and organize your ideas.

1 What did the manager at the bank do?

2 What actions were employees encouraged to do?

3 What did some employees do?

4 What were the results of the employees' actions?

Responding   Make your response by using the above information.

The professor talks to the class about

She states that

This happens when

Unfortunately,

What happened is that

As a result,

Comparing   Listen to a sample response and compare it with yours.

03 - 22

Exercise Read, listen, and answer the question following each step.

Reading Read the following passage about an academic subject.

The End-of-History Illusion

Many people have certain beliefs about their past, present, and future lives. For instance, a large number of people think that their past selves and their present selves are very different. In effect, these people claim that they have changed a great deal over the years. However, these same people often believe that their current selves will not change in the future. When asked about how they will change in the future, most people state that they will not change at all or that they will change very little. This is known as the end-of-history illusion.

📖 **Words & Phrases**

belief **n** something a person thinks or beliefs   **current** **adj** present
a great deal **phr** very much   **illusion** **n** something that is misleading in how it looks

Comprehension Answer the following questions to make sure you understand the reading.

1 What do people think about their past and present selves?

2 What do these people claim about themselves?

3 What do these same people believe about their futures?

4 What can be inferred about these people?

5 What is this phenomenon known as?

Listen to a lecture about the same topic and take notes.

✏ Note Taking

03 - 23

📖 **Words & Phrases**

range v to be assigned to a certain category

taste n an individual preference

version n a form or type of an original

tremendous adj great; very large

Q The professor discusses an experiment he conducted. Explain how it relates to the end-of-history illusion.

Organization Ask yourself the following questions and organize your ideas.

1 What did the professor do?

2 What did the professor ask the people about?

3 How did the people respond with regard to the past and the present?

4 How did the people respond with regard to the present and the future?

Responding Make your response by using the above information.

The professor discusses

He learned that

In fact, he discovered

Most of the respondents thought

This is an example of

However,

Comparing Listen to a sample response and compare it with yours.

03 - 24

Exercise Read, listen, and answer the question following each step.

Reading Read the following passage about an academic subject.

Companion Planting

Some farmers and gardeners engage in the practice of companion planting. This involves planting two or three plants close to one another—sometimes even together—in order to obtain various benefits. Among these advantages are reducing the number of pests that harm the plants and attracting beneficial insects. In other cases, companion planting is used to decrease the number of weeds that grow and to boost the growth of the plants. This practice can also be done in order to utilize all of the space available, especially for gardens that are somewhat limited in size.

📙 Words & Phrases

engage in phr to take part in; to do
obtain v to acquire; to receive

pest n an animal that causes harm or annoyance
beneficial adj helpful

Comprehension Answer the following questions to make sure you understand the reading.

1 Who engages in companion planting?

2 What is companion planting?

3 What are two advantages of companion planting?

4 What are some other advantages of companion planting?

5 Why do some people use companion planting?

✎ Note Taking

03 - 25

📖 Words & Phrases

nutritious adj healthy; good for one's body
annually adv every year

wilt v to become limp
fertilizer n something that adds nutrients to the soil

The professor discusses gardening. Explain how it relates to companion planting.

Organization Ask yourself the following questions and organize your ideas.

1 What is the professor's hobby?

2 Why does the professor plant corn and lettuce together?

3 Why does the professor plant corn and peas together?

4 Why does the professor plant tomatoes and parsley together?

Responding Make your response by using the above information.

The professor's lecture is about

She mentions that

Next, she states that

According to the professor,

The professor therefore

The professor's actions are examples of

Comparing Listen to a sample response and compare it with yours.

03 - 26

Exercise Read, listen, and answer the question following each step.

Reading Read the following passage about an academic subject.

Social Facilitation in Animals

Sometimes animals do a certain type of behavior. This could be grooming, hunting, foraging, or various other activites. In some instances, other animals of the same species may observe the first animal as it does that activity. The observers then, at times, may begin to engage in the same behavior, or the first animal may increase the intensity of the action that it is doing. This is referred to as social facilitation in animals. It has been observed and studied by researchers for the past several decades.

📖 Words & Phrases

foraging 🄝 the act of searching for food
observe 🅥 to watch, often closely

intensity 🄝 the state of doing an activity with great concentration, energy, or focus
facilitation 🄝 the act of helping bring something about

Comprehension Answer the following questions to make sure you understand the reading.

1 What are some types of behavior animals may do?

2 What may other animals do when one animal is doing a certain activity?

3 What might the observers do next?

4 What might the first animal do when it is being observed?

5 For how long have researchers observed this behavior in animals?

Listening | Listen to a lecture about the same topic and take notes.

✏ Note Taking

03 - 27

📖 **Words & Phrases**

detrimental (adj) harmful

howl (v) to make a long, loud sound such as a dog or wolf makes

cease (v) to stop

manipulate (v) to treat or move with the hands

Q The professor discusses dogs and chimpanzees. Explain how their actions relate to social facilitation in animals.

Organization | Ask yourself the following questions and organize your ideas.

1 According to the professor, what kinds of effects can social facilitation in animals have?

2 What does the professor say that his dogs sometimes do?

3 What might one chimp start to do for another?

4 What happens next?

Responding | Make your response by using the above information.

The professor says that

The first example concerns

This is an example of how

However, he then provides

This happens when

The result may be

Comparing | Listen to a sample response and compare it with yours.

03 - 28

Exercise Read, listen, and answer the question following each step.

Reading Read the following passage about an academic subject.

Risk Overestimation

When people consider various activities, they may think about how dangerous certain ones are. They may do this for strenuous activities such as scuba diving and mountain climbing as well as everyday activities such as climbing stairs and riding in a car. While all of these activities could involve some danger, the chances of something bad happening are small. Nevertheless, people frequently overestimate the amount of risk involved in these activities. This belief that certain activities are too risky can have negative effects, including anxiety and people being unwilling to do certain actions.

📖 Words & Phrases

strenuous adj energetic; requiring a great amount of energy

involve v to include

overestimate v to put a value or importance on something that is too high

risky adj dangerous

Comprehension Answer the following questions to make sure you understand the reading.

1 What do people think about when considering various activities?

2 What examples of activities are provided?

3 What is true about all of the example activities?

4 What do people often overestimate?

5 What are some negative effects of risk overestimation?

Listening   Listen to a lecture about the same topic and take notes.

  🖉 Note Taking

03 - 29

📖 **Words & Phrases**

eagerly adv enthusiastically

effective adj working well

minor adj small; not large

frighten v to scare; to make afraid

Q   The professor discusses cycling. Explain how it relates to risk overestimation.

Organization   Ask yourself the following questions and organize your ideas.

1   What did the city do for cyclists in the past?

2   What was the result of those actions?

3   What happened a few months later?

4   What did people do after the accidents happened?

Responding   Make your response by using the above information.

The professor lectures about

She points out that

This resulted in

Even though

This is an example of

This happens when

Comparing   Listen to a sample response and compare it with yours.

03 - 30

Exercise Read, listen, and answer the question following each step.

Reading Read the following passage about an academic subject.

Stopover Habitats

Each year, numerous bird species migrate to warmer climates in fall and winter. The following spring, they return to their homes when the weather there becomes warmer. Some of these birds have migrations that require traveling hundreds or even thousands of kilometers. These birds cannot make the journey nonstop. They must therefore utilize stopover habitats, which are places on their journeys where they can find food, shelter, and safety from predators. Birds may remain at stopover habitats for a few hours or even several days. Their presence lets birds reach their destinations safely.

Words & Phrases

nonstop adj without stopping or taking a break
utilize v to use

shelter n a place that offers protection from the weather
safely adv without being harmed

Comprehension Answer the following questions to make sure you understand the reading.

1 How do some birds migrate?

2 How far do some birds migrate?

3 Why do birds use stopover habitats?

4 What can birds find at stopover habitats?

5 How long do birds stay at stopover habitats?

Listen to a lecture about the same topic and take notes.

✏ Note Taking

03 - 31

📖 Words & Phrases

manage [v] to be able to do something

journey [n] a long and often difficult trip

obviously [adv] of course; as is evident

grove [n] a small group of trees growing together

Q The professor discusses the Canadian warbler. Explain how it relates to stopover habitats.

Organization Ask yourself the following questions and organize your ideas.

1 Where does the Canadian warbler fly each fall?

2 What is true about the migration?

3 What do the birds do when there is a storm during their migration?

4 What can the birds do in the places where they land?

Responding Make your response by using the above information.

The professor discusses

She remarks that

The birds cannot

There, they can find

They also

These are defined as

Comparing Listen to a sample response and compare it with yours.

03 - 32

PART IV

Integrated Speaking Task 3
Lecture

In this task, you will be presented with a short lecture about an academic topic. Typically, the professor will provide two examples of the topic being discussed. Then, you will provide a response based upon what you heard. You will be asked to discuss the examples provided in the professor's lecture. You will be given 20 seconds to prepare your answer after the question is presented, and you will have 60 seconds to respond to the question.

Integrated Speaking Task 3 |
Lecture

Overview

For this task, you will first listen to a professor present a brief lecture on an academic subject, and then you will be asked a question about what you have heard. The topics will vary but will not require you to have any prior knowledge of any field in particular. The professor will typically introduce a concept and go on to discuss examples about it. You will be asked to explain the main concept by using the given examples in the lecture.

Sample TOEFL iBT Task

Listen to a lecture about an academic subject.

Script

04-01

M Professor: Now, I'd like to talk about how to improve your acting, especially since you're going to be putting on a performance soon in which you'll need good acting to get a, well, a good grade. So when you're acting, you need to become that character. It's, uh, imperative for you to think and feel just like that character would. These acts can make your character genuine and believable.

For example, say you're going to play the title role of Shakespeare's play *Henry VIII*. Well, if you're going to be a king, then you'll have to act like one. You have to carry yourself like one. You think, no, you know that you're better than the rest of the people on stage. Henry was a proud man convinced that his actions were right. You actually need to feel that kind of confidence in order to be a convincing king. If you can't do that, then you're not going to be believable. The audience will recognize that, and your performance—and the overall play—will suffer.

Let me give you another example. Imagine you're going to play the role of Hamlet from Shakespeare's masterpiece. Well, it's a complicated role since, remember, Hamlet keeps seeing the ghost of his murdered father, and he is pretending to be insane. So you've got to feel like Hamlet. How are you going to act? You've got to appear to be insane during some scenes yet appear sane in others. You've simply got to become Hamlet in this role. Feel what he feels. Think what he thinks. Become him, and you'll have mastered the role and become a real actor.

Using points and examples from the lecture, explain what actors must do to make their acting more believable.

PREPARATION TIME
00 : 20 : 00

RESPONSE TIME
00 : 60 : 00

Sample Response

04-02

The professor provides a couple of examples of how an actor can become more convincing to the audience when playing various roles. He uses two different examples from Shakespeare in his lecture. First, he discusses Henry VIII from the play with the same name. He declares that an actor must act completely like a king in order to get that role right. Since Henry was very proud and confident, an actor must convey those same feelings in order to be a convincing king. The next example the professor uses is the role of Hamlet. He mentions that Hamlet is a complicated role since he is seeing ghosts and pretending to be insane. The professor insists that the actor must actually become Hamlet by feeling the things he feels and thinking the thoughts he thinks.

Useful Expressions for the Task

1 Expressions that can be used to tell about the subject

The professor discusses   The professor discusses why plants need light to grow.

The lecturer talks about   The lecturer talks about animals that live in caves.

The entire lecture covers   The entire lecture covers sedimentary rocks.

The topic of the lecture is   The topic of the lecture is supervolcanoes.

The majority of the talk is about   The majority of the talk is about species extinction.

The professor tells her students about   The professor tells her students about Neanderthals.

The professor's lecture mentions   The professor's lecture mentions diamond formation.

He focuses on   He focuses on online marking techniques.

The main idea is   The main idea is that dinosaurs might have been warm blooded.

The professor looks into   The professor looks into waterfall formation.

2 Expressions that can be used to tell about the first example

The first example is   The first example is a company that the professor once owned.

He first cites   He first cites an expert in economics.

First, the lecturer   First, the lecturer says that birds lay eggs in nests.

In her first example, she mentions   In her first example, she mentions the California Gold Rush.

The first is that   The first is that shipbuilding techniques improved.

First, he discusses   First, he discusses organic fertilizers.

First of all, he covers   First of all, he covers irrigation methods in ancient Rome.

She first discusses   She first discusses a problem her daughter had.

The first one he mentions is   The first one he mentions is Captain Cook.

His first explanation is   His first explanation is that camels can store water in their bodies.

3 Expressions that can be used to tell about the second example

The second example is about   The second example is about surveillance techniques.

Next, the professor mentions   Next, the professor mentions a development in motion picture cameras.

On the other hand   On the other hand, not all plants require sunlight.

The lecturer then discusses   The lecturer then discusses the formation of crystals.

Another thing she covers is   Another thing she covers is volcanic eruptions.

The second example cited is   The second example cited is product placement.

After that, the professor talks about   After that, the professor talks about how many eggs small birds lay.

The second theory is that   The second theory is that squirrels bury seeds to prevent others from stealing them.

The professor's next point is   The professor's next point is that forest fires can be beneficial.

The second explanation deals with   The second explanation deals with deep-sea exploration.

4 Expressions that can be used to tell about relations

Another similarity is   Another similarity is how the two animals hunt.

Something else similar is   Something else similar is that they have the same colors.

On the same topic   On the same topic, chestnut trees also suffered harm from disease.

This is connected to   This is connected to viral marketing.

You can see the relationship between   You can see the relationship between the two types of plants.

The two are connected by   The two are connected by their long growing seasons.

They are related because   They are related because they were both economic bubbles.

By the same token   By the same token, doctors can use the new technology in a unique way.

Another thing to consider is   Another thing to consider is how coal is mined these days.

This is just like   This is just like the earthquake that happened two hundred years ago.

5 Expressions that can be used to tell details

He declares that   He declares that polar bears are apex predators.

What happens is   What happens is that plants use their roots to extract nutrients.

However, she   However, she disagrees with this point.

As a matter of fact   As a matter of fact, whales can migrate thousands of kilometers.

The professor points out that   The professor points out that ice erosion can happen quickly.

The reason is that   The reason is that El Nino does not happen every year.

Once this happens   Once this happens, a cave begins to form.

Because of this   Because of this, print ads are still of great use.

He brings up the point that   He brings up the point that fewer people watch television nowadays.

This leads to   This leads to problems with the cleanliness of water.

Exercise Listen to a lecture and answer the question following each step.

Listening Listen to a lecture and take notes.

 Note Taking

04 - 03

📖 **Words & Phrases**

literary (adj) of or relating to literature

convention (n) a technique, practice, or device

get one's point across (phr) to explain what one means

compliment (n) praise for another

Q Using points and examples from the lecture, explain two different literary conventions and how people use them.

Organization Ask yourself the following questions and organize your ideas.

1 What is the lecture about?

2 What is exaggeration?

3 Why do people use exaggeration?

4 What is understatement?

5 Why do people use understatement?

Responding Make your response by using the organized ideas.

During the lecture,

These two conventions are

First,

On the other hand,

Comparing Listen to a sample response and compare it with yours.

04 - 04

Exercise Listen to a lecture and answer the question following each step.

Listening Listen to a lecture and take notes.

✎ Note Taking

04 - 05

📖 **Words & Phrases**

strive v to try very hard; to attempt

invasive adj encroaching into another's territory

extensive adj widespread; far-reaching

get exposed to phr to be subjected to

Q Using points and examples from the lecture, explain the two ways in which the acacia can harm other trees and plants in forests which it invades.

Organization Ask yourself the following questions and organize your ideas.

1 What is the topic of the professor's lecture?

2 What is the first physical characteristic of acacias that the professor mentions?

3 How does this characteristic affect other plant life in the forest?

4 What is the second physical characteristic of acacias that the professor mentions?

5 In what way does the acacia's height affect other plant life near it?

Responding Make your response by using the organized ideas.

The professor's lecture mentions that

To begin with,

In fact,

Because of this,

Comparing Listen to a sample response and compare it with yours.

04 - 06

Exercise Listen to a lecture and answer the question following each step.

Listening Listen to a lecture and take notes.

 Note Taking

04 - 07

📖 **Words & Phrases**

entice v to persuade; to lure
consider v to think about; to ponder

prospect n a possibility; a chance; an opportunity
enamored adj enthusiastic; interested; captivated

Q Using points and examples from the lecture, explain how giving rewards to children can have either a positive or a negative effect.

Organization Ask yourself the following questions and organize your ideas.

1 What is the main point of the professor's lecture?

2 What reward do the parents offer their daughter to clean her room?

3 How does the daughter react to her parents' offer of a reward?

4 What reward do the parents of the piano-playing girl give her?

5 What is the result of the rewards given to the piano-playing girl?

Responding Make your response by using the organized ideas.

The professor says that

In his first example,

The second example is about

This is an example of

Comparing Listen to a sample response and compare it with yours.

04 - 08

Exercise Listen to a lecture and answer the question following each step.

Listening Listen to a lecture and take notes.

✎ Note Taking

04 - 09

📖 **Words & Phrases**

pinpoint v to locate or point out with extreme accuracy
celestial adj from outer space

vulnerable adj defenseless
proliferation n an abundance; an increase

Q Using points and examples from the lecture, explain the two different theories on why the dinosaurs became extinct.

Organization Ask yourself the following questions and organize your ideas.

1 What is the topic of the professor's lecture?

2 According to the professor, what happened when a meteor or asteroid struck the Earth?

3 Why do people believe that this strike caused the dinosaurs to become extinct?

4 What do scientists say were the results of the eruption of a supervolcano?

5 How did the greenhouse effect make the dinosaurs extinct?

Responding Make your response by using the organized ideas.

The professor states that dinosaurs once

The first is that

The second theory is that

So

Comparing Listen to a sample response and compare it with yours.

04 - 10

Exercise Listen to a lecture and answer the question following each step.

Listening Listen to a lecture and take notes.

✏ Note Taking

04 - 11

📖 **Words & Phrases**

contrary to common belief `phr` opposite to what most people think

be subjected to `phr` to undergo; to suffer

rejuvenate `v` to make stronger; to enliven

crowd out `v` to push out; to force out

Q Using points and examples from the lecture, explain two ways in which forest fires can be beneficial to the forests that they burn.

Organization Ask yourself the following questions and organize your ideas.

1 What is the main point of the professor's lecture?

2 What does the professor say about pine cones?

3 How does fire help some trees become more plentiful?

4 What does the professor say about forest fires and their burning down of trees and bushes?

5 Why does the professor believe that the aftereffects of forest fires are good?

Responding Make your response by using the organized ideas.

The professor claims that

The reason is that

The second example cited is that

In addition,

Comparing Listen to a sample response and compare it with yours.

04 - 12

Exercise Listen to a lecture and answer the question following each step.

Listening Listen to a lecture and take notes.

Note Taking

04 - 13

Words & Phrases

on the contrary phr in contrast
globe n a spherical map of the Earth; a sphere

as the crow flies phr directly; straight
winding adj going back and forth; zigzag

Q Using points and examples from the lecture, explain how distances recorded on maps and globes are different from distances in reality.

Organization Ask yourself the following questions and organize your ideas.

1 What main point does the professor emphasize?

2 What example with a globe does the professor use?

3 What conclusion does the professor reach concerning measuring distances with globes?

4 What example with a map does the professor use?

5 What does the professor say about differences in distances measured on maps and in reality?

Responding Make your response by using the organized ideas.

The professor tells the class that

She first discusses

She then tells the class to observe

Comparing Listen to a sample response and compare it with yours.

04 - 14

Exercise Listen to a lecture and answer the question following each step.

Listening Listen to a lecture and take notes.

✎ Note Taking

04 - 15

📖 **Words & Phrases**

display v to show; to exhibit
prominently adv obviously
ingenious adj intelligent; brilliant; clever

symbolize v to represent something; to stand for something

 Using points and examples from the lecture, explain why stores often put their expensive and inexpensive products in different locations.

Organization Ask yourself the following questions and organize your ideas.

1 What is the main point of the professor's talk?

2 Where does the professor say that stores put their more expensive items?

3 What is the psychological importance of the location of expensive products?

4 According to the professor, where do stores often put cheaper-priced items?

5 What is the psychological importance of the location of cheaper products?

Responding Make your response by using the organized ideas.

During his lecture, the professor emphasizes

First, he discusses

The reason is that

The second explanation deals with

Comparing Listen to a sample response and compare it with yours.

04 - 16

Exercise Listen to a lecture and answer the question following each step.

Listening Listen to a lecture and take notes.

 Note Taking

04 - 17

📖 **Words & Phrases**

displace v to move from one place to another
get cast into phr to be thrown into

gorge v to eat to excess
shelter n a safe place

Q Using points and examples from the lecture, explain two benefits of floods for fish.

Organization Ask yourself the following questions and organize your ideas.

1 What is the lecture about?

2 What do fish eat during floods?

3 How much do fish eat during floods?

4 What happens to fish habitats during floods?

5 What can fish do in these new habitats?

Responding Make your response by using the organized ideas.

The professor lectures to the students about

According to the professor,

The reason is that

The second benefit the professor mentions concerns

Comparing Listen to a sample response and compare it with yours.

04 - 18

Exercise Listen to a lecture and answer the question following each step.

Listening Listen to a lecture and take notes.

✏ Note Taking

04 - 19

📖 **Words & Phrases**

stimulating adj enjoyably exciting or interesting
receptive adj open to ideas or suggestions

generally adv usually; most of the time
auditorily adv with regard to hearing

Q Using points and examples from the lecture, explain two advantages of broadcast advertisements.

Organization Ask yourself the following questions and organize your ideas.

1 What is the lecture about?

2 When do most people listen to the radio?

3 How do many people react to advertisements on the radio?

4 What is an advantage of television advertising?

5 What kinds of advertisements do companies try to create for television?

Responding Make your response by using the organized ideas.

In his lecture, the professor talks about

He then proceeds to

As a result,

Next, the professor discusses

Comparing Listen to a sample response and compare it with yours.

04 - 20

Exercise Listen to a lecture and answer the question following each step.

Listening Listen to a lecture and take notes.

 Note Taking

04 - 21

📕 **Words & Phrases**

accumulation n the buildup of something

exposure n the act of being open to or unprotected from extreme weather

sheer adj being very steep

enormous adj huge; very large

Q Using points and examples from the lecture, explain two ways that cliffs are formed.

Organization Ask yourself the following questions and organize your ideas.

1 What main point does the professor emphasize?

2 What is the first way that cliffs are formed?

3 How do cliffs form this way?

4 What is the second way that cliffs are formed?

5 How do cliffs form this way?

Responding Make your response by using the organized ideas.

In his lecture, the professor talks about

According to the professor,

The second way that

As a result,

Comparing Listen to a sample response and compare it with yours.

04 - 22

Exercise Listen to a lecture and answer the question following each step.

Listening Listen to a lecture and take notes.

📝 **Note Taking**

04 - 23

📖 **Words & Phrases**

confine Ⓥ to keep within a certain place
on the lookout for phr searching for

graze Ⓥ to eat to excess
drought ⓝ a period of time with little or no precipitation

Q Using points and examples from the lecture, explain how zebras in zoos and zebras in the wild have different lives.

Organization Ask yourself the following questions and organize your ideas.

1 What is the lecture about?

2 Why do zebras in the wild migrate?

3 What do zebras in zoos receive?

4 What are some environmental factors that affect zebras in the wild?

5 Why do zebras in zoos not worry about environmental factors?

Responding Make your response by using the organized ideas.

The professor tells the students that

First, he notes that

On the contrary,

The professor remarks that

Comparing Listen to a sample response and compare it with yours.

04 - 24

Exercise Listen to a lecture and answer the question following each step.

Listening Listen to a lecture and take notes.

🖋 Note Taking

04 - 25

📕 **Words & Phrases**

cooperative adj relating to people working together

section n one part of something larger

peer n a person who is equal in standing to another

pair n two members

Q Using points and examples from the lecture, explain two cooperative learning methods.

Organization Ask yourself the following questions and organize your ideas.

1   What is the main point of the professor's lecture?

2   What happens in jigsaw learning?

3   What can group members do during jigsaw learning?

4   How do teachers organize peer learning?

5   What might the student doing the teaching in peer learning have to do?

Responding Make your response by using the organized ideas.

In her lecture, the professor

She then describes

First, the teacher

The second method is

Comparing Listen to a sample response and compare it with yours.

04 - 26

Exercise Listen to a lecture and answer the question following each step.

Listening Listen to a lecture and take notes.

 Note Taking

04 - 27

📙 **Words & Phrases**

vague adj lacking detail or specific information

concrete adj solid

miserably adv badly; terribly

attainable adj reachable; achievable

Q Using points and examples from the lecture, explain two necessary aspects of setting goals.

Organization Ask yourself the following questions and organize your ideas.

1 What is the topic of the professor's lecture?

2 What is the first piece of advice the professor gives?

3 What are the results of establishing a concrete goal?

4 What is the second piece of advice the professor gives?

5 What example does the professor provide?

Responding Make your response by using the organized ideas.

The professor lectures about

First, a person must

For instance,

The professor provides

Comparing Listen to a sample response and compare it with yours.

04 - 28

Exercise Listen to a lecture and answer the question following each step.

Listening Listen to a lecture and take notes.

✏ Note Taking

04 - 29

📖 **Words & Phrases**

artificial adj manmade; not natural
collide v to hit; to run into

destination n the place where one is going
nocturnal adj being active at night

Q Using points and examples from the lecture, explain how artificial light harms animals.

Organization Ask yourself the following questions and organize your ideas.

1 What is the lecture about?

2 How does artificial light in buildings harm birds?

3 What happens to birds migrating near large cities?

4 How does artificial light affect rats and mice?

5 How does artificial light affect cougars?

Responding Make your response by using the organized ideas.

The professor talks about

The first animals she discusses

She then covers

As for cougars,

Comparing Listen to a sample response and compare it with yours.

04 - 30

Exercise Listen to a lecture and answer the question following each step.

Listening Listen to a lecture and take notes.

✎ Note Taking

04 - 31

📕 **Words & Phrases**

poor adj bad; being of low quality
replace v to exchange one thing for another

rotary phone n a telephone that requires a person to dial a number to make a call
turn off v to cause a person to lose interest in something

 Using points and examples from the lecture, explain how logos can harm companies.

Organization Ask yourself the following questions and organize your ideas.

1 What is the lecture about?

2 What is the first example the professor provides?

3 Why was that logo poor?

4 What is the second example the professor provides?

5 Why was that logo poor?

Responding Make your response by using the organized ideas.

The professor's lecture is about

The first example the professor provides

The professor notes that

The second example the professor gives

Comparing Listen to a sample response and compare it with yours.

04 - 32

Actual Test

Actual Test
01

CONTINUE | VOLUME

05 - 01

Speaking Section Directions

 Make sure your headset is on.

This section measures your ability to speak about a variety of topics. You will answer four questions by speaking into the microphone. Answer as completely as possible.

In the first question, you will speak about a familiar topic. Your response will be scored on your ability to speak clearly and coherently.

In the next two questions, you will first read a short reading passage. This passage will go away, and you will then listen to a talk on the same topic. You will be asked about the information you have read and heard. You will need to combine information from the reading passage and the talk to provide a complete answer. Your response will be scored on your ability to speak clearly and coherently and how accurately you convey information about what you read and heard.

In the last question, you will listen to part of a lecture. You will be asked about what you have heard. Your response will be scored on your ability to speak clearly and coherently and how accurately you convey information about what you heard.

You may take notes while you read and while you listen to the conversations and lectures. You may use your notes to help prepare your response.

Listen carefully to the directions for each question. The directions will not be written on the screen.

For each question you will be given a short time to prepare your response (15 to 30 seconds, depending on the question). A clock will show how much preparation time is remaining. When the preparation time is up, you will be told to begin your response. A clock will show how much response time is remaining. A message will appear on the screen when the response time has ended.

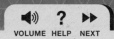
Task **1**

05 - 02

Some people like to buy books from a bookstore. Others like to borrow them from the library. Which do you prefer and why?

PREPARATION TIME
00 : 15 : 00

RESPONSE TIME
00 : 45 : 00

Sample Response ❯

05 - 03

Task **2**

05 - 04

Number of Sculpture Classes to Decrease

The Fine Arts Department has regretfully decided to cut the number of sculpture classes offered next semester from thirty to fifteen. While the department is not pleased to decrease its sculpture classes by fifty percent, there are two reasons for this choice. First, due to the department's limited number of sculpture professors, our instructors have been teaching too many classes each semester. This has disrupted their ability to provide quality individual instruction for students. Furthermore, due to cutbacks in the department's budget, there are simply not enough supplies available to offer such a large number of classes.

The man expresses his opinion of the decrease in sculpture classes. State his opinion and explain the reasons he gives for holding that opinion.

PREPARATION TIME
00 : 30 : 00

RESPONSE TIME
00 : 60 : 00

Sample Response ❯

05 - 05

Task **3**

05 - 06

Positive Externality

In business, most companies aspire to profit as much as they can. However, there are some instances where the social benefits of their actions actually outweigh the financial benefits. When something like this occurs, it is referred to as a positive externality. Positive externalities can occur in the guise of many different benefits, including education, the environment, health, and technology. As a general rule, companies do not specifically seek these benefits, but they do welcome their existence.

The professor describes the benefits of the new buses to the environment. Explain how these benefits are related to positive externalities.

PREPARATION TIME
00 : 30 : 00

RESPONSE TIME
00 : 60 : 00

Sample Response ❯

05 - 07

Task **4**

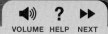
Using points and examples from the lecture, explain two documents necessary to convince people to invest in a new business.

PREPARATION TIME
00 : 20 : 00

RESPONSE TIME
00 : 60 : 00

Sample Response ❯

05 - 09

Actual Test

02

CONTINUE | VOLUME

Speaking Section Directions

05 - 10

 Make sure your headset is on.

This section measures your ability to speak about a variety of topics. You will answer four questions by speaking into the microphone. Answer as completely as possible.

In the first question, you will speak about a familiar topic. Your response will be scored on your ability to speak clearly and coherently.

In the next two questions, you will first read a short reading passage. This passage will go away, and you will then listen to a talk on the same topic. You will be asked about the information you have read and heard. You will need to combine information from the reading passage and the talk to provide a complete answer. Your response will be scored on your ability to speak clearly and coherently and how accurately you convey information about what you read and heard.

In the last question, you will listen to part of a lecture. You will be asked about what you have heard. Your response will be scored on your ability to speak clearly and coherently and how accurately you convey information about what you heard.

You may take notes while you read and while you listen to the conversations and lectures. You may use your notes to help prepare your response.

Listen carefully to the directions for each question. The directions will not be written on the screen.

For each question you will be given a short time to prepare your response (15 to 30 seconds, depending on the question). A clock will show how much preparation time is remaining. When the preparation time is up, you will be told to begin your response. A clock will show how much response time is remaining. A message will appear on the screen when the response time has ended.

Task **1**

05 - 11

Some students prefer to eat lunch in a school cafeteria. Others prefer to make a lunch at home and to take it to school. Which do you prefer and why?

PREPARATION TIME
00 : 15 : 00

RESPONSE TIME
00 : 45 : 00

Sample Response ❯

05 - 12

Task **2**

05-13

Jonathan Davis to Speak at Graduation

Central University is proud to announce Jonathan Davis will be the commencement speaker at the graduation ceremony to be held on May 15. Mr. Davis is a leader in the world of business. He took his company, DP Solutions, out of bankruptcy and promptly turned it into the most prominent financial corporation in the world. He will surely have some words of wisdom about business for our graduating seniors. Mr. Davis is also a graduate of Central University, and the school is looking forward to honoring one of its own and acknowledging his contributions to society.

The woman expresses her opinion of the school's choice of commencement speakers. State her opinion and explain the reasons she gives for holding that opinion.

PREPARATION TIME
00 : 30 : 00

RESPONSE TIME
00 : 60 : 00

Sample Response ❯

05-14

Task **3**

05-15

Long-Term Memory

Every day, the human brain processes an enormous amount of information. It discards most of this information but still retains many items. Some information is available for immediate recall. It is called short-term memory. Other information remains in the brain awaiting recall, sometimes years later. This is long-term memory. For this, the brain must catalog the information, often by sensory input or associative addressing. Thanks to long-term memory, people are able to remember not only various facts but also how to do certain actions, even ones as simple as riding a bicycle. Without long-term memory, humans would simply not be able to function.

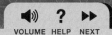

The professor describes two kinds of memory and how people utilize them. Explain how they are related to long-term memory.

PREPARATION TIME
00 : 30 : 00

RESPONSE TIME
00 : 60 : 00

 Sample Response

05-16

Task **4**

05 - 17

Using points and examples from the lecture, explain how people often read books both before and after Johannes Gutenberg's invention of movable type.

PREPARATION TIME
00 : 20 : 00

RESPONSE TIME
00 : 60 : 00

Sample Response ❯

05 - 18

Appendix

Useful Expressions
for the Speaking Tasks

This part provides some essential expressions and collocations that can be used in each unit. They will be given with sample sentences through which their applications as well as their meanings can be clarified. Once in your memory, these lexical chunks will help you give sophisticated responses.

Useful Expressions for the Speaking Tasks

1 Stating Your Preference

I prefer A to B

I prefer home-cooked meals **to** meals at restaurants.
I prefer team sports **to** individual ones.

I like A better [more] than B

I like hiking in the forest **more than** swimming in a pool.
I like to travel by plane **more than** to travel by train.

I'd rather A than B

I'd rather watch a concert on television **than** see it at a concert hall.
I'd rather take a class in person **than** take one online.

I think [believe] (that) A is better than B

I believe studying science **is better than** studying music.
I think that watching movies at home **is better than** watching them at a theater.

In my opinion, A is better than B

In my opinion, camping **is better than** staying at a hotel.
In my opinion, lifting weights **is better than** jogging.

Given the choice of A and [or] B, I would choose

Given the choice of flying to my destination **and** driving there, **I would choose** to drive.
Given the choice of staying at home **or** going out to meet my friends, **I would choose** my friends.

2 Giving Reasons

I prefer ~ because S + V

I prefer cycling to walking **because** cycling gets me to my destination faster.
I prefer history to science **because** history teaches me about the past.

There are several reasons why I prefer

There are several reasons why I prefer to travel to other countries.
There are several reasons why I prefer spicy food to bland food.

The first reason is that S + V

The first reason is that I can improve my future career.
The first reason is that I don't have to care about what to wear every morning.

The second reason is that S + V

The second reason is that I can experience new kinds of foods.
The second reason is that I can gain more knowledge.

The last [final] reason is that S + V

The last reason is that learning history is like reading an exciting story.

The last reason is that I can make more contacts with people in the industry.

3 Giving Supporting Details

Comparing & Contrasting

S + V, but S + V

Many people like long trips, **but** I think that short ones are better.

My friends prefer to play computer games, **but** I would rather play sports.

S + V while S + V

I would rather have a dog **while** many other people might prefer to have a cat.

I like to attend small classes **while** other people think large lectures are better.

On the other hand, S + V

Online classes are usually cheap. **On the other hand**, you can interact with your teacher more in an in-person class.

Playing a musical instrument is lots of fun. **On the other hand**, it can cost a lot to buy one.

Although [Though] S + V, S + V

Though cooking at home is cheap, eating at a restaurant can be more enjoyable.

Although libraries are quiet, they are not the best places to study.

Clarifying

That means (that) S + V

Some people spend their entire lives in one place. **That means** they might be exclusive.

I don't own a car. **That means that** I have to rely on public transportation.

What I'm saying is (that) S + V

What I'm saying is that it is better to travel to as many places as possible.

What I'm saying is that most people in my neighborhood are very friendly.

TASK 2 Reading & Conversation

1 Stating the Speaker's Position

Agreeing

The man [woman] agrees with / The man [woman] agrees that S + V

The man agrees with the announcement that the engineering building will be renovated.

The woman agrees with the decision to close the Sociology Department.

The man [woman] approves of

The woman approves of the decision to raise the price of a parking sticker.

The man approves of the announcement that tuition will not increase this year.

The man [woman] supports

The man supports the new café being built in the library basement.

The man supports the school's announcement that the cafeteria's hours will be expanded.

The man [woman] thinks [believes] ~ is a good idea

The woman thinks expanding the size of the main parking lot **is a good idea**.

The man believes that decreasing the average size of classes **is a good idea**.

The man [woman] likes the idea of / The man [woman] likes the idea that S + V

The man likes the idea of decreasing the amount of the fine for overdue books.

The woman likes the idea that professors should spend more time with their students.

Disagreeing

The man [woman] disagrees with / The man [woman] disagrees that S + V

The man disagrees with the decision to hire more administrators on campus.

The man disagrees with the announcement that some school clubs will be closed.

The man [woman] is against

The man is against the decision to require students take an art class.

The man is against requiring students to live on campus.

The man [woman] opposes

The woman opposes the closing of the school's art facilities.

The woman opposes making students buy physical books.

2 Talking about the Reasons

He [She] gives two reasons why he [she]

He gives two reasons why he dislikes the idea of TVs in dormitory lounges.

She gives two reasons why she disagrees with the announcement.

The [His, Her] first reason is that S + V

Her first reason is that her schedule is already too full.

The first reason is that there are already too many physics classes.

The [His, Her] other reason is that S + V

Her other reason is that she has already taken enough required courses.

The other reason is that the school is suffering a financial crisis.

3 Quoting

According to the announcement [letter, article], S + V

According to the article, a famous professor will begin teaching next semester.

According to the announcement, there will be no more guest speakers the rest of the semester.

The announcement [letter, article] says (that) S + V

The letter says that freshman orientation is too long.

The article says that student government elections have been canceled.

According to the student [man, woman], S + V

According to the woman, many professors do not spend enough time with their students.
According to the student, few people ever use the university's tutorial facilities.

He [She] mentions (that) S + V

She mentions that the library's book collection is too small.
He mentions that the campus is too big for students to get to their classes on time.

He [She] points out (that) S + V

He points out that the buildings on campus are far from one another.
She points out that the food in the cafeteria has increased in quality lately.

He [She] argues (that) S + V

She argues that the school should try to lower the prices of textbooks.
He argues that the university should ask the students before making such an important decision.

TASK 3 Reading & Lecture

1 Talking about the Topic

The reading defines A as B

The reading defines symbiosis **as** a situation in which two kinds of organisms live together.
The reading defines mimicry **as** the ability of an animal to look like something else.

According to the reading, S + V

According to the reading, a supervolcano may have killed the dinosaurs.
According to the reading, many companies use the Internet for marketing purposes these days.

The professor explains

The professor explains an action his friend took while working at a business.
The professor explains why his own actions caused a problem.

The professor talks about

The professor talks about the migration of animals in Africa.
The professor talks about a common psychological problem people have.

According to the professor, S + V

According to the professor, building a bridge can take a long time.
According to the professor, the Romans were some of the best road builders.

The lecture is about

The lecture is about reasons that some companies choose not to advertise.
The lecture is about some ways that small businesses can advertise.

According to the lecture, S + V

According to the lecture, bird nests can protect birds from bad weather.
According to the lecture, some animals can live on land and in the water.

❷ Explaining the Details

Talking about Subtopics

There are two main A of B

There are two main types **of** whales.
There are two main kinds **of** jobs.

One is A, and the other is B

One is wind erosion, **and the other is** water erosion.
One is print advertising, **and the other is** online advertising.

There are two (different) kinds of

There are two different kinds of plant roots.
There are two different kinds of mammals.

The first (one) is A, and the second (one) is B

The first is sunspots, **and the second is** solar flares.
The first one is rocky planets, **and the second one is** gas planets.

Talking about Examples

The professor talks about A as an example of B

The professor talks about dinosaurs **as an example of** extinct animals.
The professor talks about cobras **as an example of** animals that are predators.

The professor gives an example of A by discussing B

The professor gives an example of viral marketing **by discussing** a popular company's recent effort.
The professor gives an example of camouflage **by discussing** the walking stick insect.

The professor bases his [her] example on

The professor bases her example on the artwork of Michelangelo.
The professor bases his example on an experiment conducted in the 1950s.

The professor discusses ~ to demonstrate [illustrate]

The professor discusses bats **to demonstrate** how they survive in caves.
The professor discusses cognitive dissonance **to illustrate** how people can suffer from it.

The first example shows how S + V

The first example shows how some countries run their elections.
The first example shows how animals first came to live on the land.

Another example the professor gives is

Another example the professor gives is the dodo bird and how it went extinct.
Another example the professor gives is the path of human migration in the Americas.

1 Stating the Topic of the Lecture

The lecture is (mainly) about

The lecture is **mainly about** two types of volcanoes.
The lecture is **mainly about** two methods of mining coal.

The topic of the lecture is

The topic of the lecture is nutrients that plants need.
The topic of the lecture is rainforest plants.

The professor talks about

The professor **talks about** how animals defend themselves from predators.
The professor **talks about** ways that businesses can protect themselves from problems.

The professor discusses [explains]

The professor **explains** how gophers build their homes.
The professor **discusses** the effects of solar radiation.

According to the lecture [professor], S + V

According to the lecture, the Greeks made three different types of columns.
According to the professor, natural gas is a clean type of fossil fuel.

According to the lecture [professor], A refers to B

According to the lecture, cyclic population change **refers to** how animal populations constantly change.
According to the professor, animal cooperation **refers to** how different species work together.

2 Explaining the Details

Talking about Subtopics

The professor says there are two ways (for something) to

The professor says there are two ways to detect ancient ruins.
The professor says there are two ways to display items in stores.

The first (one) is A, and the second (one) is B

The first one is to dig, **and the second one is** to study historical documents.
The first is to put expensive items at the front, **and the second is** to put cheap items in other places.

According to the professor, there are two types [kinds] of

According to the professor, there are two types of fish.
According to the professor, there are two kinds of advertising.

According to the lecture, there are two factors in

According to the lecture, there are two factors in plant growth.
According to the lecture, there are two factors in eclipses.

One is A, and the other is B

One is sunlight, **and the other is** water.
One is the movement of the larger body, **and the other is** the movement of the smaller one.

The professor gives two examples of

The professor gives two examples of invasive species.

The professor gives two examples of the effects of supernovas.

The professor explains ~ by giving two examples

The professor explains the formation of islands by giving two examples.

The professor explains a problem companies have by giving two examples.

The professor talks [speaks] about A as an example of B

The professor talks about the horned frog as an example of an animal that changes its skin color.

The professor speaks about Tulip Mania as an example of an economic bubble.

The professor gives A as an example of B

The professor gives his friend's company as an example of a well-run business.

The professor gives a story from her past as an example of impression management.

The professor gives one more example that shows

The professor gives one more example that shows how crops can be irrigated.

The professor gives one more example that shows how fish benefit from floods.

The other example (of something) is

The other example is when businesses refuse to hire more workers in bad economic times.

The other example of a deciduous tree is the oak.

How to
Master Skills for the
TOEFL® iBT
SPEAKING

▌ Answers, Scripts, and Translations

Intermediate

How to
Master Skills for the

Second Edition

TOEFL® iBT

SPEAKING Intermediate

Answers, Scripts,
and Translations

Unit 01 Education

Exercise ·········· p.12

Before you start

Script 🎧 01-02

M Student: How was your day, Sue?

W Student: It was so boring. My professor just went on and on about nothing.

M: Yeah, I know what you mean. I've had a few classes like that.

W: And he's so out of touch with technology. He won't even put his lecture notes on the class website.

M: Really? Why not?

W: He said that if he did that, there would be no reason to have a lecture.

M: I guess he has a point.

W: He just knows that he's so boring that no students would come if they didn't have to.

해석

M Student: 오늘 하루 어땠니, Sue?

W Student: 너무 지겨웠어. 교수님이 중요하지도 않은 얘기를 끝도 없이 하셨거든.

M: 그래, 무슨 말인지 알아. 나도 그런 수업을 몇 번 들어본 적이 있어.

W: 그리고 그분은 과학 기술과 동떨어진 분이셔. 강의 웹사이트에 강의 노트도 올리지 않으신다니까.

M: 정말이야? 왜 그러시지?

W: 그렇게 하면 강의를 할 이유가 없다고 말하시더라고.

M: 그것도 말은 되는 것 같네.

W: 너무 재미가 없으셔서 만약 학생들이 수업에 오지 않아도 되면 아무도 수업을 들으러 오지 않을 것이라는 점을 아시는 거지.

1 Her day was boring because of a university lecture she attended.
2 She wishes he would put his lecture notes on the class website.
3 He's afraid no one will come to class if he puts his notes on the website.
4 They attend class because they need to take notes on his lectures.

Script 🎧 01-03

M Professor: The explosion of the Internet over the last ten years has led to dramatic changes in many things we do nowadays. At present, there are over 100 million websites worldwide. One of the main areas that has been influenced is education. Almost every university has a correspondence course department. This means that students can take classes online. Sometimes they can even watch lectures that have been prerecorded. Unfortunately, the Internet has led to problems with plagiarism, which is basically cheating. Students can easily find completed papers online or can copy information directly onto an essay. It is estimated that almost sixty percent of students have cheated at one point in their university lives. I strongly discourage this because it's wrong and you could get in serious trouble.

해석

M Professor: 지난 10년 동안 인터넷의 폭발적 증가로 우리가 하는 많은 일들이 극적으로 바뀌었습니다. 현재 전 세계적으로 1억 개가 넘는 웹사이트가 존재해요. 그러한 영향을 받은 주요 분야 중 하나가 교육입니다. 거의 모든 대학에 통신 교육 과정 부서가 있습니다. 이는 학생들이 온라인으로 수업을 들을 수 있다는 점을 의미해요. 때로는 미리 녹화된 강의를 볼 수도 있습니다. 안타까운 것은 인터넷 때문에 표절과 관련된 문제들이 나타났는데, 표절은 기본적으로 부정행위입니다. 학생들은 온라인에서 쉽게 완성된 논문을 찾거나 정보를 보고서에 바로 복사해 넣을 수도 있죠. 학생들 가운데 거의 60%가 대학 재학 중 한 번 정도 부정 행위를 하는 것으로 추정됩니다. 부정 행위는 잘못된 행위이며 심각한 문제를 일으킬 수도 있기 때문에, 저는 이를 강력히 반대합니다.

1 It has influenced online classes and cheating.
2 Students can watch prerecorded lectures online.
3 They should not use the Internet for cheating.
4 A student caught cheating could be expelled from school, kicked out of class, or given a low grade on the assignment.

Organization

	Choice A	Choice B
I prefer	To study in a class	To study online
First reason	The quality of studying is better.	I can save money by taking online classes.
Details	Studying with a professor and other students involves more interaction, and I can ask questions and get immediate answers.	I don't have to live on or near the campus, so I could possibly save money. I don't have to spend money and time on transportation to the campus to attend classes.

Second reason	Second reason
The professor can be a mentor.	It's more convenient to take online classes.
Details	Details
A professor can become a mentor who helps you with your studies. He can also help you in the future by providing references for graduate school or employment.	I can stay in my hometown. I can have a job at the same time that I study. I don't have to change my whole life just to take some classes.

Comparing

Sample Response I Choice A

Script 🎧 01-04

I'm the kind of person who prefers to take traditional classes when I study. To begin with, the quality of the instruction is better in traditional classes. I find it easier to understand a subject by listening to the professor lecture and by interacting with the other students in class. When I don't understand something, I can ask a question and get an immediate answer. Second of all, it helps to know your professor so that he can become your mentor. Having a mentor is very important for a student. For instance, the professor could provide references for you to get into graduate school or to get a job after graduating. So for those reasons, I would much rather take traditional classes than online classes.

해석

나는 공부를 할 때 기존 방식의 강의를 듣는 것을 더 선호하는 편이다. 우선 강의의 질에서 기존 방식의 강의가 더 낫다. 교수님의 강의를 듣고 수업 시간에 다른 학생들과 상호작용을 함으로써 주제를 이해하기가 더 쉽다. 이해가 가지 않는 부분이 있으면 질문을 해서 곧바로 답을 들을 수 있다. 두 번째로는 그렇게 하면 교수님을 알게 될 수 있고 교수님께서 나의 멘토가 되어 주실 수도 있다. 멘토가 있다는 것은 학생에게 매우 중요한 점이다. 예를 들어 교수님께서 졸업 후 대학원 진학이나 취업에 필요한 추천장을 써 주실 수도 있다. 따라서 이러한 이유들로 나는 온라인 강의보다 기존 방식의 강의를 훨씬 더 좋아한다.

Sample Response I Choice B

Script 🎧 01-05

I would rather take online classes than traditional ones. First, online classes are cheaper, so I can save money by taking them. For example, I don't have to live near the university, where housing is usually more expensive. I also don't have to spend any time and money on transportation, which can be expensive. Second, online classes are more convenient than traditional ones. This would enable me to stay in my hometown and live with my parents while I'm studying. I can also get a job while I study and be much more flexible. In other words, I don't have to change my entire life just to get an education. So

for these reasons, I think studying online is better than studying in a traditional classroom setting.

해석

나는 기존 방식의 강의보다 온라인 강의를 좋아하는 편이다. 첫째, 온라인 강의는 비용이 적게 들기 때문에 온라인 강의를 수강함으로써 비용을 절약할 수 있다. 예를 들어 일반적으로 주거비가 비싼 대학 주변에 살지 않아도 된다. 또한 많은 비용이 들 수 있는 교통에 시간과 돈을 쓸 필요도 없다. 둘째, 온라인 강의는 기존 방식의 강의 보다 편리하다. 공부를 하는 기간에도 고향에 머물면서 부모님과 함께 지낼 수 있다. 또한 공부를 하면서 일을 할 수도 있고, 훨씬 더 유연하게 지낼 수 있다. 다시 말해서 교육을 받기 위해 내 인생 전체를 바꾸지 않아도 된다. 따라서 이런 이유들로 나는 온라인으로 공부를 하는 것이 전통적인 교실에서 수업을 받는 것보다 낫다고 생각한다.

Unit 02 Welfare

Exercise p.14

Before you start

Script 🎧 01-06

M Student: Why the long face, Catherine?

W Student: Oh, there's this homeless man who always hangs out on our street. I see him every day. I want to help him, but I don't know how.

M: You could volunteer. There's a church near here that has a soup kitchen. It needs help.

W: What's a soup kitchen?

M: It's a place that provides free meals to the poor and homeless.

W: That's nice, but it doesn't really help them overcome their difficulties.

M: You're right. In fact, a lot of them feel ashamed when they go there.

W: The city could provide training and help them find jobs.

M: Many of them can't keep steady jobs because they have problems with drugs and alcohol or have some kind of mental illness.

해석

M Student: Catherine, 왜 그렇게 표정이 우울하니?

W Student: 오, 우리 동네에 항상 돌아다니는 노숙자가 있거든. 매일 보게 되지. 도와 주고 싶지만 어떻게 해야 할지 모르겠어.

M: 자원봉사 활동을 하면 되잖아. 이 근처에 무료 급식소가 있는 교회가 있어. 그곳에 도움이 필요할 거야.

W: 무료 급식소가 뭔데?

M: 가난하고 집이 없는 사람들에게 무료로 식사를 제공하는 곳이지.

W: 그건 좋은 일이지만 그 사람들이 어려움을 극복하는데 정말로 도움이 되는 일은 아니야.

M: 네 말이 맞아. 많은 사람들이 그곳에 갈 때 수치심을 느끼니까.

W: 시에서 교육을 시켜서 그들이 일자리를 찾는데 도움을 줄 수도 있을 것 같아.

M: 그 사람들 중 많은 이들이 마약 및 알코올 중독 문제나 정신 질환 문제를 겪고 있어서 꾸준하게 일을 할 수가 없는걸.

1 She saw a homeless man and wants to help him but doesn't know how.

2 Her friend suggests that she volunteer at a place like a soup kitchen that helps poor people.

3 She thinks the city should provide training so they can get jobs.

4 They can't keep their homes because of drugs, alcohol, and mental problems.

B

Script 🎧 01-07

M Professor: It is estimated that almost thirty-five million people live below the poverty line in the United States. That's 12.5% of the population. The poverty line is the level of income a person needs to have the basic necessities, such as food, shelter, and clothing. It depends on the size of the family and the family's income. For example, a large family would require a greater income to remain above the poverty line. Last year, over 1.3 trillion dollars was spent on social welfare programs, but it is still not enough. However, some think that it is too much and that the poor don't help themselves because we help them so much.

해석

M Professor: 미국에서는 거의 3천 5백만 명이 빈곤선 이하에서 사는 것으로 추정됩니다. 전체 인구의 12.5%에 해당되는 수치이죠. 빈곤선은 의식주와 같은 기본적인 욕구를 충족시키는데 필요한 소득 수준이에요. 이는 가족의 크기와 소득에 따라 달라집니다. 예를 들어 대가족이 빈곤선 위에 있기 위해서는 소득이 더 많아야 하죠. 작년에 1.3조 달러 이상을 복지 프로그램에 썼어도 여전히 충분하지가 않습니다. 하지만 이러한 금액이 너무 많으며, 우리가 너무 많은 도움을 주기 때문에 가난한 사람들이 자립을 못한다고 생각하는 사람들도 있습니다.

1 The poverty line is the level of income needed to buy the necessities of life.

2 Three necessities of life are food, shelter, and clothing.

3 Some people believe that by giving the poor help, they don't feel the need to help themselves.

4 The poverty line would be lower for a family of three and higher for a family of seven.

Organization

Choice A	Choice B
I believe Cities should help the poor by giving them money.	**I believe** Cities should help the poor by giving them actual goods.
First reason The poor won't feel ashamed like they would when they receive items such as food.	**First reason** Addicts would spend any money given to them on their bad habits.
Details Many poor people feel ashamed of their positions. Giving them food and other items increases their feelings of shame. Giving them money instead will help them maintain their dignity.	**Details** Alcoholics and drug addicts would spend the money on their addictions. If people give them food and other items, it will ensure that they have some things, which is very important if they have children.
Second reason They can make their own decisions on what to buy.	**Second reason** It can save the city money.
Details Having money allows them to make choices. They can decide what to buy instead of simply taking what people give them.	**Details** Many people donate food and clothing to the needy. Since the city will spend less money, it can use the extra money for job training and other things to help the poor.

Comparing

Sample Response | Choice A

Script 🎧 01-08

I believe that cities should provide money to the poor rather than give them necessities like food. For starters, giving money to the poor allows them to keep some of their dignity. Most of the poor feel some shame because of their status. By directly giving them food or items, the poor might feel more ashamed. Giving them money provides them with some power and helps them get some dignity back. In addition, giving them money allows them to make their own decisions on what to buy. If people just give them items such as food and clothing, they might not like the items or might not eat the food for various reasons. Those are the two main reasons why I believe cities should give money to the poor instead of items.

해석

나는 시에서 가난한 사람들에게 식품과 같은 생필품보다는 돈을 주어야 한다고 생각한다. 우선 가난한 사람들에게 돈을 주면 그들도 어느 정도 품위를 유지할 수 있다. 대부분의 빈곤층들은 자신들의 지위 때문에 수치심을 느낀다. 그들에게 식품이나 물품을 직접 제공한다면 더 큰 수치심을 느끼게 될 것이다. 돈을 주는 경우에는 그들에게 약간의 능력이 생길 것이고 품위도 회복될 수 있다. 뿐만 아니라 돈을 주면 나름대로 무엇을 구입할지 스스로 결정을 내릴 수 있다. 만약 식품이나 의복 같은 물품을 주면 그러한 물품을 좋아하지 않을 수도 있고 또는 여러 가지 이유로 음식을 먹지 않을 수도 있다. 이러한 두 가지 이유로 나는 시에서 빈곤층에게 물품 대신 돈을 주어야 한다고 생각한다.

Sample Response | Choice B

Script 🎧 01-09

In my opinion, cities should provide useful items like food and clothing, not money, to the poor. Firstly, many poor people suffer from drug and alcohol addiction. They would just use the money on drugs and alcohol. However, by giving food and other items, we can ensure they and their families have some useful items. Secondly, many people donate food and clothing to help the poor. That way, cities won't need to spend lots of money on these items. Cities could use government money to build more homeless shelters and soup kitchens. They could also start training programs to help the poor get better jobs. For these reasons, I think cities should give the poor food and other items instead of money.

해석

내 생각에는 시에서 빈곤층에게 돈이 아닌 식품이나 의복 같은 유용한 물품을 제공해야 한다. 첫째, 많은 빈곤층이 마약 및 알코올 중독 증상을 겪고 있다. 그들은 돈을 그저 마약이나 알코올 구매에 사용할 것이다. 하지만 식품 및 기타 물품을 주면 그들과 그들의 가족들에게 유용한 물품이 전달될 것이라는 점이 보장될 수 있다. 둘째, 많은 사람들이 빈곤층을 돕기 위해 식품과 의복을 기증한다. 그렇기 때문에 시에서는 이러한 물품을 구매하기 위해 많은 돈을 쓸 필요가 없을 것이다. 시는 정부 보조금을 사용해 노숙자 쉼터나 무료 급식소를 더 많이 지을 수 있을 것이다. 또한 빈곤층이 더 나은 일자리를 구할 수 있도록 교육 프로그램을 실시할 수도 있을 것이다. 이러한 이유들 때문에 나는 시에서 빈곤층에게 돈 대신 식품이나 기타 물품들을 제공해야 한다고 믿는다.

Unit 03 School

Exercise ·· p.16

Before you start

A

Script 🎧 01-10

W Student Housing Employee: Hi. Can I help you?

M Student: Yes. My name is David Holmes. I live in War Memorial Residence on campus. I'd like to change my housing.

W: It's difficult since it's the middle of the term. Is there a problem?

M: Yes, it's my roommate. We don't get along.

W: Why's that?

M: He always stays up late at night, he never studies, and he's really messy.

W: I see. Have you talked to your dorm supervisor?

M: Yes, but there are no other rooms in our house, so I thought I could change dorms.

W: It may be possible. Have you thought about getting housing off campus?

M: Maybe next year. I can't really afford it right now.

해석

W Student Housing Employee: 안녕하세요. 도와 드릴까요?

M Student: 네. 제 이름은 David Holmes예요. 교내의 War Memorial 레지던스에서 살고 있죠. 저는 숙소를 바꾸고 싶어요.

W: 학기 중이라 곤란해요. 문제가 있나요?

M: 네, 바로 룸메이트 때문이에요. 사이가 좋지 않거든요.

W: 왜 그런가요?

M: 그는 항상 밤늦게까지 깨어 있고, 공부는 절대 하지 않으며, 그리고 정말로 정리정돈을 하지 않아요.

W: 알겠어요. 기숙사 사감 선생님께 이야기를 해 보았나요?

M: 네, 하지만 우리 숙소에는 남는 방이 없어서 기숙사를 바꿔야겠다고 생각을 했죠.

W: 가능할 수도 있을 것 같네요. 캠퍼스 밖으로 이사를 가는 것은 생각해 봤나요?

M: 내년이면 가능할 것 같아요. 지금 당장은 그럴 형편이 전혀 안 되고요.

1 He wants to change his dorm room.
2 His roommate is the problem.
3 He doesn't have enough money, so he can't afford it.
4 He probably goes to bed early, studies hard, and cleans his room.

B

Script 🎧 01-11

W Professor: The place a person lives often represents that person's personality. For example, someone who lives alone may at heart be a person who enjoys doing things by himself. Someone who shares housing may be terrified of being alone and may need the comfort of roommates to help support him. Another factor is cost. For example, the average cost of living for a university student is over 15,000 dollars a year, and that's without tuition and books. It's easier to live with others and share the costs of living. Another problem is finding suitable housing if you want to live off campus. Right here on our campus, approximately fifty-five percent of the students live in the dormitories. However, seventy-five percent of them are freshman and sophomores.

해석

W Professor: 어떤 사람이 사는 장소를 보면 종종 그 사람의 성격을 알 수가 있습니다. 예를 들어 혼자 사는 사람은 내심 일을 혼자서 하는 것을 좋아하는 사

람일 수 있어요. 주거 공간을 공유하는 사람은 혼자 있는 것을 무서워하고 자신을 도와 줄 수 있는 룸메이트로부터 안도감을 느낄 수도 있죠. 또 다른 요인은 비용입니다. 예를 들어 대학생의 평균적인 생활비가 연간 15,000달러를 넘는데, 이는 등록금과 교재비를 뺀 금액이에요. 다른 사람과 같이 살면서 생활비를 분담하는 것이 더 낫습니다. 또 다른 문제는 캠퍼스 밖에서 살고자 하는 경우 적당한 집을 찾는 일이에요. 우리 대학의 경우에는 약 55%의 학생들이 기숙사에서 살고 있죠. 하지만 이들 중 75%가 1학년생과 2학년생이에요.

1 The two factors are personality and money.
2 They enjoy doing things by themselves.
3 They have trouble finding suitable housing.
4 They probably live off campus.

Organization

Choice A	Choice B
I prefer To live in a dorm room with a roommate	I prefer To live alone near campus
First reason It doesn't cost as much to live in a dorm.	First reason The dorms have too many rules and are small.
Details I don't need to buy furniture or pay for utilities like electricity and gas. I don't need to buy food or cook.	Details Dormitories have many rules, such as when you can come home and have guests. The rooms tend to be smaller than those in regular apartments.
Second reason A roommate can be a friend.	Second reason There is no privacy in a dorm.
Details We won't be lonely. We can study together. We can talk about our problems.	Details You have to share a small space with another student and share the bathroom. Your roommate may be loud and messy.

Comparing

Sample Response I Choice A
Script 🎧 01-12

Personally, I prefer to live on campus with a roommate. For one, there is the issue of cost. Living in a dorm can be cheaper than living off campus. I won't have to buy things such as furniture or pay for electricity, gas, heat, or the Internet. I won't have to cook since I can just go to the school cafeteria, so I can save a lot of money on food, too. Additionally, my roommate can be my friend. Being in college can be a lonely experience. However, with a roommate, we can study together, talk about our problems, and just hang out together. These are the two reasons I prefer to live on campus with a roommate.

해석
개인적으로 나는 룸메이트와 함께 교내에서 지내는 것을 더 좋아한다. 먼저 비용 문제가 있다. 기숙사에서 살면 캠퍼스 밖에서 사는 것보다 비용이 적게 들 수 있다. 가구와 같은 물건을 살 필요도 없고, 전기 요금, 가스 요금, 난방 요금, 혹은 인터넷 사용료를 낼 필요도 없을 것이다. 교내 식당에 갈 수 있기 때문에 요리를 할 필요도 없을 것이며 따라서 식비에서도 많은 돈을 아낄 수 있다. 또한 룸메이트와 친구가 될 수도 있다. 대학 생활은 외로운 경험일 수 있다. 하지만 룸메이트가 있으면 함께 공부를 하고, 서로의 문제에 대해 이야기를 하고, 그리고 같이 어울려 다닐 수도 있다. 이러한 두 가지 이유로 나는 룸메이트와 함께 교내에서 사는 것을 더 좋아한다.

Sample Response I Choice B
Script 🎧 01-13

I would rather live alone near the campus than share a dorm room. First off, living in a dorm has a lot of drawbacks. Most dorms have curfews and rules about having guests. In other words, they're too strict for me. Another drawback is the sizes of dorm rooms. They can be rather small. You also have to share the bathrooms with everyone. Another reason is that a roommate can cause a lot of problems if you have different personalities. I like to have a clean room, go to bed early, and study hard. I wouldn't like a roommate who always has parties, smokes, and stays up very late. For these reasons, I prefer to live by myself near the campus.

해석
나는 누군가와 기숙사를 같이 쓰느니 캠퍼스 밖에서 혼자 사는 쪽을 택할 것이다. 먼저 기숙사 생활에는 많은 단점이 있다. 대부분의 기숙사에는 야간 외출 금지 및 손님 초대에 관한 규정이 존재한다. 다시 말해 이는 내게 너무 엄격한 규정이다. 또 다른 단점은 기숙사의 방 크기에 있다. 기숙사 방들은 다소 작을 수 있다. 또한 모든 사람들과 욕실을 공유해야 한다. 또 다른 이유는 룸메이트와 성격이 다를 경우 룸메이트로 인해 많은 문제가 생길 수 있기 때문이다. 나는 방을 깨끗이 쓰고, 일찍 잠자리에 들고, 열심히 공부하는 것을 좋아한다. 늘 파티를 열고, 담배를 피우고, 그리고 매우 늦게까지 잠을 자지 않는 룸메이트는 좋아하지 않는다. 따라서 이러한 이유들 때문에 나는 캠퍼스 근처에서 혼자 사는 것을 더 좋아한다.

Unit **04** Studying

Exercise p.18

Before you start

A
Script 🎧 01-14

W Student: I can't believe it!

M Student: What's the matter, Betty?

W: I'm failing my art class. It's going to drag down my overall grade point average.

M: Why are you failing art? I think your drawings and painting are wonderful.

W: Tell that to my teacher. She doesn't think so. If my GPA is too low, I won't get a good job.

M: Perhaps you should talk to your teacher and find out what the problem is.

W: Maybe. But I don't think she likes me.

M: Why not?

W: On the first day of class, I pointed out a mistake she made about Picasso.

해석

W Student: 말도 안 돼!

M Student: Betty, 무슨 일이야?

W: 미술 수업에서 낙제하게 되었어. 전체 평점이 내려갈 거야.

M: 왜 낙제를 하는데? 나는 네 드로잉과 그림이 훌륭하다고 생각했거든.

W: 우리 선생님께 그렇게 말해 줘. 선생님은 그렇게 생각 하지 않으시던걸. 평점이 너무 낮으면 좋은 직장도 구하지 못할 거야.

M: 선생님께 말씀을 드려서 무엇이 문제인지 알아봐야 할 것 같은데.

W: 그럴 수도 있겠지. 하지만 선생님이 나를 좋아하지 않으시는 것 같아.

M: 왜?

W: 수업 첫날에 선생님께서 피카소에 대해 실수하신 점을 내가 지적했거든.

1 She and her teacher don't get along well.

2 It could lower her grade point average and make it difficult for her to get a good job.

3 Her friend thinks they are wonderful.

4 She is angry with Betty for pointing out her mistake about Picasso.

B

Script 🎧 01-15

M Professor: One of the great controversies in education now is the type of curriculum to offer at universities. In the 1960s and 1970s, many universities offered courses that students were interested in but which had no practical value. Courses such as Tibetan Buddhist chanting had no practical application in the workplace. In the 1980s, Harvard University led the way in reforming its curriculum by making a strict core program that all students had to follow. It has aspects of many disciplines, including the arts, languages, and sciences. No course is considered more important than another. All are considered necessary to produce well-educated graduates.

해석

M Professor: 교육에서 가장 큰 논란거리 중 하나는 대학에서 제공하는 교과과정의 유형입니다. 1960년대와 1970년대에는 많은 대학에서 학생들의 관심

은 끌지만 실용적인 가치는 없는 강의들이 제공되었어요. 예컨대 티베트 성불과 같은 과목은 직장에서 실제로 써먹을 수 없는 것이었죠. 1980년대 하버드 대학은 모든 학생들이 거쳐야 하는 엄격한 핵심 교양 프로그램을 만듦으로써 교과 과정의 개혁에 앞장섰습니다. 여기에는 미술, 언어, 그리고 과학을 포함해 많은 과목이 들어 있었어요. 모든 과목이 똑같이 중요하다고 생각되었습니다. 균형 잡힌 졸업생을 배출하기 위해서는 다 필요하다고 생각되었던 것이죠.

1 The professor discusses the type of curriculum some universities offer.

2 They offered specialized courses that had no practical use in the workplace.

3 It changed its curriculum so that students had to follow a certain program of classes.

4 They were more prepared to enter the workforce.

Organization

Choice A	Choice B
I agree Music and art should have the same value as other courses.	I disagree Music and art should not have the same value as other courses.
First reason Music and art are parts of our culture.	First reason They won't help a person find a job in the future.
Details An understanding of music and art can build character and make you a better person. The subjects can also make you more valuable in the workforce.	Details They have no practical application. No one cares if a person is a musician or artist when that person applies for a job.
Second reason Music and art are part of some core programs at universities.	Second reason The classes are not fair to untalented people.
Details Some universities require students to take a core program of classes. Studying music and art can give these students more career opportunities.	Details Many people have no talent for music or art. Low grades in these classes could ruin their chances of entering a good university or even to graduate from university.

Comparing

Sample Response l Choice A

Script 🎧 01-16

I think music and art should have the same value as other courses. Firstly, they are part of our society. Appreciating music and art can make you a well-rounded person. On the other hand, if all we studied was math and science, we'd be like robots and never appreciate the beauty of our world. Secondly, studies have shown that people with comprehensive educations are more valuable in the workforce. Many universities now require students to take a core curriculum before they pick a major. This gives them some knowledge in many areas and provides them with flexibility when choosing their careers. For these reasons, I believe art and music should have the same value as other courses.

해석

나는 음악과 미술이 다른 과목들과 동일한 가치를 인정받아야 한다고 생각한다. 첫째, 이들은 우리 사회의 일부이다. 음악과 미술을 감상함으로써 균형 잡힌 인간이 될 수 있다. 반면에 수학과 과학만 공부한다면 우리는 로봇처럼 될 것이고 세상의 아름다움을 감상할 수 없을 것이다. 둘째, 연구에 따르면 종합적인 교육을 받은 사람이 직장에서도 더 높은 평가를 받는다. 현재 많은 대학에서 학생들로 하여금 전공을 고르기 전에 핵심 교양 과목을 먼저 듣도록 하고 있다. 이로써 학생들은 여러 분야의 지식을 얻을 수 있고 직업을 선택할 때 유연성을 갖추게 된다. 하여금 이러한 이유로 나는 음악과 미술이 다른 과목들과 동일한 가치를 인정받아야 한다고 믿는다.

Sample Response I Choice B

Script 🎧 01-17

I believe art and music shouldn't have the same value as other courses. First of all, they have no practical use in the real world. Simply put, no one cares if I can play the piano or draw well when I apply for a job, so art and music shouldn't be considered important classes. Another important thing is that some people have no talent for art and music, so giving grades in these classes is unfair. If a student with little artistic or musical talent got a bad grade in a class, it might affect that person's chances of getting into college or even graduating from college. Therefore, for these reasons, I think art and music shouldn't have the same value as other courses.

해석

나는 음악과 미술이 다른 과목과 동일한 가치를 인정받아서는 안 된다고 생각한다. 먼저 이들은 현실 세계에서 실용성이 없다. 간단히 말해서 내가 일자리에 지원하는 경우 내가 피아노를 잘 치는지 혹은 그림을 잘 그리는지는 아무도 신경쓰지 않기 때문에 음악과 미술이 중요한 수업으로 간주되어서는 안 된다. 또 다른 중요한 점은 음악과 미술에 재능이 없는 사람들도 있다는 점에서 이러한 과목에서 성적을 매기는 것은 불공평하다. 음악적인 재능이나 미술적인 재능이 거의 없는 학생이 수업에서 나쁜 성적을 받는다면 이 사람의 대학 입학이나 심지어는 대학 졸업의 기회에 영향이 미칠 수도 있다. 따라서 나는 이러한 이유들로 음악과 미술이 다른 과목들과 동일한 가치를 인정받아서는 안 된다고 생각한다.

Exercise ·· p.20

Before you start

A

Script 01-18

W Student: What are you going to do for your spring break vacation, Henry?

M Student: I haven't made any plans yet.

W: There's a group from our dorm going skiing in Vermont.

M: Sounds good. Who's going?

W: Let's see. I think there are ten people going. David, Alan, Joe, Steve, Tom . . .

M: Tom? No way. I'm not going anywhere with him.

W: Why not?

M: He's cheap and never wants to spend any money. Besides, he can never make up his mind about anything. Anyway, in a group that size, there are bound to be problems.

W: Maybe you're right. So what are you going to do?

M: I think I might just go home to see my family.

해석

W Student: 봄 방학 때 뭘 할 거니, Henry?

M Student: 아직 아무런 계획이 없어.

W: 우리 기숙사에서 버몬트로 스키 여행을 갈 거야.

M: 멋지네. 누가 가는데?

W: 잠깐만. 열 명이 갈 것 같아. David, Alan, Joe, Steve, Tom…

M: Tom? 이럴 수가. 그와는 아무데도 안 갈 거야.

W: 왜?

M: 그는 구두쇠라서 절대로 돈을 쓰려고 하지 않아. 게다가 항상 결정을 내리지 못하지. 어쨌거나 그 정도 인원이라면 반드시 문제가 생길거야.

W: 아마 네 말이 맞을 수도 있겠네. 그러면 넌 어떻게 할 거야?

M: 가족들을 보러 집에 가면 될 것 같아.

1 They are discussing their plans for spring break.

2 They are planning to go skiing in Vermont.

3 He doesn't want to go because of Tom's character and because the group is too big.

4 Yes, he enjoys skiing because he says it sounds like a good idea.

B

Script 🎧 01-19

W Professor: Tourism is big business all over the world. The package trip with a tour group is the most popular way to travel for the elderly with almost eighty-five percent of tour group travelers being fifty years of age or older. Many hotels give discounts of up to twenty percent for large groups. On the other hand, for young travelers, backpacking remains popular, especially in Europe. Some travel alone while others go with friends, but young travelers almost never join tour groups. According to a recent survey, the main reasons for not joining tour groups are the cost and the desire to have a flexible schedule. However, young travelers, especially women, are advised to travel with others to avoid danger.

해석

W Professor: 관광은 전 세계에서 거대한 비즈니스입니다. 단체로 하는 패키지 여행은 노년층에게 가장 인기 있는 여행 방식으로 단체 여행객 중 거의 85%가 50세 이상입니다. 많은 호텔들이 대규모 단체 관광객들에게 최대 20%까지 할인을 해 주죠. 반면 젊은 여행객들에게는 배낭 여행이 인기가 높은데, 특히 유럽에서 그렇습니다. 혼자 여행하는 사람도 있고 친구들과 함께 여행하는 사람도 있지만, 젊은 여행객들이 단체 여행을 하는 경우는 거의 없어요. 최근 조사에 따르면 단체 여행을 하지 않는 주된 이유는 비용 및 유연한 일정에 대한 바람 때문입니다. 하지만 젊은 여행객들도, 특히 여성인 경우, 위험한 경우가 생기지 않도록 다른 사람들과 함께 여행하는 것이 권장됩니다.

1 She compares elderly and young travelers.

2 Large groups can get discounts at hotels.

3 They should travel with others to avoid the dangers of traveling alone.

4 It isn't flexible.

Organization

Choice A	Choice B
I prefer To take a trip by myself	I prefer To take a trip with others
First reason I can be more flexible when making decisions.	First reason It's safer to travel in a group.
Details I can decide where I want to go. I can change my mind if I want to go somewhere different. I don't have to follow a tight schedule.	Details It's safer to be with others when traveling. A tour group leader could help us.
Second reason I may not get along with the others in my group.	Second reason We can have some shared experiences and memories.
Details We may have different personalities. We could have arguments about many things. I might lose a friend if I argue with one.	Details It's more interesting to travel with others. We can have some experiences that will provide good memories forever.

Comparing

Sample Response | Choice A

Script 🎧 01-20

Of the two options, I would choose to travel alone than in a group. Firstly, by traveling alone, I can decide where to go and what to do. I don't have to agree to do something just to make others happy. I can also be more flexible and change my mind. My trip can be more exciting and interesting than it would be if I had to follow a tour group's set schedule. Secondly, I may not get along with the other people I'm traveling with. Everyone has different personalities. Some are lazy or cheap, and others can never make up their minds. If we have an argument, it could ruin the trip or even our friendship. So I prefer to travel alone.

해석

두 가지 옵션 중에서 나는 단체 여행보다 혼자서 하는 여행을 택할 것이다. 첫째, 혼자서 여행을 하면 어디에 갈 것인지 그리고 무엇을 할 것인지를 내가 결정할 수 있다. 다른 사람을 기쁘게 하기 위해 무언가를 하겠다고 동의할 필요가 없다. 또한 융통성이 더 많아지며 마음도 바꿀 수도 있다. 단체 여행의 정해진 일정을 따르는 경우에 비해 여행이 훨씬 더 재미있고 흥미진진해질 수 있다. 둘째, 같이 여행을 하는 사람들과 잘 어울리지 못하는 경우도 있을 수 있다. 사람은 누구나 성격이 다르다. 게으르고 돈을 쓰기 싫어하는 사람도 있고 결코 결정을 내리지 못하는 사람도 있다. 논쟁이 생기는 경우에는 여행을 망칠 수도 있고 우정에 금이 갈 수도 있다. 따라서 나는 혼자서 여행하는 것을 더 좋아한다.

Sample Response | Choice B

Script 🎧 01-21

I'd rather travel in a group than alone. To begin with, traveling in a group is safer than traveling alone. If I were alone, I might have some problems, yet no one could help me, especially in a foreign country where I don't speak the language. If I'm with a tour group, the leader almost always speaks the local language. In addition, traveling with a group can give you and your travel partners many shared experiences and lots of good memories from the trip. Since it's more interesting to travel with others, you can get memories from your trip that will last a lifetime. That is why I prefer traveling with a group of people.

해석

나는 혼자서 하는 여행보다 단체 여행을 선호한다. 우선 단체 여행을 하는 것이 혼자서 여행을 하는 것보다 더 안전하다. 혼자 있는 경우에는 문제가 생겨도 아무도 나를 도와 줄 사람이 없는데, 특히 의사소통이 불가능한 외국에 있는 경우가 그렇다. 단체 여행을 하는 경우에는 인솔자가 거의 항상 해당 지역의 언어를 할 수 있다. 게다가 단체 여행을 하면 여행객들이 여행에 대한 많은 경험과 좋은 기억을 공유할 수 있다. 다른 사람과 함께 여행하는 것이 더 즐겁기 때문에 여행에 대한 기억이 평생 동안 지속될 수도 있다. 바로 이러한 점 때문에 나는 단체 여행을 선호한다.

Unit 06 Money

Exercise ···································· p.22

[Before you start]

A

Script 🎧 01-22

W Student: Oh, I'm glad today is payday. I'm so broke.

M Student: Really, Joanne? I always have a little money put aside.

W: I don't know how you can do it. My money just flies out of my pocket.

M: You know, you should think about the future.

W: What do you mean?

M: Well, someday, you may have an emergency. There may be an accident, or someone in your family might get sick.

W: I never think of that. I just want to have fun now while I'm young. Going out to clubs and restaurants is expensive, you know.

M: You're not going to be young forever. You might also lose your job someday.

W: Maybe you're right. With the economy the way it is, I should start thinking more about what could go wrong.

해석

W Student: 오, 오늘이 월급날이라 다행이야. 돈이 한 푼도 없거든.

M Student: 정말이야, Joanne? 난 항상 비상금을 챙겨 둬.

W: 어떻게 그럴 수 있는지 모르겠네. 나는 돈이 들어오자마자 나가 버리는데.

M: 알겠지만 나중을 생각해야지.

W: 무슨 말이니?

M: 음, 나중에 비상 사태가 생길 수도 있을 거야. 사고가 날 수도 있고 가족 중에 누군가 아플 수도 있어.

W: 그런 생각은 한 번도 안 해 봤네. 나는 젊을 때 재미있게 살고 싶을 뿐이야. 너도 알다시피 클럽과 레스토랑에 가면 돈이 많이 들거든.

M: 영원히 젊을 수는 없잖아. 게다가 언젠가는 일자리를 잃을 수도 있고.

W: 네 말이 맞을 수도 있겠군. 현재와 같은 경제 상황에서는 문제가 생기는 경우에 대해 더 많이 생각을 해야 할 것 같아.

1 Today is payday, and she has no money.

2 Joanne's friend warns her that she could get sick, have an accident, or lose her job.

3 She wants to have fun while she is young.

4 She may try to save some of it.

B

Script 🎧 01-23

M Professor: Personal savings represent a large, untapped portion of our national economy. Billions of dollars are saved for future rainy days. Many people also have several types of insurance, with life, health, auto, and house insurance being the most common. Unfortunately, a great many people either choose not to save money or cannot because their incomes are so low. The younger a person is, the less likely it is that the person will have any savings. A survey done recently showed that many people under the age of thirty live from paycheck to paycheck. As a person acquires more responsibilities, such as a family, a car, and a house, the person is more likely to think about needing some income for a future emergency.

해석

M Professor: 개인 저축은 국가 경제에서 큰 비중을 차지하는 미사용 부분입니다. 나중의 불행을 대비하기 위한 수십억 달러가 저축되어 있죠. 또한 많은 사람들이 여러 종류의 보험에 가입되어 있는데, 이들 중 생명 보험, 건강 보험, 자동차 보험, 주택 보험 등이 가장 흔한 편입니다. 안타깝게도 임금 수준이 매우 낮은 상당수의 사람들은 저축을 하지 않거나 저축을 할 수가 없습니다. 나이가 어릴수록 아무런 저축도 하지 않을 확률이 큽니다. 최근에 진행된 조사에 따르면 30세 미만의 많은 사람들이 그날 벌어서 그날 쓰고 있어요. 가족, 자동차, 그리고 주택과 같이 더 많은 책임을 떠안게 되는 것들이 많아지면 미래의 위급 상황을 대비하기 위한 수입이 필요하다고 생각할 가능성이 높아집니다.

1 Personal savings are a large part of the national income.

2 They choose not to, or they can't because their incomes are low.

3 The professor mentions life, health, auto, and house insurance.

4 The younger the person is, the fewer responsibilities he has.

[Organization]

Choice A	Choice B
I prefer To save all my extra money	I prefer To spend my extra money on the things I want
First reason There could be an unexpected emergency in the future.	First reason I love shopping and having the best of everything.

Details	Details
Having extra cash gives me peace of mind. Someone in my family or I could have an accident or get sick unexpectedly.	It's fun to go shopping and to spend money. I like having the best clothing and other items.
Second reason	Second reason
The future is uncertain, so I could possibly lose my job.	I'm young and have an active social life.
Details	Details
I could lose my job in the future. I need to have some money saved to pay for the basic necessities while I look for a new job.	I'm young and healthy and have no responsibilities. I need money to have an enjoyable social life.

Comparing

Sample Response I Choice A

`Script` 🎧 01-24

I believe that it's better to save any extra money I have. Having that extra cash saved gives me some peace of mind. For instance, someone in my family or I could have an emergency and need the extra money since hospitals can be expensive. The future is also uncertain, so I could possibly lose my job. If I lost my job and had no savings, I wouldn't be able to pay for my apartment, food, or anything. Some people recommend that you have at least three month's salary saved in case you lose your job. These are the main reasons I think it's better to save extra money than to spend it.

해석

나는 여윳돈을 저축하는 것이 더 낫다고 생각한다. 여윳돈을 저축해 두면 마음이 편안해진다. 예를 들어 가족 중의 누군가나 내게 긴급 상황이 발생하는 경우 병원비가 비쌀 수 있기 때문에 여윳돈이 필요할 수 있다. 또한 미래는 불확실해서 내가 일자리를 잃을 수도 있다. 만약 일자리를 잃었는데 저축해 둔 돈도 없다면 주거비, 식비, 혹은 그 어떤 비용도 지불할 수 없을 것이다. 어떤 사람들은 일자리를 잃는 경우에 대비해 최소한 석 달치 월급을 저축해 두라고 충고한다. 이러한 이유들 때문에 나는 여윳돈을 쓰는 것보다 저축해 두는 것이 더 낫다고 생각한다.

Sample Response I Choice B

`Script` 🎧 01-25

My preference is to spend any extra money I have rather than save it. I enjoy shopping and like to have the best of everything, such as clothing and the latest technology like computers and cell phones. Additionally, I am young, so I don't have any responsibilities. I'm not married, I don't have children, and my parents have enough to take care of themselves. I'm healthy, so I never worry about being sick. I also have an active social life. In other words, I like to go out with my friends to nightclubs and good restaurants.

For these reasons, I prefer to spend any extra money I have.

해석

나는 여윳돈을 저축하는 것보다 쓰는 것을 선호한다. 나는 쇼핑을 좋아하며 가장 좋은 제품, 예컨대 의류와 컴퓨터 및 휴대 전화와 같은 최첨단 제품들이 갖고 싶다. 게다가 나는 젊기 때문에 책임져야 할 것들이 없다. 나는 미혼이고, 자녀도 없으며, 부모님들은 스스로 지내실 수 있을 만큼 형편이 좋으시다. 나는 건강하기 때문에 병에 걸리는 것에 대해서도 걱정을 하지 않는다. 또한 나는 사교 생활도 활발히 한다. 다시 말해서 친구들과 함께 클럽 및 좋은 식당에 가는 것을 좋아한다. 이러한 이유들 때문에 나는 여윳돈을 쓰는 것을 선호한다.

Unit 07   Computers

`Exercise` p.24

Before you start

A

`Script` 🎧 01-26

M Student: Okay. You can open your eyes now, Alicia.

W Student: Wow! A new tablet PC!

M: Happy birthday.

W: Thanks, Jeff. Can I try it?

M: Of course. It can do anything you want. It has word processing software and an encyclopedia, and we also got you a compact printer for your reports.

W: What about the Internet?

M: It has a high-speed Internet connection, and you can use the Web for research and to email or chat with your friends.

W: Does it come with any games?

M: No. I guess you don't want to waste your time playing games.

해석

M Student: 됐어. 이제 눈을 떠도 좋아, Alicia.

W Student: 와! 새 태블릿 PC구나!

M: 생일 축하해.

W: 고마워, Jeff. 켜 봐도 될까?

M: 물론이지. 원하는 건 다 할 수 있을 거야. 워드 프로세서와 백과사전이 들어 있는데, 너를 위해 보고서 작성을 위한 휴대용 프린터도 샀어.

W: 인터넷은?

M: 고속 인터넷이 연결되니까 인터넷을 이용해서 조사도 할 수 있고 친구들에게 이메일을 보내거나 친구들과 채팅도 할 수 있지.

W: 게임도 들어 있니?

M: 아니. 네가 게임을 하느라 시간을 허비하고 싶어하지는 않을 것 같은데.

1 She got a new tablet PC.
2 It has word processing software, an encyclopedia, a printer, and high-speed Internet capability.
3 She might do some research and email or chat with her friends.
4 He believes that games are a waste of time.

B

Script 🎧 01-27

W Professor: The computer has embedded itself into our society to the extent that we can't imagine our lives without it. It has increased the speed at which the world operates. People use computers to find information, to provide entertainment, and to communicate with others. However, this great tool has caused some serious problems. Addictions to computer games and Internet surfing are two of the most serious. A small but growing segment of society lives on the Internet for most of their waking moments. It is estimated that over five million Americans can be called computer addicts. There is also the growing problem of Internet fraud. Several billion dollars were lost to Internet fraud just last year.

해석

W Professor: 컴퓨터 없는 삶은 상상이 되지 않을 정도로 컴퓨터는 우리의 사회 속에 깊이 자리잡고 있습니다. 컴퓨터로 인해 세상이 돌아가는 속도가 빨라졌어요. 사람들은 컴퓨터를 이용해 정보를 찾고, 오락 거리를 제공하며, 다른 사람들과 의사소통을 합니다. 하지만 이 훌륭한 도구가 몇 가지 심각한 문제를 야기하기도 했어요. 가장 심각한 문제 중 두 가지는 컴퓨터 게임 중독과 인터넷 서핑 중독입니다. 소수이기는 하지만 점점 많은 사회 구성원들이 깨어 있는 대부분의 시간을 인터넷 상에서 보내고 있어요. 5백만 명이 넘는 미국인들이 컴퓨터 중독자일 것으로 추정되고 있죠. 또한 인터넷 사기도 점점 더 큰 문제가 되고 있습니다. 작년에만 인터넷 사기로 몇 십억 달러가 사라졌습니다.

1 They can be used to find information, to provide entertainment, and to communicate with others.
2 There are the problems of game and Internet addiction and Internet fraud.
3 Over five million people are believed to be computer addicts.
4 It will increase since the lecturer mentions that Internet fraud is growing.

Organization

	Choice A	Choice B
	I agree	I disagree
	Computers have made our lives better.	Computers haven't made our lives better.

First reason	First reason
It's easier to do research and write reports with them.	People waste time on their computers and become addicted to using them.
Details	**Details**
We can use the Internet to find lots of information. Word processing programs make it easier to write reports.	Using computers to play games and to surf the Internet wastes a lot of time. Some people have no social lives and become addicted to their computers.
Second reason	**Second reason**
Computers provide better entertainment and communications capabilities.	There is a lot of Internet crime nowadays.
Details	**Details**
We can listen to music, watch movies, and play games on computers. Email and chat rooms make it faster and easier to communicate with people around the world.	Experts can get people's private information from their computers. A lot of people try to trick others into sending them money.

Comparing

Sample Response | Choice A
Script 🎧 01-28

In my opinion, computers have made our lives better. First of all, now it's easier for people to conduct research with computers and to write reports on them. For example, we can use the Internet to get information about all kinds of subjects. Plus, word processing programs make it easy to type our papers on computers. A second reason is that computers have better entertainment and communication capabilities. Thanks to computers, we can now listen to music, watch movies, and play games on computers. We also have email and chat rooms, which make it faster and easier for people to communicate with others around the world. Computers have clearly made our lives much better.

해석

내 생각에는 컴퓨터가 우리의 삶을 더 나아지게 만들었다. 우선 컴퓨터로 조사를 해서 그에 대한 보고서를 쓰는 일이 더 쉬워졌다. 예를 들어 인터넷을 이용하면 온갖 주제에 관한 정보를 얻을 수 있다. 게다가 워드 프로세서로 인해 컴퓨터로 보고서를 타이핑하는 일도 쉬워졌다. 두 번째 이유는 컴퓨터 덕분에 오락물과 의사소통 능력이 향상되었다는 점에 있다. 컴퓨터 덕분에 현재 음악을 들고, 영화를 시청하고, 그리고 컴퓨터 게임을 할 수도 있다. 또한 이메일을 보내고 채팅도 할 수 있는데, 이로써 전 세계의 다른 사람들과 의사소통하는 일이 더 빠르고 쉬워졌다. 컴퓨터는 확실히 우리의 삶을 더 나아지게 만들었다.

Script 🎧 01-29

I think that computers have not made our lives better. To begin with, many people waste their time using computers to play games and to use the Internet. Simply put, they have no friends or social lives outside of their computers. Some people even lose their jobs or fail their classes because they spend all of their time using their computers for fun. Secondly, there are the problems of privacy and Internet crime. Hackers can attack your computer and get your private information, such as your bank account and credit card numbers, from it. In addition, there are a lot of people trying to trick others into giving them money by making false claims. Overall, these reasons prove that computers have not made our lives better.

해석

나는 컴퓨터가 우리의 삶을 더 나아지게 만들지는 않았다고 생각한다. 우선 많은 사람들이 컴퓨터로 게임을 하거나 인터넷을 사용하느라 시간을 허비한다. 간단히 말해서 컴퓨터 밖에서는 그들의 친구나 사회 생활이 존재하지 않는다. 심지어 모든 시간을 재미를 위한 컴퓨터에 쓰기 때문에 일자리를 잃거나 수업에서 낙제를 하는 사람들도 있다. 두 번째로 사생활 침해와 인터넷 범죄의 문제가 있다. 해커들이 컴퓨터를 공격해서 은행 계좌나 신용카드 정보와 같은 개인 정보를 빼낼 수도 있다. 또한 많은 사람들이 다른 사람들을 속이고 사기를 쳐서 돈을 보내도록 만들려고 한다. 전체적으로, 이러한 이유들 때문에 컴퓨터가 삶을 더 나아지게 만들지는 않았다는 점을 알 수 있다.

Unit 08 Job Applications

Exercise p.26

Before you start

A

Script 🎧 01-30

W Student: Is that a copy of your résumé? Why did you put your photograph on it?

M Student: Lately, a lot of companies are asking job applicants to submit pictures with their applications.

W: Really? I didn't know that. How do you feel about that?

M: I don't mind at all. I mean, the company will find out what I look like at the job interview.

W: But aren't you worried that someone might be biased by how you look?

M: Not really. My picture is all over my social media pages. So I can't hide how I look.

W: Oh, that's a good point. I hadn't considered that.

M: And for people such as performers, how they look can help them get a job.

해석

W Student: 그게 네 이력서 사본이니? 왜 거기에 사진을 넣었어?

M Student: 최근에 많은 기업들이 입사 지원자들로 하여금 지원서에 사진을 넣을 것을 요구하고 있거든.

W: 정말이야? 나는 모르고 있었어. 그에 대해 어떻게 생각하니?

M: 나는 전혀 신경이 쓰이지 않아. 내 말은 면접에서 내가 어떻게 생겼는지 기업이 알게 될 것이라는 뜻이야.

W: 하지만 외모 때문에 누군가가 선입견을 가질 수도 있다는 점은 걱정되지 않니?

M: 그렇지는 않아. 내 사진은 내 소셜 미디어 페이지에도 다 나와 있는 걸. 그러니 내 외모를 숨길 수가 없어.

W: 오, 좋은 지적이네. 그 점은 생각 못했어.

M: 그리고 배우 같은 사람들에게는 외모가 취업에 도움이 될 수도 있지.

1 He put a picture of himself on his résumé.

2 He does not mind sending companies a picture of himself.

3 His picture is on his social media pages, so he cannot hide how he looks.

4 It is necessary for them to put their pictures on their job applications.

B

Script 🎧 01-31

M Professor: In some countries, it's common for people applying for jobs to put pictures of themselves on their applications. However, it's not common practice in some countries, such as the United States. There are a few reasons for this. The primary one is that the people in charge of hiring might be biased for or against applicants if they see pictures of these individuals. By that, I mean that an unattractive yet highly qualified person might not get an interview whereas a good-looking but unqualified person might get interviewed. That's not fair, is it? Another important thing to remember is that most résumés are one page long. A picture can take up valuable space on a résumé. What would you rather put on yours, a picture of yourself or important information about your work experience?

해석

M Professor: 몇몇 국가에서는 입사 지원자들이 지원서에 자신의 사진을 넣는 일이 일반적입니다. 하지만 미국과 같은 일부 나라에서는 흔한 일이 아니죠. 여기에는 몇 가지 이유가 있습니다. 첫 번째 이유는 고용 담당자들이 그러한 개인들의 사진을 보는 경우 지원자에 대한 호감이나 반감을 가질 수 있기 때문이에요. 이 말은 매력적이지는 않지만 자격 조건을 갖춘 사람이 면접을 보지 못할 수도 있고, 반면에 외모는 훌륭하지만 자격 조건이 부족한 사람은 면접을 볼 수도

있다는 뜻입니다. 공정하지 않죠, 그렇죠? 기억해야 할 또 다른 중요한 점은 대부분의 이력서가 1페이지 분량이라는 점이에요. 이력서에서 사진이 귀중한 공간을 차지할 수도 있습니다. 여러분들은 이력서에 무엇을, 여러분의 사진과 여러분의 경력에 관한 중요한 정보 중에서, 무엇을 넣고 싶으신가요?

1 In some countries, it is common for job applicants to put pictures of themselves on their applications.
2 The main reason is that it could cause bias in the people who hire applicants.
3 A picture can take up space on a résumé that could be used to provide important information.
4 The person might not be considered for a job.

Organization

Choice A	Choice B
I agree Job applicants should put their pictures on their applications.	I disagree Job applicants should not put their pictures on their applications.
First reason There is no reason to hide what they look like.	First reason A picture can create bias in the person considering job applications.
Details Most job applicants have pictures of themselves on their social media pages, so they have no reason to hide what they look like.	Details Some people doing hiring might give interviews to attractive but unqualified people and ignore those people who are well qualified but unattractive.
Second reason Looks are important for some jobs.	Second reason It can take up space on an application.
Details How people look is important for those individuals applying for jobs such as actor.	Details There is only so much room on a job application, and that space should be used for personal information that can get a person a job, not on a picture.

Comparing

Sample Response I Choice A
Script 🎧 01-32

I agree with the statement that people should attach photographs when applying for jobs. One reason I believe this is that there is no need for people to hide what they look like since they almost certainly have social media pages. People in charge of hiring usually check job applicants' social media pages, so they can easily find out what applicants look like. Another thing to consider is that there are many jobs in which looks are crucial. For instance, my cousin is an actress. When she applies for jobs, she always attaches a picture of herself. Directors typically want a certain kind of look in their performers. So if a director sees her picture and thinks my cousin will fit a role, the director can contact her.

해석
나는 사람들이 입사 지원을 할 때 사진을 부착해야 한다는 주장에 동의한다. 그렇게 생각하는 한 가지 이유는 사람들이 거의 다 자신의 소셜 미디어 페이지를 가지고 있어서 자신의 외모를 숨길 필요가 없기 때문이다. 채용 담당자들은 보통 입사 지원자들의 소셜 미디어 페이지를 살펴보기 때문에 지원자들의 외모를 쉽게 알아낼 수 있다. 또 다른 고려 사항은 외모가 중요한 직업들이 많기 때문이다. 예를 들어 내 사촌은 배우이다. 그녀는 일을 구할 때 항상 자신의 사진을 부착한다. 감독들은 보통 특정한 외모를 갖춘 배우들을 원한다. 따라서 감독이 그녀의 사진을 보고 내 사촌이 역할에 맞는다고 생각한다면 그녀에게 연락을 취할 것이다.

Sample Response I Choice B
Script 🎧 01-33

I disagree with the statement and do not want people to attach photographs to their job applications. Something to think about is that the people in charge of hiring could become biased when they see pictures. They might want to work with attractive people, so they could interview good-looking but unqualified people. At the same time, they might ignore qualified yet people who aren't attractive. One more thing to remember is that most job applications are short. They might be a single page long. It would be better to include information such as job experience or education in that space than simply to put a photograph there. My brother didn't include a photograph on a recent job application, and he got an interview. So that worked for him.

해석
나는 그러한 주장에 동의하지 않으며 사람들이 입사 지원서에 사진을 부착하는 것을 찬성하지 않는다. 생각해 보아야 할 점은 채용 담당자들이 사진을 보고 편견을 가질 수 있다는 점이다. 그들은 아마도 매력적인 사람들과 함께 일하고 싶어할 수도 있기 때문에 외모가 훌륭하지만 자격 조건은 부족한 사람들을 면접할 수 있다. 동시에 그들은 자격 조건을 갖추었지만 매력적이지 않은 사람들은 무시할 수도 있다. 기억해야 할 또 다른 점은 대부분의 입사 지원서가 짧다는 것이다. 단 1페이지 분량일 수도 있다. 그러한 공간에 단순히 사진을 넣기보다는 경력이나 학력과 같은 정보를 포함시키는 것이 더 나을 것이다. 우리 형은 최근 입사 지원서에 사진을 넣지 않았는데 면접을 보게 되었다. 사진을 넣지 않아도 효과가 있었다.

Unit 09 Free-Time Activities

Exercise ··· p.28

Before you start

A

Script 🎧 01-34

M Student: What are you planning to do on the weekend?

W Student: I haven't thought about that yet. What about you?

M: I'm going to play basketball with my friends again.

W: You seem to do that frequently.

M: Well, it's really fun to play sports with my friends. It's also great exercise.

W: That's a good point. I don't play sports very much.

M: You should try them sometime. Even if you aren't good, you can run around and enjoy yourself.

W: Okay. Maybe I'll see if some of my friends want to do something similar this weekend. Thanks.

해석

M Student: 주말 계획이 어떻게 되니?

W Student: 아직 생각을 못 해 봤어. 너는 어떤데?

M: 나는 친구들과 함께 또 농구를 할 생각이야.

W: 농구를 자주하는 것 같구나.

M: 음, 친구들과 함께 스포츠를 하는 것이 정말로 재미있어. 또한 운동도 되고.

W: 맞는 말이야. 나는 운동을 그다지 많이 하지 않는 편이거든.

M: 너도 조만간 해 봐. 운동을 잘하지 못해도 뛰면서 재미를 느낄 수 있을 거야.

W: 좋아. 이번 주말에 그와 비슷한 걸 하고 싶은 친구가 있는지 알아볼 수도 있겠군. 고마워.

1 He plans to play basketball with his friends.

2 He thinks it is fun to play sports with his friends, and it is also great exercise.

3 He suggests that she try playing sports sometime.

4 She will play sports with some of her friends in the future.

B

Script 🎧 01-35

W Professor: There are many people who claim that computer games are bad for young people. They state that computer games are addictive and can make people violent. However, I disagree with them. As a matter of fact, computer games provide a number of benefits for many people. First of all, some games, such as shooting games, teach hand-eye coordination. This can help

gamers in real life when they play sports or do other activities. In addition, there are many multiplayer games. In order to win, gamers have to work together with their partners. As a result, they learn about teamwork and gain leadership skills. These two abilities are vital for people when they enter the workplace. So you see, computer games can be quite helpful at times.

해석

W Professor: 어린 사람들에게 컴퓨터 게임은 나쁘다고 주장하는 사람들이 많습니다. 컴퓨터 게임은 중독성이 있고 사람들을 폭력적으로 만들 수 있다고 주장하죠. 하지만 저는 동의하지 않습니다. 실제로 컴퓨터 게임은 많은 사람들에게 다수의 이점을 가져다 주어요. 먼저 슈팅 게임과 같은 몇몇 게임들은 손과 눈의 협응력을 길러 줍니다. 이는 게이머들이 현실에서 스포츠 경기나 기타 활동을 할 때 도움이 되죠. 또한 다중 플레이어 게임들이 존재합니다. 이기기 위해서는 게이머들이 파트너와 함께 협력을 해야만 해요. 따라서 팀워크에 대해 배우고 리더쉽을 기르게 됩니다. 이 두 가지 자질은 취직을 할 때 매우 중요한 것이에요. 따라서, 아시겠지만, 컴퓨터 게임은 때때로 매우 유익할 수 있습니다.

1 They say that computer games are addictive and can make people become violent.

2 She believes that they can be beneficial to people.

3 They improve gamers' hand-eye coordination, which can help them with sports and other activities.

4 Gamers can learn about teamwork and improve their leadership skills when they play multiplayer games.

Organization

	Choice A	Choice B
I prefer	To play sports	To play computer games
First reason	I have fun doing activities with my friends.	I can improve my hand-eye coordination.
Details	We get to spend time together playing a sport, and we also have fun laughing and talking while we play.	I love to play shooting games, and that improves my hand-eye coordination. As a result, my real-life skills have also improved.
Second reason	Playing sports is good exercise.	I have learned about teamwork by playing computer games.
Details	I can exercise while playing sports, which can help me get in shape and also lose weight.	I enjoy playing multiplayer games with my friends. I have learned to be a good teammate, so that helps us win a lot of games.

Sample Response | Choice A

Script 🎧 01-36

I definitely prefer to play sports instead of computers games. For one thing, playing sports is a fun activity that I can do together with my friends. My friends and I often play soccer or basketball together on the weekend. We enjoy spending a lot of time together, and we also have fun when we play. We don't take the games too seriously but instead laugh and joke around with one another. Second of all, playing sports is really good exercise. When I first started playing sports a couple of years ago, I was a bit overweight. Now, however, I have lost a lot of weight and am in good shape. In my opinion, the reason for that is that I play sports so often.

해석

나는 컴퓨터 게임 대신 스포츠 활동을 하는 것을 크게 선호한다. 첫째, 스포츠는 친구들과 함께 할 수 있는 재미있는 활동이다. 나는 종종 주말에 친구들과 함께 축구나 농구를 한다. 우리는 즐겁게 많은 시간을 함께 보내며 또한 경기를 할 때 재미를 느낀다. 경기에 지나치게 진지하게 임하지는 않으며, 대신 서로 웃고 농담을 주고 받는다. 둘째, 스포츠 활동은 정말로 좋은 운동이 된다. 2년 전 처음 스포츠를 하기 시작했을 때 나는 약간 과체중이었다. 하지만 지금은 살이 많이 빠졌고 건강한 편이다. 나는 바로 그러한 이유에서 내가 종종 스포츠 활동을 한다고 생각한다.

Sample Response | Choice B

Script 🎧 01-37

For me, playing computer games is preferable to playing sports. I really enjoy playing a wide variety of computer games. One type of game that I often play is shooting games. Because I have to shoot small objects on the screen, I have improved my hand-eye coordination. This, in turn, has turned me into a better baseball player. I also have other skills that have improved thanks to these shooting games. Another reason is that I have learned a lot about teamwork by playing multiplayer computer games. If my teammates and I want to win the game, we have to work together and not be individuals. So I have learned how to work more closely with others thanks to computer games.

해석

나로서는 컴퓨터 게임을 하는 것이 스포츠 활동을 하는 것보다 더 좋다. 나는 매우 다양한 종류의 컴퓨터 게임을 하는 것을 정말 좋아한다. 내가 종종 하는 게임 중 하나는 슈팅 게임이다. 화면의 작은 물체들을 쏘아 맞춰야 하기 때문에 나는 손과 눈의 협응력을 기를 수 있었다. 이로써 내 야구 실력 역시 향상되었다. 또한 이들 슈팅 게임 덕분에 다른 능력들도 향상되었다. 또 다른 이유는 다중 플레이어 컴퓨터 게임을 함으로써 팀워크에 대해 많은 것을 배우기 때문이다. 팀원들과 내가 경기에서 이기고자 한다면 우리는 협력을 해야 하며 개인 플레이를 해서는 안 된다. 따라서 나는 컴퓨터 게임 덕분에 다른 사람들과 더 많이 협동하는 법을 배우게 되었다.

Unit 10 The Internet

Exercise ··· p.30

Before you start

A

Script 🎧 01-38

M Student: You don't look very happy, Wendy. What's going on?

W Student: I just got my bill from my Internet service provider. It's so expensive, and the price is going up next month.

M: I totally understand what you mean. I have the same problem.

W: All of these companies that provide Internet service are ripping off their customers.

M: You're right. They charge too much, and they don't provide good service.

W: I know. My Internet went out last month, and it took three days to get service back. The company just didn't care about getting me back online.

M: I'm sorry to hear that. You should try another company.

W: Why bother? They are all pretty much the same.

해석

M Student: 표정이 그다지 좋지 않구나, Wendy. 무슨 일이니?

W Student: 조금 전에 인터넷 서비스 업체로부터 청구서를 받았어. 매우 비싼 편인데 다음 달에 가격이 오를 예정이야.

M: 무슨 말인지 전적으로 이해해. 나도 동일한 문제를 겪고 있지.

W: 이러한 인터넷 서비스 회사들 모두가 소비자들에게 바가지를 씌우고 있어.

M: 네 말이 맞아. 요금을 너무 많이 부과하면서 좋은 서비스도 제공하지 않잖아.

W: 나도 알아. 지난 달에는 인터넷이 끊겼는데, 다시 서비스가 재개되기까지 3일이 걸렸어. 회사는 인터넷 복구에 신경을 쓰지 않더군.

M: 그런 말을 들으니 유감이야. 다른 회사를 알아 보는 것이 좋겠어.

W: 굳이? 모두 다 비슷비슷한 걸.

1 She got an expensive bill from her Internet service provider.

2 She says that they are ripping off their customers.

3 Her Internet went out, and it took three days to get service back.

4 She will stay with her current Internet service provider.

B

Script 🎧 01-39

W Professor: Nearly everyone is online these days. If people don't have desktop or laptop computers, they get online with their phones or tablets. Unfortunately, getting online is not cheap. It can cost too much for many people. That's one reason why people say that the government should provide free Internet service for everyone. Basically, people say that Internet service is a right that everyone should have, so nobody should have to pay for it. So many activities are done online today. For instance, people work, study, and play online and also do shopping and banking. As a result, it's necessary for people to have access to the Internet in order to participate in society. And that's why the government should provide it for free for everyone.

해석

W Professor: 요즘은 거의 모든 사람들이 인터넷에 접속해 있습니다. 데스크톱이나 노트북 컴퓨터가 없더라도 전화기나 태블릿 PC로 온라인에 접속해 있죠. 안타깝지만 온라인에 접속하는 비용은 싸지 않습니다. 많은 사람들에게 과도한 요금이 부과될 수 있어요. 바로 이러한 점 때문에 사람들이 정부가 모든 사람들에게 무료로 인터넷 서비스를 제공해야 한다고 말을 합니다. 기본적으로 인터넷 서비스는 모든 사람이 가지고 있는 권리이며, 따라서 그에 대한 비용은 누구도 낼 필요가 없다고 말을 하죠. 오늘날 많은 활동들이 온라인에서 이루어지고 있어요. 예를 들어 사람들은 온라인으로 업무를 보고, 공부를 하고, 게임을 하며, 또한 쇼핑도 하고 은행 업무도 보죠. 따라서 사회에 몸담기 위해서는 사람들이 인터넷에 접속해야 합니다. 그리고 바로 그러한 이유에서 정부가 모든 사람들에게 무료로 서비스를 제공해야 하는 것이죠.

1 They can use desktop or laptop computers, phones, and tablets.
2 They say it is a right that all people should have.
3 People work, study, and play online and also do shopping and banking.
4 It's necessary for people to have access to the Internet in order to participate in society.

Organization

Choice A	Choice B
I agree I agree that the government should provide Internet service for free.	**I disagree** I disagree that the government should provide Internet service for free.
First reason People have a right to access the Internet.	**First reason** There are many places where online access is already free.
Details People do many activities online, so it's necessary to have access to the Internet to participate in society.	**Details** People can visit libraries, restaurants, coffee shops, and other places that do not charge anything for Wi-Fi Internet access.
Second reason Internet service is too expensive.	**Second reason** Taxes would increase.
Details Many people cannot afford to pay the high monthly fees for Internet service.	**Details** If the government provides Internet service, taxes will rise because the government will need money to pay for the costs associated with Internet service.

Comparing

Sample Response I Choice A
Script 🎧 01-40

I agree with the statement that the government should provide free Internet service for everyone. I feel strongly about this for a couple of reasons. To begin with, people do so many activities online nowadays. For instance, I study, communicate with others, play games, and shop online while other people work and do banking online. The Internet has become something like a public utility, so everyone needs access to it. In addition, the price of Internet service for a person's home is extremely expensive nowadays. I know people who pay around one hundred dollars a month for Internet service. For them, that's a lot of money. It would be much better if the government paid for Internet service. Then, people could spend their money on other necessities.

해석

나는 정부가 모든 사람들에게 무료로 인터넷 서비스를 제공해야 한다는 주장에 찬성한다. 두 가지 이유에서 강력히 찬성한다. 우선, 오늘날 사람들은 온라인에서 너무나 많은 활동을 하고 있다. 예를 들어 나는 온라인으로 다른 사람들과 소통하며, 게임을 하고, 쇼핑을 하는데, 온라인으로 일을 하고 은행 업무를 보는 사람들도 있다. 인터넷은 공공재와 같은 것이 되었기 때문에 모든 사람들이 인터넷에 접속해야 한다. 게다가 현재 한 가정의 인터넷 서비스 요금이 매우 비싸다. 나는 인터넷 서비스 비용으로 한 달에 100만 달러 정도를 지불하는 사람들을 알고 있다. 그들에게 이는 큰 금액이다. 정부가 인터넷 서비스 요금을 부담한다면 훨씬 더 좋을 것이다. 그러면 다른 생필품들에 대한 소비가 이루어질 수 있다.

Sample Response I Choice B
Script 🎧 01-41

I do not believe that the government should pay for everyone to have Internet service, so I disagree with the statement. For starters, it is possible for people to gain access to the Internet for free in many places. In my country, buses and subways have free Wi-Fi, and so do many public buildings, restaurants, and coffee shops. If I need to use the Internet but don't have access at home, I can just go out and use it for free somewhere. It's not a major inconvenience. A second point I would like to make is that taxes would increase if the government provided everyone with Internet service. After all, the government would have to pay the Internet providers for their services. The government would need to raise money, so taxes would increase.

해석

나는 정부가 모든 사람들의 인터넷 서비스 요금을 부담해야 한다고 생각하지 않기 때문에 그러한 주장에 동의하지 않는다. 우선, 많은 장소에서 사람들이 무료로 인터넷에 접속할 수 있다. 우리 나라에서는 버스와 지하철에 무료 와이파이가 제공되고 있으며 많은 공공 건물, 식당, 그리고 커피숍에도 와이파이가 제공된다. 인터넷을 사용해야 하지만 집에서 인터넷 연결이 안 되는 경우, 나는 밖에 나가서 무료로 인터넷을 사용할 수 있다. 이는 크게 불편한 일이 아니다. 내가 제시하고 싶은 두 번째 이유는 정부가 인터넷 서비스를 모두에게 제공한다면 세금이 인상될 것이기 때문이다. 어쨌거나 정부는 서비스에 대해 인터넷 공급업체들에게 비용을 내야 한다. 정부가 돈을 마련해야 하기 때문에 세금이 인상될 것이다.

Unit 11 The Elderly

Exercise p.32

Before you start

 A

Script 🎧 01-42

M Student: You won't believe this about my family.

W Student: What's going on? Is everything okay?

M: Well, my grandfather has decided to start mountain climbing. He's getting in shape because he wants to climb Mount Kilimanjaro in Africa next year.

W: Good for him. I hope he can manage to do it.

M: Yeah, but he's seventy-five years old. He's way too old to be doing something that difficult. He shouldn't do activities better done by young people.

W: I disagree. I think it's great to see someone who is willing to try something difficult despite his age.

M: I just don't see it that way.

W: It's better that he do this than just stay at home and watch TV all day.

해석

M Student: 우리 가족 얘기를 들으면 믿지 못할 걸.

W Student: 무슨 일인데? 별일 없는 거지?

M: 음, 우리 할아버지께서 등산을 하기로 결심하셨어. 내년에 아프리카의 킬리만자로산을 오르시려고 체력을 기르시는 중이야.

W: 할아버지께는 좋은 일이네. 해내실 수 있기를 바라.

M: 그래, 하지만 연세가 75세셔. 그렇게 힘든 일을 하기에는 나이가 너무 많으시다고. 젊은 사람들이 할 수 있는 일을 하시면 안 되지.

W: 난 네 말에 동의할 수 없어. 고령에도 불구하고 힘든 일을 기꺼이 하려는 사람들을 보면 멋지다고 생각하거든.

M: 난 그렇게 생각하지 않아.

W: 하루 종일 집에서 TV나 보시는 것보다는 나을 것 같아.

1 He is getting in shape to climb Mount Kilimanjaro in Africa next year.

2 He wants his grandfather to avoid doing activities young people do.

3 She thinks it is great to see him try something difficult.

4 She is pleased the man's grandfather is trying to be active.

B

Script 🎧 01-43

M Professor: These days, many elderly people are engaging in activities they did not do in the past. For instance, some go scuba diving, hang-gliding, or roller-skating while others run marathons or do various extreme sports. People have different opinions about this.
Some claim that the elderly shouldn't take risks or do dangerous activities. They say it is too easy for the elderly to get injured or even die doing these activities. They note that the children and grandchildren of very active elderly people suffer stress from worrying about them too much. Others, however, support the elderly taking part in these activities. In their opinions, it is nice to see the elderly being active and not simply staying at home and waiting to die.

해석

M Professor: 요즘 많은 노인들이 과거에는 하지 않았던 일들을 하고 있습니다. 예를 들어 스쿠버 다이빙, 행글라이딩, 혹은 롤러스케이팅을 하는 사람들도 있고, 마라톤이나 다양한 익스트림 스포츠에 참여하는 사람들도 있죠. 이에 대한 사람들의 의견은 각자 다릅니다. 노인들이 위험을 무릅쓰거나 위험한 활동을 해서는 안 된다고 주장하는 사람들이 있어요. 노인들은 그러한 활동을 하다가 쉽게 다칠 수도 있고 심지어 목숨을 잃을 수도 있다고 말을 합니다. 매우 활동적인 노인들을 걱정하느라 그 자식과 손주들은 스트레스를 받는다고도 이야기하죠. 하지만 노인들이 그러한 활동에 참여하는 것을 지지하는 사람들도 있습니다. 그들의 생각으로는 노인들이 단순히 집에서 죽기만을 기다리는 것보다 활동적인 모습을 보이는 것이 반가운 일이죠.

1 They go scuba diving, hang-gliding, and roller-skating, run marathons, and do various extreme sports.

2 They think the elderly shouldn't take risks or do dangerous activities because they could get hurt or die.

3 They suffer stress from worrying too much.

4 They think it is nice to see the elderly being active and not simply staying at home and waiting to die.

Organization

Choice A	Choice B
Agree	**Disagree**
The elderly should not take risks or take part in difficult activities like young people do.	The elderly should be able to do any activities that they want.
First reason	**First reason**
Many elderly people get hurt or killed doing activities their bodies are no longer capable of doing.	Many elderly live sad, lonely lives.
Details	**Details**
My grandfather ran a marathon when he was seventy-five. He hurt both of his knees so now has trouble walking.	It's wonderful to see them leaving their homes to do various activities. They can be happy and spend time with others.
Second reason	**Second reason**
The families of these individuals suffer from their actions.	Doing physical activities is good for the elderly.
Details	**Details**
My parents had to take care of my grandfather. It was stressful, and they spent lots of time and money helping him.	Being active can help them stay in good shape. That will make their bodies healthier.

Comparing

Sample Response | Choice A

Script 🎧 01-44

I strongly believe the elderly should not take risks or take part in difficult activities like young people do. I have two reasons for feeling that way. First, many elderly people get seriously hurt or killed doing activities their bodies are no longer capable of doing. For instance, my grandfather decided to run a marathon when he was seventy-five. Unfortunately, he hurt both of his knees, so now he has trouble walking. He should have just stayed home and enjoyed his retirement. In addition, the children and grandchildren of these individuals suffer from their actions. My parents had to take care of my grandfather for more than a year. It was extremely stressful for them, and they had to spend too much time and money helping him.

해석

나는 노인들이 위험을 무릅쓰거나 젊은 사람들이 하는 힘든 활동에 참여해서는 안 된다고 굳게 믿는다. 두 가지 이유에서 그렇게 생각한다. 첫째, 많은 노인들이 자신의 신체가 더 이상 감당하지 못하는 활동을 하다가 심한 부상을 입거나 목숨을 잃는다. 예를 들어 우리 할아버지께서는 75세 때 마라톤을 하기로 결심하셨다. 불행하게도 할아버지께서는 양쪽 무릎을 다치셨고, 현재 걷는데 불편을 겪고 계신다. 할아버지께서는 집에 머무시면서 은퇴 생활을 즐기셔야 했다. 또한 그러

한 사람들의 자식 및 손주들은 그들의 활동으로 고생을 한다. 우리 부모님께서는 1년 이상 할아버지를 돌봐 드려야만 했다. 이는 부모님들께 엄청난 스트레스가 되었고, 부모님들은 할아버지를 돌보시느라 막대한 시간과 돈을 쓰셔야 했다.

Sample Response | Choice B

Script 🎧 01-45

I side with the second group of people. I think that the elderly should be able to do any activities that they want. For one thing, many elderly live sad, lonely lives. This is especially true when their spouse passes away. So it's wonderful to see them leaving their homes and doing various activities. That gives them the opportunity to be happy and to spend time with others. That can improve the quality of their lives a great deal. Another thing is that doing physical activities is good for the elderly. Playing a sport or doing another similar activity can help them stay in good shape. That will help their bodies become healthier, so they will be able to live longer lives.

해석

나는 두 번째 사람들과 생각이 같다. 나는 노인들도 자신이 원하는 활동을 할 수 있어야 한다고 생각한다. 우선 많은 노인들이 우울하고 외로운 삶을 살고 있다. 특히 배우자가 세상을 떠난 경우에 그렇다. 따라서 그들이 집을 나서서 다양한 활동을 하는 모습을 보이는 것은 매우 좋은 일이다. 그럼으로써 행복해질 기회와 다른 사람들과 함께 시간을 보낼 수 있는 기회가 생긴다. 그러면 삶의 질이 크게 나아질 수 있다. 또 다른 이유는 노인들에게 신체적인 활동을 하는 것이 바람직하기 때문이다. 스포츠를 하거나 그와 비슷한 활동을 하면 건강을 유지하는데 도움이 된다. 그러면 신체가 더 건강해져서 노인들이 보다 오래 살 수 있을 것이다.

Unit 12 Robots

Exercise p.34

Before you start

A

Script 🎧 01-46

W Student: Did you see the news report about that factory? It will mostly be operated by robots, and there will be few human workers.

M Student: I can't believe that's happening.

W: I know. It's awful.

M: Robots are getting smarter and smarter, so they are starting to replace humans at many places.

W: I agree with you. I heard that some robots can even perform operations. I think that's terrible.

M: I read an article about that as well. Now, doctors are going to lose their jobs and be replaced by robots.

W: Do you think that will actually happen?

M: As technology improves, robots will also improve. I believe there's a big chance robots become even smarter and more talented than humans in the future.

해석

W Student: 저 공장에 관한 뉴스를 봤어? 주로 로봇에 의해 가동될 것이고 인간인 노동자들은 거의 없을 거야.

M Student: 그런 일이 일어나다니 믿을 수가 없군.

W: 그래. 끔찍해.

M: 로봇이 점점 더 똑똑해지고 있기 때문에 많은 곳에서 인간을 대체하게 될 거야.

W: 나도 같은 생각이야. 심지어 수술을 하는 로봇도 있다고 들었어. 말도 안 된다고 생각해.

M: 나 또한 그에 관한 글을 읽었어. 이제 의사들은 일자리를 잃을 것이고 대신 그 자리에 로봇이 들어가게 될 거야.

W: 그런 일이 실제로 일어날 거라고 생각하니?

M: 기술이 발전할 수록 로봇도 발전하겠지. 나는 미래에 로봇이 더 똑똑해지고 더 많은 재능을 갖게 될 가능성이 크다고 믿어.

1 It will mostly be operated by robots, and there will be few human workers.
2 She thinks it is awful.
3 He says that robots are getting smarter, so they are starting to replace humans at many places.
4 He believes robots will improve as technology improves, so there's a big chance robots will become smarter and more talented than humans.

B

Script 🎧 01-47

W Professor: I know many people are concerned that due to improvements in modern technology, robots will improve in quality. As a result, they will become smarter and more talented than people. Let me reassure you that there's nothing to worry about. Robots will never be smarter than humans. For one thing, the human brain is incredibly complex. We cannot come close to equaling it, so we'll never make super-smart robots. For another thing, most robots these days do menial jobs that are dirty or dangerous. Nobody is trying to make robots that can create art or write novels or do anything else that requires real intelligence and talent. Since nobody is trying to make that kind of robot, it's obvious that smart and talented robots will never exist.

해석

W Professor: 많은 사람들이 현대 기술의 발전에 덕분에 로봇의 성능이 우수해질 것이라는 점을 걱정하고 있다는 점은 저도 알고 있습니다. 그 결과 로봇이 사람보다 더 똑똑하고 더 뛰어난 재능을 갖게 될 것이죠. 하지만 걱정할 점이 전혀 없다는 점을 제가 다시 한번 확인시켜 드릴게요. 로봇은 인간보다 결코 더 똑똑해질 수 없습니다. 우선, 인간의 뇌는 믿을 수 없을 정도로 복잡해요. 우리는 그

근처에도 갈 수 없기 때문에 엄청나게 똑똑한 로봇은 결코 만들 수가 없을 것입니다. 또 다른 점으로, 오늘날 대부분의 로봇은 더럽거나 위험한, 하찮은 일들을 하고 있습니다. 예술품을 만들어 내거나, 소설을 쓰거나, 혹은 진정한 지능과 재능을 요구하는 기타 활동을 할 수 있는 로봇을 만들려는 사람은 없어요. 아무도 그러한 로봇을 만들려고 하지 않기 때문에 분명 똑똑하고 재능이 많은 로봇은 결코 존재할 수 없을 것입니다.

1 They are concerned that robots will become smarter and more talented than people.
2 We cannot equal the human brain, so we will never make super-smart robots.
3 They mostly do menial jobs that are dirty or dangerous.
4 She says that nobody is trying to make robots that require intelligence and talent, so they will never exist.

Organization

Choice A	Choice B
Agree Robots will never become smarter and more talented than humans.	**Disagree** Robots will become superior to humans someday.
First reason Robots are not being designed to be smart.	**First reason** It will soon be possible to create highly intelligent robots with many talents.
Details They are mostly being made to do mindless, repetitive work in factories.	**Details** Robots will be much smarter than humans and will be able to do activities with great skill.
Second reason Creating art, writing novels, and composing operas are things only humans can do.	**Second reason** AI is improving, and some robots will be equipped with powerful AI someday.
Details Making them involves inborn talent, something no machine can replicate.	**Details** Robots will have all knowledge available to them, so they will be much smarter than humans.

Comparing

Sample Response | Choice A
Script 🎧 01-48

I believe robots will never become smarter and more talented than humans, so I agree with the statement. First, robots are not being designed to be smart. They are mostly being made to do mindless, repetitive work in factories. For instance, they might help make cars or manufacture computer chips. Both activities require neither intelligence nor talent. Another point I'd like to make is that creating art, writing novels, and composing operas are things only humans can do. Making them involves inborn talent, something no machine can replicate. Sure, a robot could probably draw a picture, write a book, and make a song, but the quality will be nothing like what a human can do.

해석

나는 로봇이 결코 인간보다 더 똑똑하고 더 많은 재능을 갖게 될 것이라고 생각하지 않기 때문에 그러한 주장에 동의한다. 첫째, 똑똑한 로봇은 만들어지지 않고 있다. 주로 공장에서 머리를 쓸 필요가 없고 반복적인 일들을 할 수 있는 로봇들이 만들어지고 있다. 예를 들어 이들은 자동차를 만들거나 컴퓨터 칩을 생산하는데 도움이 될 것이다. 이러한 두 가지 일 모두 지성이나 재능을 요구하지 않는다. 내가 제기하고 싶은 또 다른 논점은 예술품을 만들고, 소설을 쓰고, 오페라를 작곡하는 것은 인간만이 할 수 있는 일이라는 점이다. 이를 위해서는 타고난 재능이 필요한데, 이는 기계가 결코 따라 할 수 없는 것이다. 분명 로봇이 그림을 그리고, 책을 쓰고, 그리고 노래를 만들 수는 있겠지만, 결코 그 퀄리티는 인간의 것과 비교될 수 없을 것이다.

Sample Response | Choice B
Script 🎧 01-49

I disagree with the statement because I believe robots will become superior to humans someday. As computers continue to become smaller and more powerful, it will soon be possible to create highly intelligent robots with many talents. These robots will be much smarter than any human and will be able to do a wide variety of activities with great skill. Additionally, artificial intelligence is improving, and some robots will be equipped with powerful AI someday. These robots will have all human knowledge available to them, so they will be much smarter than any human could ever be. I hope something like this never happens, but I am afraid that it will someday soon.

해석

나는 로봇이 언젠가 인간보다 우수해질 것이라고 믿기 때문에 그러한 주장에 동의하지 않는다. 컴퓨터는 더 작고 강력해지고 있으므로 곧 많은 재능과 고도의 지능을 갖춘 로봇이 만들어질 수 있을 것이다. 이러한 로봇들은 인간보다 훨씬 더 똑똑할 것이며 매우 능숙하게 다양한 일들을 처리할 수 있을 것이다. 또한 인공 지능이 발전하고 있는데, 언젠가 일부 로봇에는 강력한 AI가 탑재될 것이다. 이러한 로봇들은 인류의 모든 지식을 이용할 수 있을 것이기 때문에 어떤 인간보다도 훨씬 더 똑똑할 것이다. 나는 그러한 일이 결코 일어나지 않기를 바라지만 가까운 미래에 그런 일이 일어날 것 같아 두렵다.

Exercise p.36

Before you start

A

Script 🎧 01-50

W Student: I just read an article in the student newspaper. The school is shutting down its computer labs this summer.

M Student: That's smart. There's no need to have them.

W: Why do you say that?

M: Well . . . when was the last time you visited a computer lab?

W: Never. I have my own computer in my dorm room.

M: It's the same for me. In fact, I don't know a single student who has ever visited a lab.

W: Hmm . . . I see your point. Maybe the school will sell the computers. I should see if I can get a good deal since mine is getting old.

M: I hope the school turns the lab rooms into classrooms. We need more classrooms on campus.

해석

W Student: 얼마 전에 학생 신문에서 기사를 하나 읽었거든. 학교측이 이번 여름에 컴퓨터실을 폐쇄할 예정이래.

M Student: 현명한 결정이군. 있을 필요가 없지.

W: 왜 그런 말을 하는 거니?

M: 음… 너는 마지막으로 컴퓨터실에 간 것이 언제였어?

W: 가 본 적 없어. 기숙사에 내 컴퓨터가 있거든.

M: 나도 마찬가지야. 사실 나는 컴퓨터실에 가 본 학생을 한 명도 본 적이 없어.

W: 흠… 무슨 말인지 알겠어. 아마도 학교측이 컴퓨터를 팔아 버릴 수도 있겠네. 내 컴퓨터가 오래되어서 나도 좋은 조건에 하나 구할 수 있는지 알아봐야겠어.

M: 학교측이 컴퓨터실을 교실로 바꾸면 좋을 것 같아. 캠퍼스에 교실이 더 필요하니까.

1 The school is shutting down its computer labs this summer.

2 They have never visited the computer labs.

3 She will try to buy one of the computers from a computer lab.

4 He believes getting more classrooms is more important than having computer labs.

Script 🎧 01-51

M Professor: I'm sure many of you are aware that the school has closed down all of its computer labs. It has transformed them into classrooms and other spaces available to students. In my opinion, that's a bad idea. Let me tell you why. Now, I realize most of you have your own computers. However, that's not true about all students on campus. There are many students who rely on the computers in the labs to do their assignments. The school has now deprived those individuals of computers. They'll either have to buy computers of their own or borrow computers from their friends. That is a major inconvenience for them. It could cause their grades to go down, and that could harm their chances of future employment.

해석

M Professor: 여러분 중 다수가 학교측이 모든 컴퓨터실을 폐쇄했다는 점을 알고 있을 것으로 확신합니다. 교실 및 학생들이 이용할 수 있는 다른 공간으로 바뀌었죠. 제 생각으로, 이는 좋지 못한 아이디어입니다. 그 이유를 말씀드릴게요. 자, 저는 여러분 중 대부분이 컴퓨터를 소유하고 있다고 알고 있어요. 하지만 교내의 모든 학생들이 그런 것은 아닙니다. 컴퓨터실의 컴퓨터를 이용해서 과제를 하는 학생들도 많아요. 학교측은 현재 그러한 개인들로부터 컴퓨터를 빼앗아 갔습니다. 그들은 컴퓨터를 구입하거나 친구에게서 컴퓨터를 빌려야만 할 것입니다. 그들에게 상당히 불편한 일이 되겠죠. 성적이 떨어질 수도 있으며, 이후 취업 과정에서 불이익을 받게 될 수도 있을 거예요.

1 It has turned them into classrooms and other spaces available to students.

2 He thinks it is a bad idea.

3 They must buy computers or borrow computers from their friends.

4 It could cause their grades to go down, and that could harm their chances of future employment.

Organization

	Choice A	Choice B
	Agree I believe schools should close their computer labs.	**Disagree** I don't think that schools should close down their computer labs.
	First reason Few students use these labs.	**First reason** Not every student can afford a computer.
	Details Most students have their own computers, so the labs are wastes of resources.	**Details** Many students have to use computers that schools provide for them.
	Second reason Computer labs are expensive.	**Second reason** Some students have to do group projects.
	Details Schools must purchase computers, printers, and software, which cost a lot of money.	**Details** Students can work much better if the group members have their own computers.

Comparing

Sample Response | Choice A

Script 🎧 01-52

I agree with the statement and believe schools should close their computer labs. The first reason is that few students use these labs. Most students have their own computers, so they never need to visit the labs. As a result, the labs are wastes of resources. The second reason is that computer labs are expensive. Schools must purchase computers, printers, and software, and all of them cost a lot of money. However, few people are using these labs, so schools are just wasting their money. Schools should instead spend their money on other things that could actually benefit students. For instance, schools could buy more books for their libraries. That would be much better and helpful to students.

해석

나는 그러한 주장에 동의하며 학교측이 컴퓨터실을 폐쇄해야 한다고 생각한다. 첫 번째 이유는 이러한 컴퓨터실을 이용하는 학생이 거의 없기 때문이다. 대부분의 학생들이 자신의 컴퓨터를 소유하고 있기 때문에 컴퓨터실을 방문할 필요가 없다. 그 결과 컴퓨터실은 자원 낭비가 된다. 두 번째 이유는 컴퓨터실에 많은 비용이 들기 때문이다. 학교측은 컴퓨터, 프린터, 그리고 소프트웨어를 구입해야 하는데, 이들은 모두 비싼 것들이다. 하지만 이러한 컴퓨터실을 이용하는 사람이 거의 없어서 학교측은 돈을 낭비하고 있다. 대신 학교측은 돈을 실제로 학생들에게 도움을 줄 수 있는 다른 곳에 사용해야 한다. 예를 들어 학교측은 책을 더 많이 사서 도서관에 둘 수도 있을 것이다. 그렇게 하는 것이 학생들에게 더 좋고 더 큰 도움이 될 것이다.

Sample Response | Choice B

Script 🎧 01-53

I don't think that schools should close down their computer labs, so I disagree with the statement. Let me explain why. First, not every student has enough money to buy a computer. Many students have to use computers that schools provide for them. Instructors nowadays insist that homework and papers be typed. So if students don't have their own computers and there are no labs, they won't be able to do their work. Second, some students have to do group projects. They can do their work much better if the group members have their own computers. This means that working together in a computer lab is ideal for students working on group projects. Having labs will therefore help them considerably.

해석

나는 학교측이 컴퓨터실을 폐쇄해서는 안 된다고 생각하기 때문에 그러한 주장에 동의하지 않는다. 그 이유를 설명하겠다. 첫째, 모든 학생들이 컴퓨터를 구입할 수 있을 정도의 충분한 돈을 가지고 있는 것은 아니다. 많은 학생들은 학교에서 제공되는 컴퓨터를 사용해야만 한다. 현재 교수들은 과제와 보고서에서 타이핑 작업을 요구한다. 따라서 컴퓨터를 가지고 있지 않은데 컴퓨터실도 없다면 학생들은 과제를 할 수 없을 것이다. 둘째, 일부 학생들은 조별 과제를 해야 한다. 조원들이 컴퓨터를 가지고 있으면 과제를 더 잘 할 수 있다. 이는 컴퓨터실에서 함께 과제를 하는 것이 조별 과제를 하는 학생들에게 이상적임을 의미한다. 따라서 컴퓨터실이 있으면 그들에게 커다란 도움이 될 것이다.

Unit 14 Movie Reviews

Exercise p.38

[Before you start]

A

Script 🎧 01-54

M Student: How about seeing a movie this weekend? What do you want to see?

W Student: That's a good idea. Let me read some movie reviews to decide what we should see.

M: Movie reviews? You read them?

W: Sure. I do that all of the time. I read reviews of every movie that comes out.

M: Why? I mean, uh, what use do movie reviewers have?

W: Well, I can find out which movies people think are good and which ones are bad.

M: You trust the reviewers and think that their opinions are valid?

W: I sure do. They can provide extra information about the acting, the soundtrack, the special effects, and other things. I find movie reviews really helpful.

해석

M Student: 이번 주말에 영화를 보는 것이 어떨까? 어떤 영화를 보고 싶니?

W Student: 좋은 생각인데. 영화 리뷰들을 좀 보고 어떤 걸 볼지 결정하자.

M: 영화 리뷰? 영화 리뷰를 읽어?

W: 물론이지. 항상 읽는 걸. 나는 출시되는 모든 영화의 리뷰를 읽고 있어.

M: 왜? 내 말은, 어, 영화 리뷰가 어떤 쓸모가 있는데?

W: 음, 사람들이 어떤 영화가 좋고 어떤 영화가 별로라고 생각하는지 알 수가 있거든.

M: 리뷰를 쓰는 사람들을 믿고 그들의 의견이 옳다고 생각하는 거지?

W: 그래. 그들은 연기, 사운드트랙, 특수 효과, 그리고 기타 등등에 대한 추가적인 정보를 제공해 줄 수 있어. 나는 영화 리뷰가 정말로 도움이 된다고 생각해.

---

1 She will read some movie reviews to decide what movie to see.

2 She reads reviews of every movie that comes out.

3 They can provide extra information about the acting, the soundtrack, the special effects, and other things.

4 He never reads movie reviews.

B

Script 🎧 01-55

W Professor: For decades, movie reviewers have been popular. They watch movies and then present their opinions of the plots, the acting, and other aspects of movies. People use them to determine which movies to watch. However, I'd like to tell you that reading movie reviews simply isn't necessary. For example, visit some websites for movie reviews. In many cases, reviews by regular people and those by professional reviewers have exactly opposite opinions. Why is that? Well, movie reviewers often let their personal and political opinions determine which movies they praise and which ones they criticize. So they are actually biased and not openminded about many films. As a result, they aren't providing their honest opinions about movies. That makes their reviews worthless.

해석

W Professor: 수십 년 동안 영화 리뷰어들이 인기를 얻어 왔습니다. 그들은 영화를 보고 구성, 연기, 그리고 기타 영화의 측면들에 대한 자신들의 의견을 나타내죠. 사람들은 영화 리뷰를 이용해 어떤 영화를 볼 것인지 결정합니다. 하지만 저는 영화 리뷰를 읽는 것이 필요하지 않다고 말씀을 드리고 싶군요. 예컨대 몇몇 웹사이트를 방문해서 영화 리뷰를 찾아보세요. 많은 경우, 보통 사람들이 쓰는 리뷰와 전문가들이 쓰는 리뷰는 정확히 반대되는 견해를 나타냅니다. 왜 그럴까요? 음, 영화 리뷰어들은 종종 개인적인, 그리고 정치적인 의견에 따라 어떤 영화는 호평하고 어떤 영화는 혹평을 합니다. 즉 실제로는 편견을 가지고 있으며 여러 영화에 대해 편협한 자세를 취합니다. 그 결과 영화에 대한 솔직한 자신의 의견을 나타내지 않아요. 따라서 리뷰들은 쓸모가 없습니다.

1 They watch movies and then present their opinions of the plots, the acting, and other aspects of movies.

2 Reading movie reviews isn't necessary.

3 They let their personal and political opinions determine which movies they praise and which ones they criticize.

4 Movie reviewers don't provide their honest opinions about movies.

[Organization]

Choice A	Choice B
Agree	Disagree
I love to read movie reviews before seeing a movie.	I never read movie reviews before I see movies.

First reason Movie reviews let me know which movies are good and which are bad.	First reason I love the movies reviewers hate and hate the movies reviewers love.
Details I read some reviews about a movie and learned the acting is terrible. I avoided watching it and saw a different movie.	Details The style of entertainment movie reviewers prefer is different from mine.
Second reason I can learn about the plots of movies.	Second reason Movie reviewers tend to be biased against certain actors, directors, and movie genres.
Details I like knowing what movies are about before seeing them.	Details They cannot review certain movies impartially. There's no point in reading a review if I think the reviewer is biased about the movie.

Comparing

Sample Response | Choice A

`Script` 🎧 01-56

I'm the kind of person who loves to read movie reviews before seeing a movie. To begin with, movie reviews let me know which movies are good and which are bad. Just last week, I wanted to see a movie. I read some reviews about it and learned the acting is terrible. I therefore avoided watching it and saw a different movie. However, some of my friends watched the other movie. They hated it. If they had read some reviews, they would have known to avoid it. An additional reason I like reviews is that I can learn about the plots of movies. I like knowing what movies are about before seeing them. For me, that's important information.

해석

나는 영화를 보기 전에 영화 리뷰를 읽는 것을 선호하는 사람 중 하나이다. 우선 영화 리뷰로 인해 어떤 영화가 좋고 어떤 영화가 별로인지 알 수 있다. 지난 주에 나는 한 영화가 보고 싶었다. 그에 관한 몇몇 리뷰를 읽었는데, 연기가 형편없다는 점을 알게 되었다. 따라서 나는 그 영화를 보지 않고 다른 영화를 보았다. 하지만 내 친구들 중 몇 명은 그 영화를 보았다. 그들은 영화를 혹평했다. 만약 그들이 리뷰를 읽었더라면 그 영화를 보지 말아야 한다는 점을 알았을 것이다. 내가 리뷰를 좋아하는 또 다른 이유는 영화의 구성에 대해 알 수 있기 때문이다. 나는 영화를 보기 전에 그 영화가 어떤 내용인지 알고 싶다. 이는 나에게 중요한 정보이다.

Sample Response | Choice B

`Script` 🎧 01-57

I never read movie reviews before I see movies, so I am the second kind of person. In the past, I used to read movie reviews. But over time, I noticed that I usually

loved the movies reviewers hated and hated the movies reviewers loved. The style of entertainment that movie reviewers prefer is much different from mine. That makes movie reviews useless to me. I have also noticed that movie reviewers tend to be biased against certain actors, directors, and movie genres. This means they cannot review certain movies impartially. So to me, there's no point in reading a review if I think the reviewer is biased about some aspect of the movie. Essentially, the review will be worthless.

해석

나는 영화를 보기 전에 결코 영화 리뷰를 읽지 않기 때문에 두 번째 부류에 속한다. 예전에는 영화 리뷰를 읽곤 했다. 하지만 시간이 지나면서 나는 주로 영화 리뷰어들이 싫어하는 영화를 좋아하고, 영화 리뷰어들이 좋아하는 영화를 싫어한다는 점을 알게 되었다. 영화 리뷰어들이 선호하는 스타일의 영화는 내 경우와 상당히 다르다. 따라서 영화 리뷰는 나에게 도움이 되지 않는다. 나는 또한 영화 리뷰어들이 특정 배우, 감독, 그리고 영화 장르에 대해 편견을 가지는 경향이 있다는 점을 알게 되었다. 이는 특정 영화에 대해서 그들이 공정하게 리뷰를 할 수 없다는 점을 의미한다. 따라서 리뷰어가 영화의 몇 가지 측면에 대해 편견을 가지고 있다는 생각이 드는 경우, 리뷰를 읽는 것은 내게 아무런 의미가 없다. 기본적으로 그러한 리뷰는 쓸모가 없는 것이다.

Unit 15 Electronic Devices

Exercise p.40

Before you start

A

`Script` 🎧 01-58

W Student: I can't wait for my birthday. My parents have promised to buy me a smartphone.

M Student: Congratulations, but try not to use it too much.

W: Try not to use my phone too much? What are you talking about?

M: Look around you. So many young people are addicted to their phones and other electronic devices. It's a shame what is happening with them.

W: Do you really think so?

M: Of course, I do. Their addiction to these devices is harming them in many ways. For instance, many young people have trouble dealing with others in person.

W: What else?

M: Some young people neglect their homework in favor of going online or using their devices for other reasons.

W Student: 내 생일이 몹시 기다려지는 걸. 부모님께서 스마트폰을 사 주신다고 약속하셨거든.

M Student: 축하하고, 하지만 너무 많이 사용하지는 마.

W: 너무 많이 사용하지 말라고? 무슨 말이야?

M: 주위를 둘러 봐. 너무나 많은 젊은 사람들이 전화기 및 기타 전자 기기에 중독되어 있잖아. 안타까운 일이 벌어지고 있어.

W: 정말로 그렇게 생각해?

M: 물론이지. 그러한 기기에 중독되면 여러 가지 측면에서 피해를 입게 돼. 예를 들면 많은 젊은 사람들이 다른 사람들과 직접 만나는데 어려움을 겪고 있어.

W: 그리고 또?

M: 일부 젊은 사람들은 온라인에 접속하거나 다른 이유들로 기기를 사용하느라 과제를 소홀히 하지.

1 She will get a smartphone for her birthday.
2 She should try not to use her new smartphone too much.
3 Many young people have trouble dealing with others in person.
4 Some young people neglect their homework in favor of going online or using their devices for other reasons.

B

Script 🎧 01-59

M Professor: You often hear about smartphone addiction and other types of addictions to electronic devices. But I don't think it's a big problem. For one thing, parents realize the potential problems with these devices. They therefore restrict the amount of time their children use their electronic devices. For instance, I have two teenagers. They can use their phones for an hour a day, but then they must give the phones to me when time is up. By doing that, I help them avoid addiction. Secondly, many young people need to use their devices a lot. Schools require most work to be submitted online. Students need to do research, too. So in some ways, I don't think young people are addicted. They are using their devices to finish their homework.

M Professor: 여러분은 종종 스마트폰 중독 및 기타 전자 기기의 중독에 대한 이야기를 들을 것입니다. 하지만 저는 그것이 큰 문제라고 생각하지 않아요. 우선, 부모들이 그러한 기기의 잠재적인 문제를 알고 있습니다. 따라서 자녀들이 전자 기기를 사용하는 시간을 제한하죠. 예를 들면, 제게 십대인 두 명의 아이들이 있습니다. 이들은 하루에 한 시간 동안 전화기를 사용하고 시간이 다 되면 전화를 제게 주어야만 해요. 그렇게 함으로써 저는 아이들이 중독되지 않도록 할 수 있습니다. 둘째, 많은 젊은 사람들이 기기를 자주 사용해야 합니다. 학교에서는 대부분의 숙제를 온라인으로 제출하라고 요구를 해요. 또한 학생들은 리서치도 해야 합니다. 따라서 몇 가지 측면에서 저는 젊은 사람들이 중독되어 있다고 생각하지 않습니다. 기기를 이용해서 과제를 하고 있는 것이죠.

1 He thinks it's not a big problem.
2 They restrict the amount of time their children use their electronic devices.
3 He restricts them to using their phones for one hour a day.
4 They submit work online and do research, too.

Organization

Choice A	Choice B
Agree Many young people are addicted to their electronic devices.	Disagree I don't believe many young people are addicted to their electronic devices.
First reason My brother is addicted to his tablet computer.	First reason I rarely use my smartphone.
Details He does many activities on it and looks lost and confused without it.	Details I can control my urges and use it only when it's necessary. My friends are similar to me.
Second reason My brother has changed since he got his tablet computer.	Second reason My friends and I do activities without our devices.
Details He doesn't meet his friends much, and his grades have gone down.	Details We play sports and hang out. While we meet, we don't look at our devices.

Comparing

Sample Response | Choice A
Script 🎧 01-60

It's true that many young people are addicted to their electronic devices, so I agree with the statement. My brother has a tablet computer, and he can't take his eyes off it. He carries it everywhere he goes. He plays games on it, talks to his friends on it, and does other activities with it. When he can't use it, he looks lost and confused. It's sad how addicted he is to it. Another problem is that my brother has changed greatly since he got his tablet computer. He doesn't meet his friends after school much. Instead, he rushes home to use his tablet. His grades at school are suffering, too. I hope my parents help him with his addiction problem.

많은 젊은 사람들이 전자 기기에 중독되어 있는 것은 사실이기 때문에 나는 그러한 주장에 동의한다. 내 동생은 태블릿 컴퓨터를 가지고 있는데, 그것에서 눈을 떼지 못한다. 어디를 가더라도 항상 가지고 다닌다. 그것으로 게임을 하고, 친구들과 이야기하며, 기타 다른 일들을 한다. 사용할 수 없는 경우에는 멍해지고 혼란스러워 보인다. 그것에 중독된 모습을 보면 안타깝다. 또 다른 문제는 동생이 태블릿 컴퓨터를 얻고 난 이후로 크게 달라졌다는 점이다. 그는 방과 후에 친구들을 자주 만나지 않는다. 대신 집으로 달려 와서 태블릿을 사용한다. 학교 성적 또한 낮아지고 있다. 나는 중독 문제와 관련해서 부모님들이 동생을 도와 줄 수 있기를 바란다.

Sample Response | Choice B

Script 🎧 01-61

I disagree with the statement because I don't believe many young people are addicted to their electronic devices. For instance, I have a smartphone but rarely use it. I can control my urges and only use it when absolutely necessary. Most of my friends act like me. They know the dangers of addiction and do their best to avoid it. In addition, my friends and I often do activities that don't involve electronic devices. We meet after school to play sports and just hang out. While we do different activities, none of us looks at our devices. Instead, we focus on what we are doing. In that way, we keep ourselves from becoming addicted to our devices.

해석

나는 많은 젊은 사람들이 전자 기기에 중독되어 있다고 생각하지 않기 때문에 그러한 주장에 동의하지 않는다. 예를 들어 나는 스마트폰을 가지고 있지만 거의 사용하지 않는다. 나는 내 충동을 조절할 수 있고 반드시 필요한 경우에만 스마트폰을 사용한다. 내 친구들도 대부분 나처럼 행동한다. 중독의 위험성을 알고 있으며 중독에 빠지지 않기 위해 최선을 다한다. 또한 친구들과 나는 종종 전자 기기가 필요하지 않는 활동들을 한다. 방과 후에 모여서 스포츠 활동을 하거나 함께 시간을 보낸다. 다양한 활동을 하는 경우 우리 중에서 기기를 쳐다 보는 사람은 아무도 없다. 대신 우리는 우리가 하는 일에 집중한다. 그렇게 함으로써 우리는 기기에 중독되지 않을 수 있다.

Unit **16** School Facilities I

Exercise p.48

Reading

해석

대학 과외 지도 시스템

8월 22일부터 대학의 새로운 과외 지도 시스템이 시작됩니다. 학생들은 더 이상 대면 과외 수업을 받을 수 없습니다. 대신 온라인 과외 지도 시스템이 실시될 것입니다. 컴퓨터 기반의 과외 지도 시스템을 통해 학생들은 정규 수업 시간뿐만 아니라 주 7일 하루 24시간 동안 언제나 과외 지도를 받을 수 있습니다. 과외 지도 교사와 만날 수 있는 시간이 더 많아짐으로써 학생들에게 혜택이 돌아갈 것입니다. 뿐만 아니라 컴퓨터 시스템 덕분에 학생들은 혼잡한 과외 지도 센터에서 비롯되는 스트레스에서 벗어나게 될 것입니다. 학생들은 더 이상 과외 지도를 받기 위해 학교에 오는 수고를 하지 않아도 됩니다. 인터넷과 연결된 컴퓨터를 사용해서 컴퓨터 기반의 시스템에 접속할 수 있습니다.

Comprehension

1 The notice is about how the university will change from face-to-face tutoring to a computer-based tutoring system.
2 One reason for the changes is that only offering tutoring services during regular school hours is not enough for the students.
3 Students will have access to tutoring twenty-four hours a day, seven days a week.
4 Another reason for the change in the tutoring system is that it will eliminate crowded, stressful tutoring centers.
5 Students will be able to access the tutoring network from any computer with an Internet connection.

Listening

Script 🎧 02-03

M Student: This new tutoring system will be great.

W Student: I'm not so sure about that.

M: Really? What do you mean?

W: First of all, a lot of students don't even know how to type very fast. Some cannot even type at all. This will make the tutoring sessions really slow.

M: Right. Typing skills will be really important.

W: Sure they will. When students are tutored face to face, they don't have to worry about typing though. They can just focus all of their energy on what they're learning. I think that's more efficient.

M: You might be right.

W: There's something else, too. Students must have a good computer at home in order to access the computer-based system. Many students will have to upgrade their current computer or even buy a new one. I know a lot of students who don't even have their own personal computer. It will be very expensive for a lot of students to get access to tutoring now.

M: That's a good point.

W: I think it might be better to stick with the old system.

해석

M Student: 이번 새 과외 지도 시스템은 정말 좋은 것 같아.

W Student: 난 잘 모르겠는걸.

M: 정말? 무슨 뜻이야?

W: 우선, 많은 학생들이 어떻게 타이핑을 빨리하는지 모르고 있어. 타이핑을 전혀 할 줄 모르는 학생들도 있고. 그래서 과외 수업이 정말 느리게 진행될 거야.

M: 맞는 말이군. 타이핑 능력이 정말 중요할 것 같아.

W: 그렇고 말고. 학생들이 대면 수업을 할 때에는 타이핑 걱정을 할 필요가 없지. 배우는 내용에만 온 에너지를 집중하면 되니까. 난 그게 더 효과적이라고 생각해.

M: 어쩌면 네 말이 맞을지도 몰라.

W: 다른 이유도 있어. 컴퓨터 기반의 시스템에 접속을 하려면 집에 있는 컴퓨터가 좋아야만 해. 많은 학생들이 갖고 있는 컴퓨터를 업그레이드하거나 혹은 컴퓨터를 새로 사야만 할 수도 있지. 내가 알기로는 집에 개인용 컴퓨터가 없는 학생들도 많아. 많은 학생들이 과외 지도 시스템에 접속하려면 상당한 비용을 내야 할 거야.

M: 좋은 지적이군.

W: 기존 시스템을 유지하는 것이 더 나을 것 같다는 생각이 들어.

Organization

1 The woman does not think it is a good idea for the university to switch to a computer-based tutoring system.

2 The woman says that some students either cannot type or type very slowly.

3 She claims the lack of typing skills will make the tutoring system slow.

4 The woman states that students will either have to upgrade their computers or else purchase new ones.

5 She thinks upgrading or purchasing new computers will be too expensive for students.

Comparing

Sample Response

Script 🎧 02-04

The notice describes a new university tutoring system. The woman is against the university's decision to replace face-to-face tutoring with a computer-based tutoring system. First, she believes that students will require excellent typing skills in order to take advantage of the new tutoring system. However, she states that many students lack the ability to type well enough, so the new tutoring system will be much slower than the face-to-face system. To her, the inability to type well will hinder the learning process for some students. Second of all, she believes many students will have to upgrade their computers or even buy new ones. According to the woman, this will be very expensive for many students. She believes the former face-to-face method of tutoring is better for students than the new computer-based tutoring system.

해석

공지에는 새로운 대학 과외 지도 프로그램이 소개되어 있다. 여자는 대면 과외 지도 수업을 컴퓨터 기반의 과외 지도 시스템으로 대체하겠다는 대학측의 결정에 반대한다. 먼저, 그녀는 새로운 과외 지도 시스템을 이용하기 위해서는 학생들의 뛰어난 타이핑 능력이 요구된다고 생각한다. 하지만 많은 학생들의 타이핑 속도가 충분히 빠르지 않기 때문에 새로운 과외 지도 방식은 대면 방식보다 훨씬 느리게 진행될 것이라고 주장한다. 일부 학생들의 경우 타이핑을 하지 못해서 학습 과정에 차질이 생길 것이다. 두 번째로, 그녀는 많은 학생들이 컴퓨터를 업그레이드하거나 컴퓨터를 새로 사야 할 수도 있다고 생각한다. 여자의 말에 따르면 이는 많은 학생들이 매우 큰 부담이 될 것이다. 그녀는 학생들에게 새 컴퓨터 기반의 과외 지도 시스템보다 기존의 대면 과외 지도 방식이 더 낫다고 생각한다.

Unit 17 University Construction

Exercise ·· p.50

Reading

해석

미술관 벽 철거

대학 당국은 미술관 건물과 대학 극장 사이에 위치한 벽을 철거하기로 결정했습니다. 철거는 5월 말에 완료될 예정입니다. 벽이 철거되면 두 건물 간의 이동이 용이해질 것입니다. 더 이상 학생 및 방문객들이 벽을 돌아가기 위해 한 블록을 걸어갈 필요가 없을 것입니다. 또한 이 벽은 애초에 미대 학생들의 작품을 전시할 목적으로 만들어졌습니다. 최근에는 벽에 그래피티만 난무합니다. 이로 인해 캠퍼스의 흉물이 되었고, 학교 당국은 캠퍼스를 아름답게 꾸미고자 합니다. 철거 기간 중 학생들이 겪게 될 불편함에 대해서는 사과의 말씀을 드립니다.

Comprehension

1 The notice describes how the university will remove a wall of art between two buildings on campus.

2 Taking down the wall will create better access between the art building and the university theater.

3 The wall is being taken down because it often merely has graffiti instead of student artwork.

4 Students will benefit from the wall's removal because they will no longer have to walk far to get around it.

5 The school will benefit because the campus will be beautified.

Listening

Script 🎧 02-05

W Student: So the wall of art will be down by May.

M Student: Yeah, I know. I can't believe the school is actually going through with the removal.

W: Really? How come?

M: Well, for one thing, it is one of the oldest original parts of our university.

W: Oh, I didn't know that.

M: Sure. It is very historic. If the school knocks the wall down, there will be nothing left on campus that was built during the university's first construction period. There will just be a bunch of new buildings.

W: Hmm.

M: Yeah. And there's something else. It has always been a kind of showcase for student artists. It's a way for them to show their work to the public for free. Now, they aren't going to have that opportunity anymore. I think it will really limit the exposure of some of the wonderful work of art majors.

W: Right. I didn't think about that.

M: Well, all I can say is that if the school goes through with it, it will hurt the university in more ways than one.

해석

W Student: 그러니까 미술관 벽이 5월이면 철거되겠구나.

M Student: 그래, 나도 알아. 학교측이 실제로 철거를 하려고 한다는 점이 믿어지지가 않아.

W: 정말이야? 어째서?

M: 음, 우선 그 벽은 우리 대학에서 가장 오래 된 초기 건축물 중 하나야.

W: 오, 그 점은 내가 몰랐네.

M: 진짜야. 아주 역사가 깊어. 학교측이 벽을 철거한다면 대학 초기에 지어진 건축물 중 캠퍼스에 남아 있는 건 아무것도 없게 되지. 새 건물들 천지가 될 뿐이야.

W: 흠.

M: 그래. 게다가 다른 이유도 있어. 그 벽은 항상 미대생들에게 일종의 전시회장이었어. 일반인들에게 무료로 자신의 작품을 보여 줄 수 있는 수단이었지. 이제 더 이상 그럴 수 있는 기회가 없어질 거야. 미술 전공자들의 훌륭한 작품이 소개되는 경우가 줄어들 것이라고 생각해.

W: 맞아. 나도 그 생각은 못 해 봤어.

M: 음, 내가 하고 싶은 말은 만약 대학측이 철거를 감행한다면 여러 가지 측면에서 대학에 해가 될 것이라는 점이야.

Organization

1 The man believes the university should not demolish the wall of art.

2 He states that the wall is one of the oldest parts of the school and is therefore an historic area.

3 The wall's age is important because if the school knocks it down, none of the university's original structures will still exist.

4 Many of the school's art students have used the wall to showcase their work to the public.

5 Without the wall, students will no longer have a free place to exhibit their work, which will cut down on the exposure art students receive.

Comparing

Sample Response

Script 🎧 02-06

The male student opposes the university tearing down the wall of art on campus. One reason he gives is that its destruction will further reduce the historic parts of the university. He claims the wall is one of the original parts of the university, making it historic and important. Without it, a vital piece of the university's history will be lost forever. Another reason he gives is that art students will no longer have a place to display their works to the public for free. He believes that once the wall is gone, it will be difficult for art majors to have an opportunity to exhibit their works, thereby limiting their exposure. For these reasons, the male student believes the destruction of the wall of art will do much more harm than good to both the university and its students.

해석

남학생은 캠퍼스 내 미술관 벽을 철거하기로 한 대학측의 결정을 반대한다. 그가 제시하는 한 가지 이유는 벽이 철거되면 대학의 역사적인 부분이 더욱 줄어들 것이라는 점이다. 그는 그 벽이 대학의 초기 건축물 가운데 하나이며 역사적이고 중요한 건축물이라고 주장한다. 그 벽이 사라지면 대학 역사의 중요한 일부가 영원히 사라지게 될 것이다. 그가 제시하는 또 다른 이유는 미술 전공자들이 더 이상 일반인들에게 무료로 자신들의 작품을 선보일 장소가 없어지게 된다는 점이다. 그는 벽이 없어지면 미술 전공자들이 작품을 전시하는 일이 힘들어질 것이며, 그 결과 작품을 선보이는 기회가 줄어들 것이라고 생각한다. 이러한 이유들 때문에 남학생은 미술관 벽을 철거하는 일은 대학 및 학생들 모두에게 도움을 주기보다 막대한 피해를 가져다 줄 것이라고 생각한다.

Exercise ··· p.52

Reading

해석

인문대 학장 임명

William Reynolds 박사님께서 인문대의 새 학장으로 임명되셨습니다. Reynolds 박사님께서는 15년간 인문대 부교수로 재임하셨습니다. 박사님께서는 학자로서 전국적으로 유례없는 명성을 얻으셨습니다. 박사님의 부임으로 해당 분야의 최고의 교수진을 끌어들이고 인문대의 위상을 높이는데 도움이 될 것입니다. Reynolds 박사님께서는 또한 지난 5년 간 본교에서 우수 교수상과 지도 교수상을 수상하셨기 때문에 학생들은 학업 및 미래의 목표에 대한 훌륭한 조언을 받게 될 것입니다. 모두들 Reynolds 박사님의 학장 임명을 축하해 주시기 바라며 새 직위를 맡게 되신 박사님께 지지를 부탁드립니다.

Comprehension

1 Dr. Reynolds has been appointed the new dean of the Humanities Department.

2 The first reason he has been appointed dean is that his reputation as a scholar is excellent.

3 The second reason for his appointment is that he has won awards for his teaching and advising skills.

4 The university will benefit because other professors in his field will want to teach there.

5 The university will also benefit from Dr. Reynolds's advice to students concerning their academic performances and future desires.

Listening

Script 🎧 02-07

W Student: Do you think the university is making a good move by appointing Dr. Reynolds the new dean?

M Student: Yes, I do.

W: Really? But I've heard he's a terrible advisor and seldom helps students in need.

M: I disagree completely. He's my roommate John's advisor, and John can't say enough good things about Dr. Reynolds. He says that Dr. Reynolds always has time to meet him and has given him lots of good advice. Those sound like good qualities in a dean.

W: Okay, but what about those rumors?

M: What rumors?

W: The ones that said Dr. Reynolds was going to go elsewhere if he didn't get appointed dean.

M: I don't believe them. First, Dr. Reynolds has been a teacher here for years. His family's happy here, too.

W: Yeah, but that's no reason to make him the dean.

M: Sure, you're right. But he's one of the best scholars in his field. He'll not only attract excellent professors but will also get the best students to come here. That'll definitely improve the quality of our school.

해석

W Student: 대학측이 Reynolds 박사님을 새 학장으로 임명한 것이 현명한 조치라고 생각하니?

M Student: 어, 그렇게 생각해.

W: 정말이야? 하지만 나는 그분이 끔찍한 지도 교수이고 도움이 필요한 학생들을 도와 주는 일도 거의 없다고 들었어.

M: 절대 동의할 수 없어. 그분은 내 룸메이트인 John의 지도 교수님이신데, John은 항상 Reynolds 박사님에 대해 좋은 얘기만 해. Reynolds 박사님께서 항상 자기를 위해 시간을 내 주시고 좋은 충고도 많이 해 주신다고 말하지. 학장이 될 자격이 충분한 것처럼 들려.

W: 좋아, 그렇지만 소문들은?

M: 어떤 소문인데?

W: Reynolds 박사님께서 만약 학장으로 임명이 안 되었으면 다른 곳으로 가실 생각이었다는 소문 말이야.

M: 난 믿지 않아. 우선, Reynolds 박사님께서는 수년 간 이곳에서 교편을 잡으셨어. 교수님의 가족들도 여기에서 잘 지내고 있잖아.

W: 그래, 하지만 그렇다고 해서 Reynolds 박사님께서 학장이 되어야 하는 건 아니야.

M: 물론 네 말이 맞아. 하지만 그분은 자기 분야에서 최고의 학자 중 한 사람이야. 훌륭한 교수들뿐만이 아니라 우수한 학생들도 우리 대학으로 끌어올 수 있을 테지. 그렇게 되면 확실히 학교의 위상도 높아질 거고.

Organization

1 The man supports the university's decision to appoint Dr. Reynolds the new dean.

2 The man mentions that his roommate says Dr. Reynolds always has time for him and has given him very much good advice.

3 The man says that his roommate's comments make Dr. Reynolds sound like he would be a good dean.

4 Dr. Reynolds is one of the leading scholars in his area of study.

5 Because he is such a good scholar, both top professors and students will want to be associated with the university.

Sample Response

Script 🎧 02-08

The subject of the announcement is that Dr. Reynolds will become the new dean of the Humanities Department. The man's opinion is that Dr. Reynolds is a good choice. The first reason is that his roommate has commented positively about Dr. Reynolds's ability as an advisor. To begin with, Dr. Reynolds always has time to meet the man's roommate. He has also given his advisee some good advice. In addition, the man comments that Dr. Reynolds is an excellent scholar and is actually one of the best people in his field. The man notes that this fact will attract both top professors and students to the university since they will want to be associated with the school. In the man's mind, these two reasons justify Dr. Reynolds's appointment as the new dean.

해석

공고의 주제는 Reynolds 박사가 인문대의 새 학장이 될 것이라는 점이다. 남자의 의견은 Reynolds 박사를 선택한 것이 잘한 일이라는 것이다. 첫 번째 이유는 그의 룸메이트가 Reynolds 박사의 지도 교수로서의 능력에 대해 긍정적으로 평가하기 때문이다. 우선 Reynolds 박사는 남자의 룸메이트를 위해 항상 시간을 낸다. 또한 지도하는 학생들에게 좋은 충고를 해 준다. 게다가 남자는 Reynolds 박사가 훌륭한 학자이며 자신의 분야에서 최고의 학자 중 한 명이라고 말한다. 남자는 그러한 사실로 인해 일류 교수진과 우수한 학생들이 대학에 들어오고자 할 것이기 때문에 이들이 대학에 유입될 것이라고 언급한다. 남자의 의견으로는 이러한 두 가지 이유 때문에 Reynolds 박사를 새 학장으로 임명하는 것이 정당화된다.

Unit 19 School Policies I

Exercise p.54

Reading

해석

대학 기숙사 정책

이번 봄부터 대학에서 새로운 기숙사 정책이 시행됩니다. 각 기숙사들의 층은 전공별로 분류될 것인데, 이는 같은 전공을 가진 학생들끼리 함께 생활하게 될 것임을 의미합니다. 이러한 정책으로 학생들은 보다 효과적으로 공부할 수 있을 것입니다. 서로 가까이에 거주하기 때문에 전공이 같은 학생들끼리 보다 쉽게 스터디 그룹을 결성할 수 있을 것입니다. 또한 전공이 같은 다른 학생들과 보다 긴밀한 관계를 맺게 될 것입니다. 학교측은 전공이 같은 학생들끼리 강의실 밖에서도 보다 많은 시간을 함께 해야 한다고 생각합니다. 이로써 학업적인 측면 및 사교적인 측면에서의 교류가 모두 활발해질 것입니다.

Comprehension

1 The notice mentions that students with the same majors will now live on the same floors in their dormitories.

2 The first reason for this new policy is that students will be able to study more effectively.

3 The second reason is that students will become closer to other students with the same majors.

4 Students will benefit from living close to one another since that will make it easier for them to form study groups.

5 Students will also benefit because they will spend more time together outside of class, thereby furthering their social interactions.

Listening

Script 🎧 02-09

W Student: I can't believe the school is going to start this new dorm policy.

M Student: Really?

W: Do you think it's going to improve students' grades? It might actually lower them since it will definitely limit the interactions between students with diverse interests. You can learn a lot from people in other majors you know.

M: Well, maybe. I suppose so.

W: Students need to stimulate one another. One of the best ways is when students with various interests and majors live together. It broadens their minds. With this new policy, the university is taking away one of the best parts of dorm life.

M: But don't you think it would be a good thing if every student living on one floor had the same major? Think of all of the great discussions they could have together.

W: Sorry, but I don't agree with you. Students do better when they interact with others with completely different perspectives on things. If everyone living on a dorm floor has the same major, they will all have pretty much the same perspective. That won't make them creative or think differently from others.

해석

W Student: 학교에서 이런 기숙사 정책을 새로 시행하려고 한다니 믿기지가 않아.

M Student: 그래?

W: 그러면 학생들의 성적이 더 좋아질 거라고 생각하니? 실제로 다양한 관심을 가진 학생들 사이의 교류가 확실히 줄어들 것이기 때문에 성적이 떨어질 수도 있어. 알고 지내는 타 과목 전공생들로부터 많은 것을 배울 수가 있잖아.

M: 음, 그럴 수도 있지. 그런 것 같아.

W: 학생들은 서로에게 자극이 되어야 해. 가장 좋은 방법 중 하나는 서로 다른 관심과 전공을 가진 학생들끼리 함께 사는 거야. 그래야 생각이 넓어진다고. 이번 새 정책으로 대학측이 기숙사 생활 중 가장 유익한 부분을 빼앗아가게 될 거야.

M: 하지만 같은 층에 사는 학생들의 전공이 모두 같으면 좋을 거라고는 생각하지 않니? 같이 멋진 토론을 하게 되는 경우를 생각해 봐.

W: 미안하지만 난 그렇게 생각하지 않아. 학생들은 무언가에 대해 자신과 완전히 다른 시각을 가진 사람들과 교류할 때 발전하는 법이거든. 기숙사의 같은 층에 사는 사람들의 전공이 다 같으면 모두가 서로 상당히 비슷한 시각을 갖게 될 거야. 창의적이지 못하게 되거나 다른 학생들과 다르게 생각하지 않게 될 거라고.

Organization

1 The woman thinks the university's new dormitory policy is a terrible idea.

2 She believes that the new policy will not help students improve their grades at all.

3 She thinks that if students interact with other students with different majors, it will help them learn a lot and expand their minds.

4 She believes the students will not be able to have good discussions.

5 The woman says that students with the same majors will all have the same perspectives, so they will not be creative at all.

Comparing

Sample Response

Script 🎧 02-10

According to the announcement, students with the same majors will have to live on the same floors of the university's dormitories. The woman thinks this is a terrible idea. One reason she gives is that the new policy won't improve students' academic performances. On the contrary, she fears it may cause students' performances to decrease. Likewise, the students will now have fewer interactions with students in other majors, which will not enable them to learn more or broaden their minds. The woman also points out that having diverse living conditions is more beneficial than having major-specific floors. She claims that students with the same majors have similar perspectives, meaning that they think similarly. She believes that because of the new policy, students will no longer be creative or think differently than others.

해석
공지에 따르면 전공이 같은 학생들끼리 대학 기숙사의 같은 층에 살게 될 것이다. 여자는 이것이 끔찍한 아이디어라고 생각한다. 그녀가 제시하는 한 가지 이유는 새 정책으로 인해 학생들의 성적이 향상되지는 않을 것이라는 점이다. 그와 반대로 그녀는 그로 인해 성적이 떨어질 것이라고 걱정한다. 동시에 다른 전공을 가진 학생들과의 교류가 줄어들어서 학생들이 더 많이 배우지 못하고 생각을 넓힐 수 없게 될 것이다. 여자는 또한 같은 전공자끼리 모여 사는 것보다 다양한 생활 여건을 갖는 것이 더 유익하다고 지적한다. 그녀는 전공이 같은 학생들은 동일한 시각을 갖는다고 주장하는데, 이는 그들이 비슷한 사고를 한다는 점을 의미한다. 그녀는 새로운 정책으로 인해 학생들이 더 이상 창의적이지 않고 남들과 다르게 생각하지도 않게 될 것이라고 생각한다.

Unit 20 Bus Routes

Exercise ·· p.56

Reading

해석

버스 노선 변경

가을 학기부터 대학 버스 시스템에 새로운 노선과 정류장이 추가될 예정입니다. 신설 노선은 오전 8시부터 오후 5시까지 운행될 것입니다. 오후 5시 이후에는 기존 노선에 따라 운행이 이루어질 것입니다. 신설 노선으로 인해 교내 주요 지점 간의 이동 속도가 빨라질 것입니다. 학생들이 버스 간격 때문에 3분 이상 기다리는 일은 없어질 것입니다. 또한 정류장 수가 증가함으로써 교내에서 걸어 다니는 일도 줄어들 것입니다. 학생들은 이전처럼 목적지에서 멀리 떨어진 곳에서 내리지 않아도 될 것이며, 먼 거리를 걸어야 할 필요도 없어질 것입니다.

Comprehension

1 The notice states that there will be additional bus routes and stops on campus during the daytime.

2 The first reason the routes are being changed is so that it will take less time to get to major areas on campus.

3 The second reason for the change is that pedestrian traffic on campus will decrease.

4 Students will benefit by having to wait a minimal amount of time between buses.

5 Students will also benefit by having more places to get off the buses, so they will have to walk less across campus.

Listening

Script 🎧 02-11

M Student: It looks as though the school's going to start those new bus routes pretty soon.

W Student: Yeah, I'm really looking forward to them.

M: I'm not. They're probably going to increase the noise level on campus.

W: That's true, but this is a big campus, and there aren't many buses on campus now. We really could use some more buses so that we can get to places on campus a lot quicker. Right now, I've got to walk about fifteen minutes to get to each class. Buses will cut down on that time considerably.

M: All right, but the routes won't be in effect during the evening. What about all of the night school students who won't get to make use of the program? That's not fair, is it?

W: Well, it's unfortunate, but the large majority of the students here take classes during the day. Since the school doesn't have unlimited funds, it should take care of the largest number of students. That means the day students should come first.

M: Okay, I guess I see your points.

해석

M Student: 곧 학교측이 버스 노선을 신설할 것처럼 보이는군.

W Student: 그래, 나는 정말로 기대하고 있어.

M: 나는 그렇지 않아. 아마도 교내의 소음이 더 심해질 거야.

W: 그건 사실이지만, 이곳 캠퍼스는 큰 편인데 현재 캠퍼스에는 버스가 잘 없잖아. 실제로 버스가 많아지면 교내의 목적지까지 훨씬 빨리 이동할 수 있을 거야. 지금은 내가 각 강의실까지 이동하려면 15분 정도 걸어야 해. 버스로 다니면 시간이 상당히 줄어들 거야.

M: 그래, 하지만 노선이 저녁 시간에는 운행을 하지 않을 거야. 노선을 이용하지 못하는 야간 수업 학생들은 어떻게 하지? 그건 공평하지 않아, 그렇지 않니?

W: 음, 안타까운 일이기는 하지만 대다수의 학생들은 주간에 수업을 들어. 학교 재원이 제한되어 있으니 가장 많은 수의 학생들을 고려해야 할 거야. 주간 수업 학생들을 우선시 해야 한다는 뜻이지.

M: 그래, 무슨 말인지 알겠어.

Organization

1 The woman is very pleased that there will be more buses on campus.

2 She feels that there are currently not enough buses on campus.

3 The woman currently must walk about fifteen minutes to get to each class, so the new buses will enable her to get to her classes faster.

4 She feels that it is unfortunate that night school students will not be able to use the new bus routes.

5 The woman says that the school does not have unlimited amounts of money, so it must take care of the greatest number of students first.

Comparing

Sample Response

Script 🎧 02-12

The topic of the notice is some bus route changes that the school will be making on its campus. The woman supports these changes for a couple of reasons. According to the woman, there are not enough buses on campus. She states that she needs fifteen minutes to walk to her classes; however, once she is able to take a

bus, she will be able to get to her classes much faster than she is currently. While the man points out that night school students will not benefit from these bus route changes, the woman counters by saying that the school doesn't have an unlimited amount of money. In the woman's mind, the school must take care of the day students first because they make up the majority of the student body.

해석

공지의 주제는 학교측이 교내 버스 노선을 일부 변경할 것이라는 점이다. 여자는 두 가지 이유로 이러한 조치를 찬성한다. 여자에 따르면 교내에는 버스가 부족하다. 그녀는 자신이 15분 정도 걸어야 강의실에 도착한다고 말한다. 하지만 버스를 이용할 수 있으면 현재보다 훨씬 빨리 강의실까지 갈 수 있을 것이라고 말한다. 남자가 야간 학생들은 그러한 버스 노선 변경의 혜택을 받지 못할 것이라고 지적하자 여자는 학교의 예산이 한정되어 있다고 말함으로써 반박한다. 여자의 의견으로는 주간 학생들이 학생 중 대다수를 차지하고 있으므로 학교측은 이들을 먼저 고려해야 한다.

Unit 21 Library Construction

Exercise ·· p.58

Reading

해석

도서관의 새로운 카페

대학측이 도서관 지하에 학생 카페 공사를 시작할 예정입니다. 카페는 10월 31일부터 영업을 시작할 것입니다. 카페에서 학생들은 스낵이나 음료를 쉽게 구입할 수 있을 것입니다. 식품 및 음료를 사기 위해 더 이상 캠퍼스 밖으로 나가지 않아도 됩니다. 이제 도서관 건물 내에서 가벼운 휴식을 취한 뒤 다시 공부를 시작할 수 있습니다. 또한 먹을거리들은 비싸지 않을 것입니다. 유효한 학생증을 제시하기만 하면 모든 메뉴에 대한 할인을 받을 수 있습니다. 학교측은 카페가 문을 열면 학생들이 새로운 카페를 애용할 것으로 기대합니다.

Comprehension

1 The announcement states that the university is building a student café in the basement of the library.

2 The first reason for building it is that it will provide students with a closer alternative for snacks.

3 The second reason for its construction is that it will provide students with inexpensive snacks.

4 Students will benefit by not having to leave campus for food and drinks.

5 Students will also be able to save money when they purchase food and drinks at the café.

Script 🎧 02-13

W Student: It seems they're finally putting a café in the library's basement.

M Student: Yeah, I heard. I can't understand why they're doing such a thing.

W: Really? Why do you say that?

M: Well, I heard it's only going to sell junk food like donuts, chips, and candy bars. You know, stuff like that.

W: What? No fruits or healthy alternatives?

M: Nope, just junk food, which is terrible for people and really unhealthy. The café should at least offer some good food and drinks, but it won't.

W: That's not good.

M: No, it isn't. It's also simply too close . . . Well, it's inside the library. How do you think that will affect students? I imagine that it'll give them an easy excuse to procrastinate. They'll go down there and hang out with their friends instead of focusing on their schoolwork. At least having to go off campus keeps more students in the library because the shops are far away.

W: I see your point.

M: Yeah, the more I think about it, the more I think this new café in the library isn't such a good idea.

해석

W Student: 드디어 도서관 지하에 카페가 생길 것 같아.

M Student: 그래, 나도 들었어. 그런데 왜 그런 일을 하려는지 나는 이해가 안 돼.

W: 정말이니? 왜 그런 말을 하는 거야?

M: 음, 그곳에서는 도넛, 감자칩, 그리고 초코바와 같은 정크푸드만 판매될 것이라고 들었거든. 알겠지만 그런 것들이지.

W: 뭐라고? 과일이나 건강에 좋은 건 없어?

M: 전혀 없어. 사람들에게 좋지 않고 정말로 건강에 해가 되는 정크푸드뿐이지. 카페라면 적어도 괜찮은 음식과 음료를 제공해야 하지만 그렇지는 않을 거야.

W: 그럼 안 되는데.

M: 안 되지. 게다가 너무 가까워서… 음, 도서관 내에 있잖아. 학생들한테 어떤 영향을 줄 것 같아? 나는 학생들이 빈둥댈 수 있는 좋은 핑계 거리가 생길 거라고 생각해. 공부에 열중하는 대신 친구들과 어울려 카페에 내려가서 시간을 보내겠지. 가게가 멀리 떨어져 있으면 캠퍼스 밖으로 나가는 일이 불편해서 많은 학생들이 도서관에 있게 되는데 말이야.

W: 무슨 말인지 알겠어.

M: 그래, 생각을 하면 할수록 도서관에 카페를 여는 건 그다지 좋은 생각이 아닌 것 같아.

Organization

1 The man does not think a café in the library will benefit students.

2 The male student says that the café will only be selling junk food like donuts, chips, and candy bars.

3 He claims that junk food is bad for people and will harm their health.

4 The man fears that too many students will start hanging out at the café.

5 He feels that this will cause students to procrastinate and stop focusing on their studies.

Comparing

Sample Response

Script 🎧 02-14

According to the announcement, a new café is opening in the library's basement. The male student dislikes this idea of including a student café inside the library. First of all, he says that the café will only be selling snacks and junk food like donuts, chips, and candy bars. He claims that junk food is bad for people and is too unhealthy. The second reason he gives is that because of its location, many students will start hanging out at the café. He feels this will cause students to procrastinate and stop focusing on their studies. In his opinion, to get students to study, it's better to have restaurants far away from the library instead of actually inside of it. That will convince students to stay in the library and to study instead of going out to eat.

해석

안내문에 따르면 도서관 지하에 새로운 카페가 문을 열 예정이다. 남학생은 도서관 내부에 학생 까페를 신설한다는 그러한 아이디어를 반기지 않는다. 우선 그는 카페에서 도넛, 감자칩, 그리고 초코바와 같은 정크푸드만 판매될 것이라고 말한다. 그는 정크푸드가 사람들에게 좋지 않고 건강에 해롭다고 주장한다. 그가 제시하는 두 번째 이유는 위치 때문에 많은 학생들이 카페에서 시간을 보내게 될 것이라는 점이다. 그는 이로 인해 학생들이 빈둥거리고 공부에 집중하지 않을 것이라고 생각한다. 그의 의견으로는 학생들을 공부하게 만들려면 식당을 도서관 안에 두기 보다 도서관에서 멀리 떨어진 곳에 두는 것이 더 낫다. 그러면 학생들이 밖에 나가서 무언가를 먹는 대신 도서관에 머물면서 공부를 하게 될 것이다.

Unit 22 Student Affairs

Exercise p.60

Reading

해석

학생 선거 일정 변경

학생 활동 사무소에서 학생 대표 선거 일정을 변경합니다. 과거에는 5월에 선거가 진행되었지만 이제 새 학년을 위한 대표들은 9월에 선출될 것입니다. 이로써 신입생들도 학생 대표를 선출하는데 도움을 줄 기회를 갖게 될 것인데, 이에 관해서는 신입생들의 불만이 종종 접수된 바 있었습니다. 뿐만 아니라 선거가 5월에 진행되지 않을 것이기 때문에, 학생들이 선거에 참여하지 않은 주된 변명거리였던, 학생들의 기말 고사 공부에 선거가 지장을 주는 일도 없어질 것입니다. 이로써 선거 참여율이 높아질 것입니다.

Comprehension

1 The notice mentions that student representative elections will now be held in September instead of in May.

2 The election date has changed because many freshmen complained about not being able to vote.

3 Freshmen will now be able to help elect their student representatives.

4 Many students did not participate in past elections because they were busy studying for their final exams.

5 Voter turnout should go up since the elections will not be held during an exam period.

Listening

Script 🎧 02-15

W Student: Hey, this is a spectacular idea. The school is moving elections for student representatives to September. That'll let freshmen be more involved in the elections.

M Student: Yeah, maybe. But do you know what? Lots of students are busy at the beginning of the year. They've got to fix their schedules and get used to their roommates and stuff.

W: So?

M: I'm just saying that many students might not bother to vote if the elections are held too early in the school year. I probably won't vote if I'm occupied with getting used to starting school again.

W: Okay. You have a point. But what about the freshmen? Don't you think it's great that they'll get involved in the election process?

M: Hmm . . . It's fine that they'll get to vote, but they don't really know anything about the important issues on campus. So how can they make good decisions without knowing all the facts? And they won't know much about the candidates either. They'll be voting, but they won't have much information to go with.

W: Hmm . . . I guess I see your points.

해석

W Student: 이것 봐, 정말 멋진 생각이군. 학교측이 학생 대표 선거 시기를 9월로 옮길 예정이네. 그러면 신입생들의 선거 참여율이 높아질 거야.

M Student: 그럴 수도 있겠지. 하지만 그거 알아? 많은 학생들이 학년 초에는 바빠. 시간표도 짜야 하고 룸메이트나 기타 일에도 익숙해져야 해.

W: 그래서?

M: 선거를 학년 초 너무 이른 시기에 치루면 많은 학생들이 굳이 선거에 참여하려고 하지 않을 것이라는 뜻이지. 학교 생활에 다시 익숙해지는 일에 몰두하면 나라도 아마 투표를 하지 않을 것 같아.

W: 그래. 말이 되네. 하지만 신입생은 어떻게 하고? 신입생이 선거에 참여하면 정말 좋을 것이라고 생각하지 않니?

M: 흠… 신입생들이 투표를 하는 건 좋지만 그들은 사실 주요한 학내 문제에 대해서 아무것도 모르잖아. 그러니 상황도 모르면서 어떻게 현명한 선택을 할 수 있겠어? 그리고 후보들에 대해서도 잘 모를 거야. 투표는 하겠지만 가진 정보는 별로 없을 테지.

W: 흠… 무슨 말인지 알 것 같아.

Organization

1 The man has a rather negative opinion of the decision to move the day for electing student representatives.

2 The man says that many students are busy in September since they have just come back to school.

3 He feels that many students might not be able to vote and says that even he might not vote.

4 He thinks that it is nice that freshmen get to vote.

5 He believes the freshmen will not know anything about campus issues or the candidates, so they will not be informed while they are voting.

Comparing

Sample Response

Script 🎧 02-16

The man feels negatively toward the student activities office's decision to move the date of the student representative elections from May to September. He gives two reasons for his negative feelings. First, he mentions that in September, students are still getting used to their schedules, their roommates, and simply being back at school. So many students, including the student himself, might not vote if they're too busy with back-to-school activities. Second of all, he acknowledges that while it's nice that freshmen may now vote in the elections, they will not know enough about either the important campus issues or the candidates themselves. He states that they won't know all of the necessary facts before they vote. Because of this lack of knowledge, they won't be able to make educated decisions on who to vote for.

해석

남자는 학생 대표 선거일을 5월에서 9월로 옮기겠다는 학생 활동 사무소의 결정에 부정적으로 생각한다. 그는 두 가지 이유에서 부정적인 의견을 나타낸다. 첫째, 그는 9월이 학생들이 스케줄, 룸메이트, 그리고 신학기 생활에 적응하는 시기라고 말한다. 따라서 자신을 포함한 많은 학생들이 신학기 일들로 너무 바빠서 투표를 하지 않을 수도 있다. 둘째, 그는 신입생들이 선거에 참여하게 된 것은 좋은 일이지만 그들은 학내 문제나 후보자에 대한 정보를 충분히 알지 못할 것이라고 생각한다. 그는 신입생들이 투표를 하기 전에 필요한 정보를 다 얻지 못할 것이라고 주장한다. 이러한 정보의 부족 때문에 누구를 뽑을 것인가에 대한 결정을 제대로 내리지 못할 것이다.

Unit 23 Student Activities I

Exercise ·· p.62

Reading

해석

학생 활동비

학교 당국은 학생 활동비를 인상하기로 결정했습니다. 현재 학생들은 학기마다 100달러를 납부하고 있지만 이제 그 금액이 125달러로 인상될 예정입니다. 전에는 납부가 선택 사항이었으나 이제는 의무 사항입니다. 모든 정규 학생들은 반드시 개강 전에 활동비를 납부해야 합니다. 학생 활동비는 다양한 목적으로 사용됩니다. 여기에는 교내 초청 강사 초빙, 동아리 활동 지원, 그리고 기타 다양한 학생 활동의 비용 부담이 포함됩니다. 활동비 인상은 최근의 전국적인 물가 상승에 따른 것입니다.

Comprehension

1 The announcement is about an increase in the student activity fee.
2 It is increasing from 100 dollars a semester to 125 dollars.
3 All full-time students must pay the fee.
4 It is used to secure guest speakers on campus, to pay for student clubs, and to cover the costs of various other student activities
5 It is increasing due to the recent national rise in prices.

Listening

Script 🎧 02-17

M Student: I'm really disappointed by this news.

W Student: Are you referring to the increase in the price of the student activity fee?

M: I sure am. It's just not fair that the school keeps raising the price of everything.

W: What do you mean? It's only an increase of twenty-five dollars.

M: Actually, for me, it's an increase of 125 dollars. I didn't pay it before because I don't take part in any student activities. But now that it's mandatory, I need to come up with more money.

W: Ah, sure. I see your point now.

M: And the school just raised the price of tuition this week.

W: It did? I hadn't heard that.

M: The price of tuition is going up by ten percent. It's hard for people like me to afford school when prices continue to increase so much. It's like the school only cares about how much money it can make from us. The quality of our education hasn't been increasing, but prices have.

W: Yeah, you may be right.

해석

M Student: 이번 소식은 정말 실망스러운데.

W Student: 학생 활동비 인상을 말하는 거니?

M: 그래. 학교가 모든 것에 대한 비용을 인상시키는 건 공정하지 않은 일이야.

W: 무슨 말이지? 단지 25달러만 인상되는 걸.

M: 사실 내게는 125달러가 인상된 거야. 나는 학생 활동에 참가하지 않기 때문에 전에는 활동비를 내지 않았거든. 하지만 의무 사항이 되었으니 돈을 더 마련해야만 하지.

W: 아, 그래. 이제 무슨 말인지 알겠군.

M: 그리고 학교측이 이번 주에 등록금도 인상시켰잖아.

W: 그래? 그런 말은 못 들었는데.

M: 등록금이 10% 인상될 거야. 물가가 너무 많이 올라서 나같은 사람은 학교를 다니기가 힘들어. 학교측은 우리로부터 얼만큼 돈을 뜯어낼 수 있는지에 대해서만 관심이 있는 것 같아. 교육의 질은 오르지 않았는데 비용만 오르고 있지.

W: 그래, 네 말이 맞는 것 같아.

Organization

1 The man dislikes the increase in the student activity fee.
2 He doesn't take part in any student activities.
3 It is increasing by ten percent.
4 It is difficult for him to afford to go to school.
5 He thinks that the school only cares about how much money it can make from students.

Comparing

Sample Response
Script 🎧 02-18

The announcement mentions that the student activity fee is increasing from 100 dollars to 125 dollars each semester. In addition, all full-time students must pay the fee before they take classes. The man is strongly against this decision by the school. First, he points out that he didn't pay the fee in the past because he doesn't participate in any student activities. So now he needs to pay 125 dollars extra each semester. He says that he has to come up with the money for that. He also claims that tuition is increasing. Unfortunately, he states that the quality of education at the school is not increasing. As a result, the man believes that the school only cares about how much money it can make from the students who go there.

해석

안내문에는 매 학기 학생 활동비가 100달러에서 125달러로 인상될 것이라고 나와 있다. 또한 모든 정규 학생들이 수업을 듣기 전에 활동비를 납부해야만 한다. 남자는 학교측의 이러한 결정을 강력히 반대한다. 먼저 그는 자신이 어떠한 학생 활동에도 참가하지 않기 때문에 전에는 활동비를 납부하지 않았다고 말한다. 따라서 이제 그는 학기마다 125달러를 추가로 납부해야 한다. 그는 자신이 활동비를 위한 돈을 마련해야 한다고 말한다. 그는 또한 등록금이 인상될 것이라고 이야기한다. 안타깝게도 그는 학교 교육의 질은 오르지 않고 있다고 주장한다. 그 결과 남자는 학교측이 학교에 다니는 학생들로부터 돈을 얼마나 많이 끌어낼 수 있는지만 신경을 쓴다고 생각한다.

Unit 24 | School Facilities II

Exercise p.64

Reading
해석

새로운 공원 건설 예정

대학측이 캠퍼스의 북쪽 끝자락에 있는 새로운 부지를 취득하게 되었다는 점을 알리게 되어 기쁘게 생각합니다. 30에이커가 넘는 이 땅은 학생들을 위한 공원을 건설하는데 사용될 예정입니다. 공원에는 넓은 잔디밭뿐만 아니라 연못, 테니스 코트, 그리고 2개의 야외 농구장이 들어설 예정입니다. 조깅 및 자전거용 도로 또한 건설될 예정입니다. 이 지역의 일부에는 숲이 우거져 있습니다. 나무들은 벌목되지 않고 그대로 남아 있을 것입니다. 부지 취득을 포함하여 총비용은 약 120만 달러에 이를 것으로 추산됩니다.

Comprehension

1 The notice is about the acquisition of a new tract of land and what the university will do with it.
2 It covers more than thirty acres.
3 It will be turned into a park for students.
4 The park will have a grassy area, a pond, tennis courts, two outdoor basketball courts, jogging and cycling trails, and a wooded area.
5 The total price of everything, including land acquisition, is estimated at 1.2 million dollars.

Listening
Script 🎧 02-19

W Student: I'm so excited that the school is going to construct a new park.

M Student: You are? Why is that?

W: Well, there really aren't many green areas on campus. It will be nice to have somewhere to go to relax.

M: I guess.

W: You guess? I know that you enjoy hiking and cycling. Now, you'll be able to do both without having to avoid getting hit by cars on campus.

M: Hmm . . . That's a good point, Stephanie. I hadn't considered that.

W: There's something else I like about the new park.

M: What's that?

W: I love the fact that the school is going to leave the forested area intact. It will be nice just to walk through the forest and to be among all of those trees. I really can't wait for the park to be completed. I hope that happens soon.

M: Yeah, I suppose you're right. Maybe it will be something nice.

해석

W Student: 학교에서 새로운 공원을 건설한다니 정말로 기대가 되는 걸.

M Student: 그래? 어째서?

W: 음, 교내에는 정말로 녹지가 많지 않잖아. 휴식을 취하러 갈 수 있는 곳이 있으면 멋질 거야.

M: 그럴 것 같군.

W: 그럴 것 같지? 나는 네가 하이킹과 사이클링을 좋아한다고 알고 있어. 이제 교내에서 차에 치일 걱정 없이 두 가지 다 할 수 있을 거야.

M: 흠… 좋은 지적이야, Stephanie. 그 점은 생각 못했네.

W: 내가 새 공원을 좋아하는 또 다른 이유도 있어.

M: 그게 뭔데?

W: 나는 학교측이 숲을 손대지 않고 놔둘 것이라는 사실이 마음에 들어. 숲속을 걸어 다니고 그곳 나무들 사이에 있으면 멋질 것 같아. 정말로 공원 완공이 기다려지는 걸. 빨리 그렇게 되면 좋겠어.

M: 그래, 네 말이 맞는 것 같군. 아마 멋진 곳이 될 거야.

Organization

1 The woman is excited about the school's plans to make the new park.
2 She wants to go there to relax.
3 She thinks he can go hiking and cycling in the park.
4 She is glad that it will remain intact because she wants to walk among all of the trees.
5 She hopes the park will be completed soon.

Sample Response

Script 🎧 02-20

The notice discusses the school's recent acquisition of some land near campus and its plans to build a park there. The park will have many facilities, including cycling and hiking trails, tennis courts, and basketball courts. The woman supports this decision by the school and mentions that she is very excited about the park. For starters, the woman wants to spend time in the grassy area in the park and would like to go there to relax. Another benefit of the park is the wooded area that will be in it. The woman is pleased that the school will keep all of the trees. She remarks that she is looking forward to spending time walking among the trees and hopes that the school completes construction of the park very soon.

해석

공지에 따르면 학교측이 최근 캠퍼스 인근의 부지를 확보해서 그곳에 공원을 건설할 계획이다. 공원에는 자전거 도로 및 하이킹 도로, 테니스 코스, 그리고 농구장을 포함하여 여러 시설들이 들어설 예정이다. 여자는 학교측의 이러한 결정을 찬성하며 공원에 대해 기대가 매우 크다고 말한다. 우선 여자는 공원 내 잔디밭에서 시간을 보내고 싶어하며 그곳에 가서 휴식을 취하고 싶어한다. 공원의 또 다른 혜택은 그 안에 마련될 녹지 공간에 있다. 여자는 학교측이 모든 나무를 그대로 둘 것이라는 점에 기뻐한다. 그녀는 자신이 나무들 사이를 걸어 다니며 시간을 보낼 수 있기를 고대하며 학교측이 공원 공사를 빨리 마쳤으면 좋겠다고 말한다.

Unit 25 School Policies II

Exercise p.66

Reading

해석

새로운 수업 조교 정책

현재 세미나 수업에는 교수님들을 보조하는 수업 조교가 배정될 수 있습니다. 이전에는 대학원생들만 수업 조교가 되는 것이 가능했습니다. 하지만 익명의 후원자로부터 받은 막대한 기부금 덕분에 학부생 수업 조교에게 지불할 수 있는 충분한 자금이 마련되었습니다. 수업 조교를 필요로 하는 수업의 리스트가 각 학과 사무실에 게시될 예정입니다. 4학년생들만 지원이 가능합니다. 지원 자격을 갖추기 위해서는 전체 평점이 3.40 이상이어야 합니다. 전공 평점은 3.60 이상이어야 합니다. 또한 해당 수업의 수업 조교가 되기 위해서는 반드시 그 수업을 수강한 적이 있어야 합니다.

Comprehension

1 The announcement is about a change in policy that allows undergraduate students to be teaching assistants

for professors.

2 An anonymous person donated a lot of money to provide funding to pay students.

3 A list of classes requiring teaching assistants will be posted in each departmental office.

4 Only seniors are eligible.

5 They must have an overall GPA of 3.40 and a GPA of 3.60 in their major.

Listening

Script 🎧 02-21

M Student: This is great news. I can't wait to apply to be a teaching assistant.

W Student: I'm actually displeased by this news.

M: How come?

W: There are a couple of reasons. First of all, I prefer that teaching assistants be graduate students. They usually have enough knowledge of the topic that they can be helpful to students like us. I simply don't believe undergraduate students are knowledgeable enough to be teaching assistants.

M: Hmm . . . Maybe. But I'm not sure. I think I know enough about economics.

W: Sure, but you have a perfect 4.00 GPA. Most students aren't like you.

M: What's your other reason?

W: Being a teaching assistant is a time-consuming job. One of my TAs told me that she spends up to twenty hours a week on her work as a TA.

M: What's wrong with that?

W: It's too much time for busy undergraduates. Can you imagine spending that much time and then completing your coursework? I bet your grades will go down if that happens.

해석

M Student: 좋은 소식이네. 당장 수업 조교에 지원을 해야겠어.

W Student: 사실 나는 이번 소식이 만족스럽지 않아.

M: 어째서?

W: 두 가지 이유가 있어. 무엇보다 수업 조교가 대학원생인 편이 더 좋아. 대학원생들은 보통 해당 주제에 대해 충분한 양의 지식을 갖고 있기 때문에 우리와 같은 학생들에게 도움이 될 수 있지. 나는 수업 조교가 될 만큼 학부생들에게 충분한 지식이 있다고는 생각하지 않아.

M: 흠… 그럴 수도 있겠네. 하지만 잘 모르겠어. 나는 내가 경제학을 충분히 잘 알고 있다고 생각하는데.

W: 그래, 네 평점은 4.00 만점이니까. 대부분의 학생들이 너와 같지는 않잖아.

M: 다른 이유는 뭐니?

W: 수업 조교는 시간을 잡아 먹는 일이야. 내 수업 조교 중 한 명은 자신이 수업

조교로 일을 하느라 일주일에 20시간을 쓴다고 말하더군.

M: 그게 무슨 문제인데?

W: 바쁜 학부생들에게는 너무 많은 시간이야. 그렇게 많은 시간을 쓰고 나서 수업 과제를 다 한다는 걸 상상할 수 있어? 그렇게 되면 분명 학점이 떨어질 거야.

Organization

1 The woman dislikes the announcement that undergraduate students can become teaching assistants.

2 She believes that graduate students are more knowledgeable than undergraduate students.

3 Most students do not have a perfect 4.00 GPA like he has.

4 The TA spends up to twenty hours a week on her work as a TA.

5 Spending a lot of time on being a TA is too much for undergraduates, so their grades will probably go down.

Comparing

Sample Response

Script 🎧 02-22

The notice points out that the school has a new policy regarding teaching assistants. Now, undergraduates will be eligible to become teaching assistants if they pass certain requirements. The woman opposes this decision and gives a couple of reasons explaining why. For one thing, she believes undergraduate students are not always knowledgeable in certain topics. She thinks, however, that graduate students have a lot more knowledge, so she prefers them as teaching assistants. The second reason the woman mentions is that being a TA is a time-consuming job. According to her, one of her TAs spends up to twenty hours a week on her work as a TA. The student believes that is too much time for undergraduates and that their grades will decline if they try to be TAs.

해석

공지는 수업 조교에 관한 학교측의 새로운 정책을 안내한다. 이제 특정 조건을 충족하는 경우 학부생들도 수업 조교가 될 수 있는 자격을 갖추게 된다. 여자는 이러한 결정을 반대하며 그렇게 생각하는 두 가지 이유를 제시한다. 우선 여자는 학부생들이 항상 특정 주제에 대해 해박한 것은 아니라고 생각한다. 하지만 대학원생들은 많은 지식을 가지고 있기 때문에 자신은 수업 조교로서 그들을 더 선호한다고 말한다. 그녀가 언급하는 두 번째 이유는 수업 조교가 시간을 많이 소비하는 일이라는 점에 있다. 그녀에 의하면 그녀의 수업 조교 중 한 명은 조교 업무를 하느라 일주일에 20시간을 쓰고 있다. 그녀는 이러한 시간이 학부생에게 너무 많은 시간이며, 만약 수업 조교가 되고자 한다면 학생들의 성적이 떨어질 것이라고 생각한다.

Unit 26 Graduation Requirements

Exercise ·· p.68

Reading

해석

서양 문명 수업이 필수 과목이 됩니다

가을 학기부터 모든 1학년과 2학년 학생들에게 서양 문명 1 수업이 필수 과목으로 지정됩니다. 3학년과 4학년 학생들은 이러한 졸업 요건을 적용받지 않지만 선택 과목으로서 이를 수강할 수 있습니다. 이 수업에서는 고대 그리스부터 현대에 이르기까지의 서구의 업적이 중점적으로 다루어질 예정입니다. 학생들은 수업을 통해 서구 문화의 중요한 측면들을 배우게 될 것입니다. 이 수업은 역사, 미술사, 그리고 고고학 교수님들에 의해 공동으로 진행될 것입니다. 수업에 관한 질문이 있는 경우에는 459–9039 내선 42로 전화를 주시기 바랍니다.

Comprehension

1 The announcement is about a requirement for freshmen and sophomores to take Western Civilization I.

2 Juniors and seniors are exempt.

3 It will focus on the achievements of the West from the ancient Greeks to modern times.

4 Professors in the History, Art History, Literature, and Archaeology departments will co-teach the class.

5 They can call 459-9039 extension 42.

Listening

Script 🎧 02-23

M Student: I'm really disappointed about the new course requirement.

W Student: You're talking about the Western civilization class, right?

M: That's correct. I'm a freshman, so I'm required to take it before I graduate.

W: What's wrong about learning about the history and culture of the West? I'm kind of looking forward to taking the class.

M: The problem is that I'm an engineering student. I have to take a full courseload every semester. Now that I have to add an extra class, I'll be even busier than normal.

W: Can't you just attend summer school?

M: I could, but I usually work at my parents' company during summer. I don't have time to stay here to take a single class.

W: I see.

M: Another problem is that few students are interested in the class. Most of my friends are unhappy about being forced to take another required class. It's just so upsetting for us.

W: I see your point, but I don't agree with you. It's just a single class.

M Student: 새로운 수강 요건은 정말 실망스러운데.

W Student: 서양 문명 수업을 말하는 거지, 그렇지?

M: 맞아. 나는 1학년이라서 졸업하기 전에 그 수업을 들어야만 해.

W: 서양의 역사와 문화를 배우는 것이 뭐가 문제인데? 나는 그 수업을 빨리 들어보고 싶은 걸.

M: 문제는 내 전공이 공학이라는 점이야. 매 학기마다 들어야 하는 수업들이 가득 있지. 이제 수업을 하나 더 들어야만 하니 평소보다 훨씬 더 바빠질 거야.

W: 여름 학기 수업을 들을 수는 없어?

M: 그럴 수도 있겠지만 나는 여름에 보통 부모님 회사에서 일을 해. 수업 하나를 듣기 위해서 여기에 머무를 수 있는 시간은 없어.

W: 그렇구나.

M: 또 다른 문제는 그 수업에 관심이 있는 학생이 거의 없다는 점이야. 내 친구들은 대부분 강제로 또 다른 필수 과목을 들어야 한다는 점에 불만을 갖고 있어. 우리들에게는 매우 속 터지는 일이지.

W: 무슨 말인지는 알겠는데, 나는 네 의견에 동의하지 않아. 단 한 과목일 뿐이니까.

Organization

1 He is really disappointed about it.
2 She is looking forward to taking the class.
3 He has a full courseload every semester because he is an engineering student.
4 He works at his parents' company during summer.
5 They are unhappy about being forced to take another required class.

Comparing

Sample Response
Script 🎧 02-24

The announcement notes that freshmen and sophomores have a new required class for graduation. They must take a class called Western Civilization 1. The man is against the decision to make this a required course. He provides two reasons to explain his thinking. First of all, he mentions that he is an engineering student, so he has many classes to take. Because he has to take an extra class now, it will be very difficult for him. The second reason that he discusses is that many students are not interested in the class. The man points out that a large number of his friends are very displeased about having to take another

required class. The students, like the man, are upset about this decision by the school.

공지에 따르면 1학년과 2학년 학생들에게 새로운 졸업 필수 과목이 지정되었다. 그들은 서양 문명 1이라는 수업을 들어야만 한다. 남자는 이 수업을 필수 과목으로 지정한 결정을 반대한다. 그는 두 가지 이유를 들어 자신의 생각을 밝힌다. 우선 그는 자신이 공학 전공자이기 때문에 들어야 할 수업이 많다고 말한다. 이제 추가로 수업을 하나 더 들어야 하기 때문에 그는 매우 힘들어질 것이다. 그가 언급한 두 번째 이유는 많은 학생들이 그 수업에 관심을 가지지 않고 있지 않다는 점이다. 남자는 자신의 친구들 중 상당수가 필수 과목을 하나 더 들어야 한다는 점에 큰 불만을 가지고 있다고 지적한다. 남자와 마찬가지로 그러한 학생들은 학교측의 이번 결정에 언짢아하고 있다.

Unit 27 Summer Programs

Exercise p.70

Reading

여름 스포츠 프로그램

학교에서 7월과 8월에 첫 번째 여름 스포츠 프로그램이 운영될 예정입니다. 초등학생들을 위한 여름 캠프가 열릴 것입니다. 학생들은 4주 동안 캠퍼스를 방문해서 다양한 스포츠를 배우게 될 것입니다. 캠프 참가자들의 선생님은 본교 학생들이 될 것입니다. 이는 학생들에게 실무 경험을 제공해 줄 것이고 흥미로운 여름 일자리가 될 것입니다. 관심이 있는 학생은 체육학과 사무실에서 지원할 수 있습니다. 새로운 프로그램에 따라 발생하는 모든 수익은 학교의 체육 시설을 개선하는데 사용될 예정입니다.

Comprehension

1 The announcement is about a summer sports program at a school.
2 Elementary school students can attend the program.
3 They will be students at the university.
4 They will get work experience and have an exciting job.
5 It will use the profits to improve the school's athletic facilities.

Listening
Script 🎧 02-25

W Student: Eric, are you going to apply to be an instructor for the summer sports program? That's what I'm going to do right now.

M Student: I already have a job for summer. I didn't

know you were interested in the program.

W: I want to be a teacher when I graduate, but I'd also like to coach. I'm going to apply to teach basketball at the program.

M: That sounds fun.

W: It should be fun, and being a student-instructor will look great on my résumé when I apply for jobs after graduation next year.

M: Good luck.

W: Thanks. And you know something else . . . ?

M: What?

W: If a lot of kids attend the camp, the school will make some money. The school's gym is not particularly good, so I hope that the school spends some of the money it earns on improving the gym. That will help improve the gym and let students here get in good shape.

M: Yeah, that sounds great. I hope it all works out for you.

해석

W Student: Eric, 여름 스포츠 프로그램의 교사 자리에 지원할 거니? 나는 지금 그렇게 하려고 해.

M Student: 나는 이미 이번 여름에 할 일을 구해 놓았어. 네가 그 프로그램에 관심이 있는지는 내가 모르고 있었군.

W: 나는 졸업하면 교사가 되고 싶은데, 코치 일도 해 보고 싶었거든. 프로그램에서 농구를 가르치는 일에 지원을 할 거야.

M: 재미있겠네.

W: 재미있을 거고, 학생일 때 교사로 일을 해 보면 내년 졸업 후 입사 지원을 할 때에도 이력서에 큰 보탬이 될 거야.

M: 행운을 빌어.

W: 고마워. 그리고 혹시 그것도 알아…?

M: 뭔데?

W: 많은 아이들이 캠프에 참가하는 경우 학교측은 돈을 벌게 될 거야. 교내 체육관은 그다지 상태가 좋지 않아서 나는 학교측이 거두어들이는 수익의 일부를 체육관 개선에 쓰면 좋겠어. 그러면 체육관이 좋아질 것이고, 이곳 학생들의 건강도 좋아질 거야.

M: 그래, 괜찮게 들리는군. 모든 일이 잘 되길 빌게.

Organization

1 She is going to apply to be an instructor for the summer sports program.

2 She wants to work as a teacher and also coach.

3 It will look great on her résumé when she applies for jobs.

4 The school will make some money.

5 She wants the school to improve the gym so that students can get in shape.

Comparing

Sample Response

Script 🎧 02-26

The notice describes the school's summer sports program. It involves elementary school students attending the school to learn how to play sports in summer. The instructors will be students at the university. The woman supports this decision by the school for a couple of reasons. The first reason that she provides is that she is excited to get some experience as an instructor. She wants to be a teacher and coach at a school after she graduates, so being an instructor will make her résumé look good. The second reason the woman mentions concerns the money the school will make from the program. She hopes the school will spend some money on improving the gym. She thinks that if the gym becomes better, it will let many students get in good shape.

해석

공지에는 학교의 여름 스포츠 프로그램이 안내되어 있다. 초등학교 학생들이 여름에 학교에 와서 스포츠를 배울 수 있는 프로그램이다. 강사는 대학교 학생들이 될 것이다. 여자는 두 가지 이유에서 이러한 학교측의 결정을 반기고 있다. 그녀가 제시하는 첫 번째 이유는 그녀가 강사로서 경험을 쌓고 싶어하기 때문이다. 그녀는 졸업 후 교사가 되어 학교에서 코치 업무를 해 보고 싶기 때문에 강사가 되면 그녀의 이력서에 도움이 될 것이다. 여자가 언급하는 두 번째 이유는 프로그램으로 인해 학교측이 거두어들일 수익과 관련이 있다. 그녀는 학교측이 일부 수익을 체육관 개선에 쓰기를 바란다. 그녀는 체육관이 개선되면 많은 학생들의 건강이 좋아질 것으로 생각한다.

Unit 28 Student Activities II

Exercise p.72

Reading

해석

교내 동아리에 대한 지원 중단

학교측은 다양한 관심사를 아우르는 다수의 동아리들을 인정하고 있습니다. 일부 동아리는 많은 회원을 보유하고 있는 반면에 최소한의 회원만 보유하고 있는 동아리들도 있습니다. 학교측은 이러한 모든 동아리들에게 지원을 해 주고 있습니다. 하지만 바로 지금부터 회원수가 10명 미만인 모든 동아리들에게는 지원이 중단될 것입니다. 여전히 동아리로서 인정은 받을 것이고 교내에서 모임을 가질 수 있습니다. 하지만 더 이상 동아리 활동에 대한 금전적인 지원은 받지 못하게 될 것입니다. 이로써 보다 인기 있는 교내 동아리들이 필요한 자금을 지원받게 될 것입니다.

Comprehension

1 The announcement is about some school clubs that will

lose their funding.

2 It provides funding for these clubs.

3 Clubs with fewer than ten students will lose their funding.

4 They can still meet on campus.

5 It will ensure that the more popular clubs receive the funding they require.

Listening

Script 🎧 02-27

W Student: I'm really disheartened by this news. My club is going to get defunded.

M Student: What club are you in?

W: I'm a member of the knitting club. We only have seven members, but we have tons of fun.

M: Isn't there any way you can get new members?

W: It's just not a popular activity, so many people aren't into it. But I've been a member for four years, and I've made some really good friends in it. The other members and I will almost surely be lifelong friends.

M: Well, you can't really spend much money, can you?

W: On the contrary, our supplies cost a lot of money. The material we knit with is expensive, and we have to buy other equipment, too. The school used to pay for it, but now that won't happen. Some of us can't afford to pay for the materials.

M: Hmm . . . Maybe you can get some new members.

W: I guess. It seems like it's our only solution.

M: I hope that you can do it.

해석

W Student: 이번 뉴스 때문에 난 정말로 낙심했어. 우리 동아리에 대한 지원이 끊길 거야.

M Student: 어떤 동아리에 가입해 있는데?

W: 나는 뜨개질 동아리 회원이야. 회원은 7명뿐이지만 무척 재미있어.

M: 새로운 회원을 구할 수 있는 방법은 없어?

W: 인기 있는 활동이 아니라서 많은 사람들이 그다지 좋아하지 않아. 하지만 나는 4년째 회원이고, 이곳에서 정말 좋은 친구들을 사귀었어. 다른 회원들과 나는 분명 평생 동안 친구로 지내게 될 거야.

M: 음, 실제로 많은 돈을 쓸 수는 없잖아, 그렇지?

W: 그와 반대로 물품에 대한 비용이 많이 들어. 뜨개질 재료들은 값이 비싸고, 우리는 기타 장비들도 사야 해. 학교측이 그에 대한 비용을 지불해 주곤 했지만 이제 그런 일은 없을 거야. 우리들 중 몇몇은 재료비를 감당할 수가 없어.

M: 흠… 아마 새로운 회원을 모집할 수도 있을 거야.

W: 그럴 수도 있겠지. 그게 우리의 유일한 해결책인 것 같아.

M: 그럴 수 있기를 바랄게.

Organization

1 The woman is disheartened by the decision.

2 She belongs to the knitting club.

3 She has been a member for four years and has made some lifelong friends.

4 The club's materials and other equipment are expensive.

5 Some of the members cannot afford to pay for their own supplies.

Comparing

Sample Response

Script 🎧 02-28

The notice states that clubs with fewer than ten members will have their funding cut off. The clubs can still exist, but the school will not pay for anything. It will instead focus on funding clubs with larger memberships. The woman dislikes this decision. She remarks that she belongs to the knitting club, which has seven members. First, she says that the members are likely to be lifelong friends. So even though the club is small, its members are close to one another. Next, she comments that the materials used by the knitting club are expensive. She says the school pays for the materials. However, since funding will be cut off, the members will have to pay. But she mentions that some members cannot afford to do that.

해석

공지는 회원수가 10명 미만인 동아리에 대한 지원이 중단될 것이라는 점을 알리고 있다. 동아리는 계속 존재할 수 있지만 학교측이 자금을 지원해 주지는 않을 것이다. 대신 보다 회원이 많은 동아리에 지원이 집중될 것이다. 여자는 이러한 결정을 반기지 않는다. 그녀는 자신이 속해 있는 뜨개질 동아리의 회원이 7명이라고 언급한다. 첫째, 그녀는 회원들끼리 평생 친구가 될 것이라고 말한다. 따라서 동아리가 작기는 하지만 회원들이 서로 매우 친하게 지낸다. 다음으로, 그녀는 뜨개질 동아리에서 사용되는 재료가 비싸다고 언급한다. 그녀는 학교측이 재료비를 지불해 준다고 말한다. 하지만 지원이 중단된 후에는 회원들이 비용을 내야 할 것이다. 하지만 그녀는 일부 회원들에게 그럴 수 있는 여력이 없다고 언급한다.

Unit 29 Residential Life

Exercise ·· p.74

Reading

해석

신입생들의 1인실 입실 허용

가을 학기를 시작으로 교내 세 곳의 기숙사의 1인실에서 신입생들의 거주가 허용될 예정입니다. 이는 룸메이트와 지내지 않고 학업에 집중하고자 하는 신입생들에게 좋은 기회일 것입니다. 보다 내성적인 학생들 또한 이러한 기회를 반길 수도 있을 것입니다. 신입생에게 배정된 1인실은 100개입니다. 1인실의 비용은 2인실보다 대략 50% 더 비쌉니다. 신입생들을 위한 1인실은 선착순에 따라 배정됩니다. 더 많은 정보가 필요한 경우 893–1293으로 Kendra Beck에게 연락을 주시기 바랍니다.

Comprehension

1 The announcement is about single rooms in dormitories being available for freshmen.
2 Freshmen interested in focusing on their studies and introverts might be interested in a single room.
3 There are 100 single rooms reserved for freshmen.
4 It costs around fifty percent higher than a double room.
5 They are available on a first-come, first-served basis.

Listening

Script 🎧 02-29

M Student: I can't say that I approve of this decision to let freshmen live in single rooms.

W Student: Why do you say that? I would have loved that when I was a freshman.

M: Think back to your freshman year.

W: Okay. What about it?

M: You probably stayed up late at night talking to your roommate on many occasions, didn't you?

W: Yeah, that's right.

M: So did I. My roommate was my first friend here. We did lots of activities together that year. Freshmen who live in singles won't get that opportunity. Having a roommate is the easiest way to make a friend at school.

W: I see your point.

M: In addition, lots of freshmen suffer from loneliness. After all, most of them are away from home for the first time in their lives. Without a roommate to talk to, these lonely freshmen could suffer from depression or other mental health issues that could have negative effects on them.

W: Huh. You may be right. Maybe the school needs to reconsider this decision.

해석

M Student: 1인실에 신입생들의 거주를 허용하는 이러한 결정에 내가 찬성한다고는 말하지 못하겠어.

W Student: 왜 그런 말을 하는 거니? 내가 신입생이라면 난 좋아할 것 같은데.

M: 네가 신입생이었을 때를 생각해 봐.

W: 좋아. 그게 왜?

M: 아마도 밤 늦게까지 룸메이트와 이야기를 했던 경우가 많았을 거야, 그렇지?

W: 그래, 맞아.

M: 나도 그랬어. 내 룸메이트와 나는 이곳에서 가장 친한 사이야. 우리는 그 해에 함께 많은 일들을 했어. 1인실에서 사는 신입생들은 그런 기회를 갖지 못하게 될 거야. 룸메이트와 지내는 것은 학교에서 친구를 사귈 수 있는 가장 손쉬운 방법이지.

W: 무슨 말인지 알겠어.

M: 게다가 많은 신입생들이 외로움으로 고생해. 어찌되었든 대부분의 신입생들은 생애 처음으로 집에서 멀리 떨어져 사니까. 이야기를 나눌 수 있는 룸메이트가 없으면 이처럼 외로운 신입생들은 우울증이나 기타 부정적인 영향을 끼칠 수 있는 정신 건강상의 문제를 겪을 수도 있어.

W: 허. 네 말이 맞는 것 같아. 이번 결정을 학교측이 재고해야 할 수도 있겠군.

Organization

1 The man does not approve of the decision.
2 He says that his roommate was his first friend and that they did many activities together.
3 They will lose the opportunity to be good friends with a roommate.
4 They suffer from loneliness.
5 He says they could suffer from depression or other mental health issues.

Comparing

Sample Response
Script 🎧 02-30

The notice states that incoming freshmen are now eligible to live in single rooms in dormitories. It announces that freshmen who want to concentrate on studying and who are introverted may want to avoid having a roommate. The man is against this decision by the school. He points out to the woman that he was good friends with his freshman-year roommate and that they did many activities. Then, he adds that freshmen living in singles will not have this chance. He also reminds the woman that many freshmen become lonely since they are living away from their families for the first time. He says that freshmen without roommates could become depressed or suffer some other kind of mental health problem. This could negatively affect some freshmen.

해석

공지는 신입생들도 이제 기숙사의 1인실에서 생활할 수 있게 되었다는 점을 알리고 있다. 공지에 따르면 학업에 집중하고자 하는 신입생들과 내성적인 신입생들은 룸메이트 없이 지내는 것을 원할 수도 있다. 남자는 학교측의 이러한 결정을 반대한다. 그는 자신이 신입생이었을 때 룸메이트와 친하게 지냈고 함께 많은 활동을 했다는 점을 여자에게 이야기한다. 그런 다음에 1인실에 사는 신입생들은 그러한 기회를 갖지 못하게 될 것이라고 말한다. 그는 또한 여자에게 많은 신입생들이 처음으로 가족들과 떨어져 살게 되기 때문에 외로워 할 것이라고 말한다. 그는 룸메이트가 없는 신입생들은 우울증이나 기타 정신 건강상의 문제를 겪을 수도 있다고 주장한다. 이러한 점은 일부 신입생들에게 부정적인 영향을 미칠 수도 있다.

Unit 30 School Facilities III

Exercise ···································· p.76

Reading

해석

식물원 학생 출입 금지

지금부터 Harriet Woodrow 식물원에서 모든 학생들의 출입이 금지됩니다. 이 식물원은 Hamilton 홀 뒤에 위치해 있으며 약 10에이커의 면적을 차지하고 있습니다. 많은 교수님들께서 그곳에서 중요한 실험을 하고 계십니다. 이러한 실험들 중 일부는 3년이나 4년 정도 지나야 끝이 납니다. 안타깝게도 최근에 몇몇 학생들이 식물원의 통로를 벗어나서 이러한 실험들에 피해를 끼쳤습니다. 지금부터 허가를 받은 사람만이 식물원에 출입을 할 수 있습니다. 캠퍼스 근처에 몇 군데의 공원과 다른 식물원이 있습니다. 자연에서 시간을 보내고 싶어하는 학생들에게는 그러한 곳들을 방문할 것을 추천합니다.

Comprehension

1 The announcement is about students being prohibited from the school's botanical garden.
2 They conduct experiments that may take three or four years to conclude.
3 They damaged some professors' experiments.
4 Only authorized individuals may visit the botanical garden.
5 It advises them to visit the parks or the botanical garden located near the school.

Listening

Script 🎧 02-31

W Student: Andrew, you visit the school botanical garden a lot, right?

M Student: That's right.

W: How do you feel about not being allowed to go there anymore?

M: That's a good question, Sienna. I guess you could say that I have mixed feelings about it.

W: How so?

M: Well, students are causing a lot of harm to ongoing experiments. I've even seen some students destroying flowers and breaking branches off trees in the past. That

kind of behavior can't be allowed. So I understand why the school is banning students.

W: But . . .

M: But the botanical garden is such a beautiful and relaxing place to visit. My friends and I go there a lot just to get away from everything and to enjoy nature. Now, we'll have to go somewhere else.

W: The announcement referred to some other parks nearby.

M: They aren't that close. We'll have to take a bus or ride our bikes for thirty minutes to get to the closest one, so that will be inconvenient for us.

해석

W Student: Andrew, 너는 교내 식물원에 자주 가지, 그렇지?

M Student: 맞아.

W: 이제 더 이상 그곳에 가지 못하는 것에 대해 어떻게 생각해?

M: 좋은 질문이네, Sienna. 그에 대해 심경이 복잡하다고 할 수도 있을 것 같아.

W: 어째서?

M: 음, 학생들이 진행 중인 실험에 피해를 끼치고 있잖아. 심지어 나는 몇몇 학생들이 꽃을 훼손시키고 나뭇가지를 꺾는 모습도 전에 본 적이 있어. 그러한 행동이 허용되어서는 안 되지. 그래서 나는 학교측이 학생들 출입을 금지시키는 이유를 이해할 수 있어.

W: 하지만…

M: 하지만 식물원은 정말로 멋지고 휴식을 취하러 가기에 좋은 곳이야. 내 친구들과 나는 모든 일에서 벗어나 자연을 즐기기 위해 그곳을 자주 방문하는 편이거든. 이제는 다른 곳에 가야 할 테지만.

W: 공지에도 근처에 있는 공원들이 나와 있잖아.

M: 그렇게 가깝지는 않아. 가장 가까운 곳에 가려고 해도 버스나 자전거로 30분 정도 가야 하기 때문에 우리한테는 불편한 일이 될 거야.

Organization

1 He has mixed feelings about the announcement.
2 He has seen students destroying flowers and breaking branches off trees.
3 He understands why the school is banning students from the botanical garden.
4 He thinks it is a beautiful and relaxing place to visit.
5 He says that they are actually far from the school and that he will need to take a bus or ride a bike to get to them.

Comparing

Sample Response

Script 🎧 02-32

The announcement informs people that students are no

longer permitted to visit the school's botanical garden. It points out that professors do long-term experiments there and that some students have damaged the experiments. As a result, only certain people may visit the garden in the future. The man states that he has mixed feelings about this decision by the school. First, he understands what is happening because he has seen students destroying flowers and harming trees in the garden. He thinks the school is right to ban students. However, he and his friends enjoy visiting the garden. Now, they will have to take a bus or ride their bikes to get to a park when they want to enjoy nature. So in that regard, he dislikes the decision.

해석

공지는 학생들이 더 이상 교내 식물원에 출입할 수 없다는 점을 알리고 있다. 공지에 따르면 그곳에서는 교수들이 장기간의 실험을 진행하고 있으나 일부 학생들이 실험에 피해를 주고 있다. 그 결과 앞으로는 특정 개인들만이 식물원을 방문할 수가 있다. 남자는 자신이 학교측의 이러한 결정에 복잡한 심경을 느낀다고 말한다. 먼저 그는 학생들이 식물원에서 꽃에 피해를 주고 나무에 손상을 가하는 것을 본 적이 있기 때문에 현 상황을 이해한다. 그는 학교측이 학생들의 출입을 금지시키는 것은 정당하다고 생각한다. 하지만 그와 그의 친구들은 식물원에 가는 것을 좋아한다. 이제는 그들이 자연을 즐기고자 할 경우 버스나 자전거를 타고 공원에 가야만 할 것이다. 따라서 이러한 점에 있어서는 결정을 반기지 않는다.

Unit 31 Biology I

Exercise p.84

Reading

해석

핵심종

일부 동물들은 여러 가지 이유로 환경에 불균형적인, 그러나 긍정적인 효과를 미친다. 과학자들은 이러한 동물들을 핵심종이라고 부른다. 이러한 이름이 붙여진 이유는, 아치에서 쐐기돌이 아치가 무너지지 않도록 중요한 역할을 하는 것과 같이, 핵심종이 없으면 특정 서식지가 종종 나쁜 쪽으로 크게 변화하기 때문이다. 동물들은 여러 가지 이유로 핵심종이 될 수 있다. 가장 중요한 핵심 종은 포식 동물이지만 기타 동물들도 다른 방식으로 서식지를 긍정적으로 변화시킬 수 있다. 예를 들어 몇몇 동물들은 환경을 변화시키거나 서식지 전체에 영양분을 퍼뜨리기도 한다.

Comprehension

1 A keystone species is an animal that has a greater-than-normal effect on its environment.

2 The keystone is the most important stone in an arch, so a keystone species is the most important animal in its environment.

3 A habitat would change in a negative way without its keystone species.

4 The major way animals serve as keystone species is as predators.

5 Other ways animals can be keystone species are by changing their environments and by spreading nutrients in their areas.

Listening

Script 🎧 03-03

M Professor: We've talked about some of the animals in Africa and the roles they play in their environments, but let me tell you about the most important one. Are you ready? It's . . . the elephant. Really. I'm serious. Actually, the elephant is a keystone species in its part of Africa. Here, let me explain it.

First, elephants have prodigious appetites. Do you know how much they eat daily? They chow down about 500 pounds of vegetation. Thanks to elephants, the areas in which they live don't get overrun with plants. Why is this important? Well, if elephants weren't there, their habitat would be filled with vegetation, which would cause most other animal species either to migrate or simply to become extinct. They wouldn't be able to handle the resulting new environment.

Since they eat lots, elephants also defecate a lot. Because elephants are somewhat nomadic, they spread nutrients for the soil to absorb, and through their waste, they essentially plant seeds, which will grow up to be plants that other animals can feed upon. Clearly, then, elephants are crucial to their environment.

해석

M Professor: 아프리카의 몇몇 동물들과 그들이 자신의 환경에서 하는 역할에 대해 이야기했는데, 이제 가장 중요한 동물이 무엇인지 알려 드리도록 하죠. 준비가 됐나요? 바로… 코끼리입니다. 진짜예요. 농담이 아닙니다. 실제로 코끼리는 아프리카 지역의 핵심종이에요. 이제 그 이유를 설명해 드리죠.

우선, 코끼리는 엄청난 식욕을 갖고 있어요. 하루에 얼마만큼 먹는지 아시나요? 약 500파운드의 초목을 먹어 치웁니다. 코끼리 덕분에 코끼리가 사는 곳은 식물들로 우거지지가 않죠. 그런데 이러한 점이 왜 중요할까요? 음, 만약 코끼리가 없다면 서식지가 초목으로 가득 찰 것이며, 이로써 대부분의 기타 종들이 다른 곳으로 이동하거나 멸종하게 될 수도 있습니다. 그에 따라 비롯된 새로운 환경에 대처할 수가 없는 것이죠.

엄청난 양을 먹기 때문에 코끼리의 배설물의 양도 엄청납니다. 코끼리는 다소 방랑성이 있는 편이라 토양이 흡수할 수 있는 양분을 퍼뜨리고 배설물을 통해 식물의 씨앗이 자라게 만드는데, 씨앗이 자라서 식물이 되면 다른 동물들이 이를 먹을 수 있게 됩니다. 분명 코끼리는 환경에 핵심적인 존재인 것이죠.

Organization

1 Elephants are the keystone species in Africa.
2 Elephants eat vegetation and keep plants from overrunning the region, which makes for a comfortable environment for many animals.
3 When elephants defecate in different places, they provide the soil with nutrients, and they spread different plants' seeds, which will grow and then feed other animals.
4 Without elephants, Africa would be a drastically different place, so this makes them a keystone species.

Comparing

Sample Response

Script 🎧 03-04

The professor begins by telling the students that the keystone species in Africa is the elephant. He states that a keystone species is defined as an animal that has an incredibly large effect on its environment. While the most common keystone species are predators, there are other ways in which animals can serve as a keystone species. This is the case of the elephant. To begin with, elephants eat around 500 pounds of vegetation a day. This keeps the forest from expanding too much, something which

would inconvenience other animals to the point that they would either migrate from the region or merely die off. In addition, when elephants wander and defecate, they enrich the soil and plant seeds that will become other plants and trees. Animals can then use these new plants as food sources.

해석

교수는 학생들에게 아프리카의 핵심종이 코끼리라고 말하면서 강의를 시작한다. 그는 핵심종이란 환경에 막대한 영향을 미치는 동물로 정의된다고 말한다. 대부분의 핵심종은 포식 동물이지만 다른 방식으로 핵심종이 될 수 있는 동물들도 있다. 코끼리의 경우가 그러하다. 우선, 코끼리는 매일 약 500파운드의 초목을 먹는다. 이로 인해 숲이 과도하게 확대되는 것을 막을 수 있는데, 만약 그렇게 된다면 다른 동물들에게 피해가 발생하여 이들이 해당 지역을 떠나거나 멸종하는 상황이 발생할 수도 있다. 또한 코끼리는 돌아다니면서 배설을 하기 때문에 토양을 기름지게 만들고 식물 및 나무로 성장할 씨앗을 심어 놓는다. 이후 동물들이 이러한 새로운 식물을 먹이로 삼을 수 있다.

Unit 32 Business I

Exercise ·· p.86

Reading

해석

비상 대응 계획

간혹 예상하지 못한 일들이 발생한다. 이러한 일은 지진, 허리케인, 그리고 산불과 같은 자연 재해일 수 있다. 또한 사람에 의해 일어나는 것일 수도 있다. 예를 들어 때때로 전쟁, 경제 위기, 폭동이 발생할 수 있다. 이러한 일들은 모두 기업에 막대한 영향을 끼칠 수 있다. 그러한 이유로 많은 기업들이 비상 대응 계획을 수립한다. 이 경우 사업가들은 자신에게 영향을 미칠 수 있는 잠재적인 문제들에 대해 생각한다. 그런 다음 각각의 문제에 어떻게 대응할 것인지에 관한 계획을 세운다. 다양한 비상 상황에 대한 준비를 함으로써 기업은 재난에 대한 대비를 할 수 있기 때문에 다양한 사건으로 입을 수 있는 피해를 줄이게 된다.

Comprehension

1 They can be earthquakes, hurricanes, and fires.
2 They include wars, economic problems, and riots.
3 Unexpected events can have a tremendous effect on businesses.
4 It involves people thinking of what events can affect them and then developing plans on how to react to these events.
5 Businesses can be prepared for disasters, so they will suffer less harm from them.

M Professor: As you all know, this area got hit by a really bad storm during the summer. It wasn't a hurricane, but its effects were similar to one. The power went out at lots of places, and that caused problems for many local businesses. Some establishments, however, were okay during the blackout because they had prepared for unexpected events ahead of time.

For instance, my brother owns a grocery store in this city. Now, uh, when the power goes out, that can cause huge problems for grocery stores. Why is that? Well, the meat, dairy products, and frozen food products stop being refrigerated. As a result, if the power stays off for an extended period of time, all of that food can go bad and spoil. Imagine the financial losses that would be incurred when that happens.

Fortunately, my brother is a smart businessman, so he had a contingency plan. He was prepared for a blackout because he had purchased a generator powerful enough to run all the fridges and freezers at his store. This meant that the food at his store didn't have to be thrown away. Other grocery stores didn't have contingency plans though, so they lost a lot of food. One even went out of business because it couldn't handle the financial loss it suffered.

해석

M Professor: 모두들 아는 것처럼 여름에 매우 극심한 폭풍우가 이곳을 강타했습니다. 허리케인은 아니었지만 그 영향은 허리케인과 비슷했죠. 많은 지역에서 정전이 발생했고 그로 인해 많은 지역 기업들에게 문제가 발생했습니다. 하지만 일부 업체들은 정전이 발생해도 괜찮았는데, 그 이유는 그들이 예상치 못한 사건들에 대해 미리 준비를 해 두었기 때문이에요.

예를 들어 제 남동생은 이곳 시내에서 식품점을 운영하고 있습니다. 자, 어, 정전이 되면 식품점에 막대한 피해가 발생할 수 있어요. 왜일까요? 음, 육류, 유제품, 그리고 냉동 식품이 저온 상태에 있지 못하게 됩니다. 그 결과 장시간 정전이 계속되면 그러한 모든 식품들이 상해서 먹지 못하게 될 수 있죠. 그런 일이 일어나는 경우에 발생할 금전적인 손해를 생각해 보세요.

다행히 제 동생은 똑똑한 사업가라서 비상 대응 계획을 가지고 있었습니다. 매장 내의 모든 냉장고 및 냉동고의 가동에 필요한 충분한 전력을 발생시키는 발전기를 구입해 두었기 때문에 정전에 대한 대비가 되어 있었어요. 이는 매장의 식품들을 폐기할 필요가 없다는 점을 의미했죠. 하지만 다른 식료품 매장들은 비상 대응 계획을 가지고 있지 않았기 때문에 많은 식품들을 버려야 했습니다. 심지어 한 매장은 금전적인 손실을 감내할 수가 없어서 파산을 하기까지 했어요.

Organization

1 The area got hit by a really bad storm, so there was a blackout.
2 The meat, dairy products, and frozen food products stop being refrigerated, so they can spoil.

3 The professor's brother bought a generator powerful enough to run all the fridges and freezers at his store.
4 The food at his grocery store did not have to be thrown away.

Comparing

Sample Response

Script 🎧 03-06

The professor mentions a powerful storm that hit the city and caused a blackout. He adds that his brother owns a grocery store in the city. When there are blackouts, grocery stores have problems because much of their food doesn't get refrigerated, so it can spoil. The professor states his brother had a contingency plan. That's a plan for an unexpected event. It allows the person to be prepared and to suffer little or no harm it something bad happens. His brother's contingency plan was to buy a generator that could run the fridges and freezers at his store. This meant that none of the food there went bad, so his brother didn't suffer any financial losses. Other stores didn't have contingency plans, so some of them lost money when their food went bad.

해석

교수는 도시를 강타하여 정전을 일으켰던 강력한 폭풍우를 언급한다. 그는 덧붙여 자신의 동생이 시내에서 식료품 매장을 운영한다고 말한다. 정전이 발생하면 식료품 매장은 상당수의 식품이 냉장되지 않아서 상할 수 있기 때문에 문제를 겪는다. 교수는 자신의 동생이 비상 대응 계획을 가지고 있었다고 말한다. 이는 예상치 못한 사건을 대비한 계획이다. 이로써 준비가 되어 있기 때문에 좋지 못한 일이 발생한 경우 그로 인한 피해를 거의 입지 않거나 전혀 입지 않게 된다. 교수의 동생의 비상 대응 계획은 매장의 냉장고 및 냉동고를 가동시킬 수 있는 발전기를 구입한 것이었다. 이는 그곳의 어떤 식품도 상하지 않았다는 점을 의미했으며, 따라서 교수의 동생은 금전적인 손실을 입지 않았다. 다른 매장들은 비상 대응 계획을 가지고 있지 않았기 때문에 그들 중 일부는 상한 식품들로 인한 손실을 보았다.

Unit 33 Psychology I

Exercise ⋯⋯⋯⋯⋯⋯⋯⋯⋯⋯⋯⋯⋯⋯⋯⋯⋯⋯⋯⋯⋯ p.88

Reading

해석

인상 관리

사람들은 종종 다른 사람들이 자신을 어떻게 생각하는지에 관심을 갖는다. 많은 경우 의식적으로, 그리고 무의식적으로도 사람들은 자신들의 긍정적인 이미지를 만들기 위해 인상 관리를 한다. 인상을 관리할 수 있는 많은 방법들이 있지만 가장 일반적인 것은 본인이 드러내는 자신에 대한 정보의 흐름을 조절하는 것이다. 인상 관리를 할 때 사람들은 보통 자신의 나쁘거나 부정적인 면을 보여 주지 않는다. 이러한 방식은 한 사람을 완전히 정직하게 보여 주지는 않지만, 특히 누군가를 처음 대면할 때나 중요한 자리에서, 흔하게 사용된다.

Comprehension

1 People use impression management both consciously and unconsciously.

2 People use impression management to give others a positive image of themselves.

3 The most common way to use impression management is to control the information that a person lets others know about him.

4 A person typically does not let others know any unflattering or negative characteristics about himself.

5 People are most likely to use it when they are meeting others for the first time or attending some kind of important event.

Listening

Script 🎧 03-07

W Professor: Now, I know most of you probably think that impression management doesn't play a major role in our lives, but if you think that, you're definitely wrong. As a matter of fact, we use impression management all the time even if we aren't consciously aware of doing so. Here are some examples.

Your class presentations begin next week, right? So what are you planning to wear to them? Surely not the clothes you're wearing now. If you showed up in a T-shirt, shorts, and, uh, sandals, do you think I'd be impressed? Hardly. Instead, you're all likely to dress up in formal clothes like suits to try to impress me. Why? Well, you want me to take you seriously, so you're dressing the part. You're managing my impression of you.

Let me give you a personal example. I had some guests over for dinner at my house the other night. Now, uh, I have an office at my home, but it's usually a mess. Well, before the guests showed up, I cleaned up everything in that office. I even organized all of the papers and books on my desk. When everyone arrived and looked around the house, they were really impressed with my office. As a result, I made a good impression on them.

해석

W Professor: 자, 저는 여러분 대부분이 인상 관리가 삶에서 중요한 역할을 하지 않는다고 생각하는 것을 알고 있지만, 그렇게 생각하는 것은 완전히 잘못된 것이에요. 사실 우리는 우리가 의식하지 못하는 때에도 항상 인상 관리를 하고 있죠. 몇 가지 예를 들어 보겠습니다.

수업 발표가 다음 주부터 시작이죠, 그렇죠? 그래서 그날 어떤 옷을 입을 생각인가요? 분명 지금 입고 있는 옷은 아닐 거예요. 만약 티셔츠, 반바지, 그리고, 어, 샌들을 신고 나타난다면 제게 인상을 남길 수 있을 것으로 생각하나요? 거의 그렇지 않을 거예요. 대신 여러분 모두 제게 인상을 남기기 위해 정장과 같이 격식을 갖춘 옷을 입을 가능성이 높습니다. 왜일까요? 음, 여러분은 제가 여러분을 진지하게 봐 주길 바라기 때문에 그렇게 옷을 입을 거예요. 여러분에 대한 저의 인상을 관리하는 것이죠.

개인적인 예를 하나 들게요. 저는 며칠 전 손님들을 초대해 저희 집에서 저녁 식사를 하기로 했어요. 자, 어, 저희 집에는 사무실이 있는데 보통은 어질러져 있죠. 음, 손님들이 오기 전에 저는 사무실을 싹 다 청소했어요. 심지어 책상에 있던 서류들과 책들도 정리를 해 두었죠. 모두가 도착을 해서 집을 둘러보고는 제 사무실에 정말로 깊은 인상을 받았습니다. 그 결과 저는 그들에게 좋은 인상을 남기게 되었어요.

Organization

1 In the professor's opinion, impression management has a major role in people's lives.

2 People use impression management all of the time even though they are not necessarily aware of doing so.

3 Students should wear formal clothes to their presentation so that the professor will take them seriously, which she would not do if they wore casual clothes.

4 The professor cleaned her office and organized everything to make a positive impression on her guests.

Comparing

Sample Response
Script 🎧 03-08

In the course of the lecture, the professor provides two instances in which people are conscious of the image they are projecting. She first mentions the students' upcoming class presentations. She tells them that if they wear casual clothes like T-shirts and shorts, she won't take them seriously. Instead, they need to wear formal clothes to give her a more favorable impression of them. Likewise, she cites a personal example. Before some guests arrived at her house for dinner, she cleaned her office and organized everything in it. Both instances are related to impression management in that the people—the students and the professor—are trying to show themselves in the best possible light to create a positive impression. They are also preventing the person from finding out anything negative about them. This is another important aspect of impression management.

해석

강의에서 교수는 사람들이 자신이 남기는 이미지를 의식하는 두 가지 예를 제시한다. 그녀는 먼저 앞으로 있을 학생들의 수업 발표를 언급한다. 그녀는 학생들이 만약 티셔츠 및 반바지 같은 캐주얼 복장을 입는다면 자신이 학생들을 진지하게 받아들이지 않을 것이라고 말한다. 대신 학생들은 보다 교수에게 보다 좋은 인상을 남기기 위해 격식에 맞는 옷을 입어야 한다. 그녀는 이와 비슷한 개인적인 사례를 인용한다. 자신의 집에 저녁 식사 손님들이 도착 하기 전에 그녀는 사무실을 청소하고 모든 것들을 정리해 두었다. 두 경우 모두 학생이나 교수가 좋은 인상을 남기기 위해 최선을 다한다는 점에서 인상 관리와 관련이 있다. 그들은 또한 자신들에 관한 부정적인 면을 감추려고 노력한다. 이 역시 인상 관리의 또 다른 중요한 측면이다.

Unit 34 Biology II

Exercise ···································· p.90

Reading

해석

개체수 증가

수를 늘리기 위해 종은 개체수 증가를 해야 한다. 이는, 인간이든 다른 종이든, 종의 수가 증가하는 속도이다. 일반적으로 모든 종은 일정 속도로 증가한다. 하지만 항상 질병, 가뭄, 기근, 그리고 포식 동물과 같이 종의 개체수 증가를 제한하는 다른 요소들이 존재한다. 어떤 종의 개체수가 너무 빨리 증가하거나 감소하면 동일한 환경에서 생활하는 다른 종들이 종종 영향을 받는다. 이러한 영향은 그와 관련된 종에 따라 긍정적일 수도 있고 부정적일 수도 있다.

Comprehension

1 Species must engage in population growth in order to become more numerous.

2 Population growth is the rate that any species, including humans or others, increases.

3 Disease, drought, famine, and predators can cause a species to grow at a slower rate.

4 When a species' population grows or declines too quickly, it can affect other species that are found in the same environment.

5 The results of the rapid increase or decrease in a species' population can be either positive or negative depending upon the situation.

Listening

Script 🎧 03-09

M Professor: As we know, species increase at different rates. Of course, rapid rates of increase can have tremendous effects on their environments and how nature handles these increases. Let me cite two examples that may seem different but are actually connected.

Let me discuss the pine tree first. This is one of the

faster-growing tree species. In fact, it grows so rapidly that it can literally take over entire forests. In some cases, it has pushed out other tree species, especially because it can grow in practically any climate and any kind of soil. So what limits its population? Well, there are diseases that kill pine trees, and humans chop them down, but it's mostly fire that burns them down and slows their growth. Forest fires occur naturally, and they regularly limit pine trees' growth lest they take over entire forests.

Now, let's think about deer. The deer population can increase by thirty percent in any year. So what keeps their numbers from raging out of control? Well, as the deer population increases, so does that of predators like wolves. There are more deer to eat, so the wolves' numbers increase. Of course, as the deer population decreases, so too does the wolf population. These are just a couple of ways that nature controls the populations of species.

해석

M Professor: 여러분도 아시다시피 종마다 증가 속도가 다릅니다. 물론 증가 속도가 빠르면 자신의 환경 및 자연이 이러한 증가에 대응하는 방식에 막대한 영향을 미칠 수 있어요. 다르게 보일 수 있지만 실제로는 관련이 있는 두 가지 예를 들어 드리죠.

먼저 소나무에 대해 논의해 봅시다. 소나무는 성장 속도가 빠른 편에 속하는 종이에요. 실제로 너무 빨리 성장하기 때문에 글자 그대로 숲 전체를 뒤덮어 버릴 수 있죠. 일부 경우에는 다른 나무종을 밀어내기도 하는데, 이는 특히 소나무가 거의 모든 기후와 토양에서 자랄 수 있기 때문입니다. 그러면 소나무의 개체수를 제한하는 것은 무엇일까요? 음, 소나무를 죽게 만드는 질병도 있고, 인간이 이를 베어 내기도 하지만, 이들을 태워서 성장 속도를 늦추게 만드는 것은 주로 산불입니다. 산불은 자연적으로 발생하며 소나무가 숲 전체를 뒤덮지 않도록 소나무의 성장을 주기적으로 제한해 주죠.

이제는 사슴에 대해 생각해 봅시다. 사슴의 개체수는 1년에 30퍼센트 가량 증가할 수 있어요. 그러면 그 수가 통제 불가능한 상태가 되지 않도록 막아 주는 것은 무엇일까요? 음, 사슴의 개체수가 증가함에 따라 늑대와 같은 사슴의 천적들도 증가합니다. 먹이가 되는 사슴이 많아지면 늑대의 수도 증가하게 되죠. 물론 사슴의 수가 감소하면 늑대의 수도 감소하게 됩니다. 이들은 자연이 종의 개체수를 조절하는 두 가지 방식에 해당됩니다.

Organization

1 Depending upon how rapidly a species increases its numbers, it can have a great effect on its environment and how nature tries to control excessive population growth.

2 Pine trees can grow in any kind of climate and soil, so they are one of the most rapidly growing species of trees.

3 Diseases and humans kill some pine trees, but forest fires are the way in which pine tree population growth is mostly controlled.

4 According to the professor, deer can increase their numbers by up to thirty percent in a year.

5 Wolves and other predators also increase in numbers at the same time, so they help control the deer population by eating them.

[Comparing]
Sample Response
Script 🎧 03-10

During his lecture, the professor mentions excessive and rapid population growth by both pine trees and deer. According to the professor, pine trees can survive almost anywhere in any climate and soil, and they also grow very rapidly, which is something that causes them to take over forests. In addition, the professor mentions that deer can increase their numbers by thirty percent in a single year. This can cause overpopulation problems for forests. The reading states that population growth can be controlled by many different factors, which thereby keep the balance of nature secure. Fire, caused by nature, helps limit the number of pine trees while wolves and other predators can proliferate, thereby killing and eating the deer. These are just two methods nature uses to control the rapid population growth of various species.

해석

강의에서 교수는 소나무와 사슴의 과도하고 급격한 개체수 증가에 대해 언급한다. 교수에 따르면 소나무는 거의 모든 기후와 토양에서 생존할 수 있고 성장 속도가 매우 빨라서 소나무가 숲 전체를 뒤덮는 경우도 있을 수 있다. 또한 교수는 사슴의 수가 1년에 30퍼센트 정도 증가한다고 말한다. 이는 숲에 과잉 개체수 문제를 일으킬 수 있다. 읽기 지문에는 여러 가지 요인들이 개체수 증가를 조절할 수 있으며 이로써 자연의 균형이 유지된다고 나와 있다. 자연적으로 발생하는 산불은 소나무의 수를 제한하며, 늑대 및 기타 포식자들의 증가로 사슴이 잡아먹힐 수 있다. 이들은 자연이 다양한 종의 급격한 개체수 증가를 통제하기 위해 사용하는 두 가지 방법에 해당된다.

Unit 35 Philosophy

Exercise p.92

[Reading]
해석

오캄의 면도칼

윌리엄 오캄은 13세기와 14세기에 살았던 프란체스코회의 수도승이었다. 당시 그가 교황과의 여러 가지 논쟁에 관여했기 때문에 오늘날 그는 오캄의 면도칼이라고 알려진 원리로 기억되고 있다. 윌리엄 자신이 이 원리를 만들지는 않았지만 그가 사용했던 탓에 그의 이름이 이 원리와 연결되게 되었다. 오캄의 면도칼에서는 어떤 사람이 문제에 직면하면 그것을 해결하기 위해 불필요한 모든 것을 제거함으로써 불필요한 요소들을 모조리 "밀어" 버려야 한다고 주장한다. 최대

한 단순화시키면 오캄의 면도칼은 가장 단순한 해결책이 종종 최선의 해결책이 된다고 요약할 수 있다.

[Comprehension]

1 William of Occam was a Franciscan monk from the thirteenth and fourteenth centuries.

2 People remember him because of the principle called Occam's razor.

3 He is associated with Occam's razor because even though he did not develop it, he often utilized it.

4 Occam's razor is the principle which states that a person should eliminate every unnecessary factor while trying to solve a problem.

5 The easiest way to state Occam's razor is that the simplest solution is often the best.

[Listening]
Script 🎧 03-11

M Professor: Let me give you an example of the dangers of thinking too much. Here's a situation. You wake up and look out your window to see the tree in front of your house is burning. After extinguishing the fire, you start thinking about how it started.

You arrive at two conclusions. First, someone went to your house and set the tree on fire. Okay, let's run down this line of reasoning. Why did he do it? Does someone dislike you that much? I hope not. In addition, only the top half of the tree caught fire. So the person must have climbed up the tree and started the fire or else climbed up a ladder to start the fire at the top of the tree. And how did he manage to get away with no one seeing him on that busy street you live on?

Now, you arrive at a second conclusion. There was a thunderstorm with lots of lightning last night. Lightning must have struck the tree and started the fire. It's as simple as that. Now, which of these propositions is more logical? I'd say it's the simplest one. The first has too many variables and is highly unlikely. When you get down to it, the simplest solution also tends to be the best one.

해석

M Professor: 생각이 너무 많은 경우의 위험성에 대한 한 가지 예를 들어 드리죠. 상황을 말씀드릴게요. 여러분이 잠에서 깨어 창문 밖을 보니 집 앞에 있는 나무가 불타고 있는 모습이 보입니다. 여러분은 불을 끈 후 불이 어떻게 시작되었는지에 대해 생각하기 시작합니다.

여러분은 두 가지 결론에 도달합니다. 첫째, 누군가 여러분 집으로 와서 나무에 불을 붙인 것입니다. 좋아요, 이러한 추론을 따라가 봅시다. 왜 그랬을까요? 누군가 여러분을 그토록 싫어했을까요? 그러지 않기를 바랍니다. 게다가 나무의 위쪽 부분에만 불이 붙었습니다. 그렇다면 그 사람은 분명 나무 위로 올라가

불을 붙였거나 사다리를 타고 올라가서 나무 꼭대기에 불을 붙였을 겁니다. 그리고 어떻게 여러분이 사는 혼잡한 거리에서 아무에게도 들키지 않고 달아날 수 있었을까요?

자, 여러분은 두 번째 결론에 도달합니다. 전날 밤에 번개를 동반한 강력한 뇌우가 발생했어요. 틀림없이 나무가 번개에 맞아 불이 났을 거예요. 정말 간단합니다. 자, 이러한 가정 중에서 어느 쪽이 보다 논리적인가요? 저는 가장 단순한 쪽을 고르겠습니다. 첫 번째 경우는 변수가 너무 많고 가능성도 매우 낮습니다. 잘 생각해 보면 또한 가장 간단한 해결책이 최선의 해결책인 경우가 많죠.

다. 첫 번째는 누군가 집주인을 매우 싫어했기 때문에 집으로 와서, 나무에 기어오르고, 불을 지른 후 들키지 않고서 도망을 갔다는 것이다. 두 번째는 전날 밤 뇌우가 발생해서 나무가 번개에 맞아 불이 났다는 것이다. 읽기 지문은 오캄의 면도칼, 즉 기본적으로 가장 단순한 해결책이 최선의 해결책이라는 내용의 원리를 설명한다. 바로 이를 통해 교수는 두 번째 생각이 맞다는 결론에 도달한다. 첫 번째 결론에는 너무나 많은 변수와 가능성이 존재하기 때문에 교수는 오캄의 면도날을 이용하여 그것은 불가능한 시나리오이고 두 번째 가정이 옳다는 점을 알 수 있다.

Organization

1 The professor describes a situation in which a person wakes up in the morning to see a tree in his front yard is burning.
2 The first conclusion as to how the fire started is that someone came to the house and started the fire intentionally.
3 The professor mentions that for a person to have started the fire, he must dislike the homeowner very much, must have climbed the tree or used a ladder, and must have escaped without being seen.
4 The professor's second conclusion is that a bolt of lightning from the previous night's thunderstorm must have started the fire.
5 The professor believes that the second conclusion is more logical because it is simpler and introduces fewer variables.

Comparing

Sample Response

Script 🎧 03-12

The professor tells the class about an incident where a person wakes up to see a tree burning in his yard. He arrives at two conclusions about the fire. The first is that someone disliked the homeowner very much, so he went to the house, climbed the tree, started the fire, and escaped unnoticed. The second is that since there was a thunderstorm the previous night, a bolt of lightning must have struck the tree and started the fire. The reading passage describes Occam's razor, a principle that basically states that the simplest solution is the best. This is how the professor arrives at the decision that the second proposal is correct. There are too many variables and possibilities in the first conclusion, so by using Occam's razor, he knows it was an impossible scenario, making the second proposition right.

해석
교수는 학생들에게 어떤 사람이 잠에서 깨어 자신의 마당에 있는 나무가 불타고 있는 모습을 보는 경우에 대해 이야기한다. 그는 불에 관해 두 가지 결론에 도달한

Unit 36 Sociology

Exercise ··· p.94

Reading

해석

책임감 분산

많은 사람들은 가족, 고용주, 그리고 기타 조직에 대해 다양한 책임감을 느낀다. 하지만 일부 경우, 특히 많은 사람들이 관련된 경우에, 책임감은 특정 개인에게 지워지지 않는다. 이러한 상황에서는 책임감 분산이라는 현상이 나타난다. 대부분의 경우 책임감 분산이 일어나면 사람들은 개인적인 책임감을 덜 느끼게 된다. 일부 사람들은 자신이 원하지 않는 일을 한 스스로를 용서하기 위해, 혹은 불법적이거나, 부적절하거나, 혹은 부끄러운 행동을 한 스스로에게 면죄부를 주기 위해 이를 이용한다.

Comprehension

1 People often have responsibilities to their families, employers, and other organizations.
2 In large groups of people, it is often the case that responsibility is not assigned to one particular person.
3 The diffusion of responsibility often results in people feeling less personally responsible for various things.
4 People use the diffusion of responsibility to avoid doing things that they do not want to do.
5 People rely upon it when they have done something illegal, improper, or embarrassing.

Listening

Script 🎧 03-13

W Professor: Let's say that two bad car accidents occur in the same place. However, one accident occurs in the morning when many people are commuting to work, and the other one occurs at night when there are few people on the road. Now . . . for which accident are people more likely to stop and render assistance to the injured? The morning or night accident? Anyone?

Surprisingly enough, statistics show that the people in the, uh, night accident are more likely to receive assistance from a passing motorist. Let me explain why. It's called diffusion of responsibility. Simply put, in the morning, there are many cars going by. While some people may want to stop, they also have other obligations, like, uh, getting to work. Since there are many other drivers, they convince themselves that someone else will stop and help the injured. Of course, in most cases, no one stops because everyone has passed on the responsibility to other passersby.

For the night accident though, there are fewer people on the road. Therefore, a passing motorist may experience a stronger feeling of responsibility since the likelihood of someone else coming by is low. Again, statistics show that passing motorists on little-traveled roads are much more likely to stop. And that is how the diffusion of responsibility works.

해석

W Professor: 동일한 장소에서 두 건의 심각한 교통 사고가 발생했다고 해 보죠. 하지만 한 사고는 많은 사람들이 출퇴근을 하고 있던 오전에 발생을 했고, 다른 사고는 도로에 운전자가 거의 없는 야간에 발생을 했습니다. 자… 어떤 사고의 경우에 사람들이 멈춰 서서 다친 사람들에게 도움을 줄 것 같나요? 오전 사고일까요, 아니면 야간 사고일까요? 아는 사람이 있나요?

놀랍게도 통계 자료에 따르면, 어, 야간 사고의 경우 지나가는 운전자에게서 도움을 받을 확률이 더 높습니다. 그 이유를 설명해 드리죠. 이를 책임감 분산이라고 부릅니다. 간단히 말해서 아침에는 지나다니는 차가 많습니다. 멈추려는 사람들도 있을 수 있지만 그들에게는 예컨대, 어, 출근을 해야 하는 것과 같은 다른 일들도 있어요. 다른 운전자들도 많기 때문에 그들은 누군가 다른 사람이 멈춰 서서 부상자를 도와 줄 것이라고 확신하게 됩니다. 물론 대부분의 경우 모든 사람들이 지나가는 다른 사람에게 책임을 전가하기 때문에 아무도 멈추지 않아요.

하지만 야간 사고의 경우에는 도로에 운전자가 거의 없습니다. 그래서 다른 사람이 있을 확률이 낮기 때문에 지나가던 운전자는 강한 책임 의식을 느낄 수 있습니다. 다시 한 번 통계를 인용하자면, 거의 차가 거의 없는 도로를 지나가던 운전자가 멈춰 설 확률이 훨씬 더 높습니다. 그리고 바로 이것이 책임감 분산의 효과인 것이죠.

Organization

1 The professor describes two accidents occurring at the same place, but one takes place during the morning commute, and the other takes place late at night.

2 The person more likely to receive assistance from a passing motorist is the one injured in the night accident.

3 For the morning accident, since there are many people on the road, motorists tell themselves that another driver will stop to give the injured person assistance.

4 A person is more likely to help in the night accident because there are fewer people on the road at that time, so the passing driver feels more responsible to help the injured person.

Comparing

Sample Response

Script 🎧 03-14

The subject of the talk is two accidents that occur in the same location. However, one accident happens during the day, and the other happens late at night. According to the professor's statistics, the people injured at night are more likely to receive help than those injured during the day. This fact is strongly related to the diffusion of responsibility. This is a concept that absolves people from personal responsibility when they are in large group situations. In the morning accident, there are numerous motorists passing by, therefore no one feels a sense of individual responsibility. These people all expect or hope that someone else will stop to help. But at night, there are fewer people driving, so there is no diffusion of responsibility. A passing driver will stop to help because that person feels personally responsible for rendering assistance.

해석

강의의 주제는 동일한 장소에서 발생한 두 건의 교통 사고이다. 하지만 한 사고는 주간에 일어나고 다른 사고는 밤 늦은 시간에 발생한다. 교수의 통계 수치에 따르면 야간에 부상을 당한 사람이 주간에 부상을 당한 사람보다 도움을 받을 수 있는 확률이 더 크다. 이러한 사실은 책임감 분산과 밀접한 관계가 있다. 이는 여러 사람이 관련된 상황에서는 사람들이 개인적인 책임감을 덜 느낀다는 개념이다. 오전 사고에서는 지나다니는 운전자들이 많기 때문에 아무도 개인적인 책임감을 느끼지 않는다. 이러한 사람들은 모두 누군가 다른 사람이 멈춰 서서 도움을 줄 것이라고 예상한다. 하지만 야간에는 지나다니는 운전자가 거의 없기 때문에 책임감 분산이 일어나지 않는다. 지나가던 한 운전자가 자신이 도움을 주어야 한다는 개인적인 책임감을 느끼고 차를 세워서 도움을 줄 것이다.

Unit 37 Biology III

Exercise p.96

Reading

해석

영양 번식

대부분의 식물들은 자신들이 생산해 내는 씨앗을 통해 번식을 한다. 하지만 새로운 식물들이 자랄 수 있는 또 다른 방법들이 존재한다. 이러한 형태의 무성 생식은 영양 번식이라고 불린다. 때때로 줄기나 잎과 같은 식물의 한 부분이 모 식물로부터 분리되어 땅에 떨어질 수 있다. 그러면 거기에서 뿌리가 자라나 새로운 식물이 자라게 된다. 다른 경우, 예컨대 딸기의 경우에는, 줄기에서 가는 줄기가 자라나 식물 개체가 된다. 양파 및 마늘과 같은 일부 식물들의 경우에는 땅속에 있는 구근이 성장해서 식물이 될 수 있다.

1 Most plants reproduce through the seeds that they produce.

2 It is also called vegetative propagation.

3 Sometimes a part of a plant, such as a stem or a leaf, may be cut from the parent plant and put in the ground. It will then develop roots and grow into a new plant.

4 Runners develop from stems and become individual plants.

5 They grow bulbs underground that can develop into mature plants.

Listening

Script 🎧 03-15

W Professor: I'm a huge fan of raspberries, which are my favorite fruit. I actually have several raspberry bushes growing in my backyard garden. Interestingly, raspberries are extremely difficult to grow from seeds. In fact, few people have success trying that. Instead, raspberries typically reproduce through asexual methods.

One popular method for gardeners to acquire new raspberry plants is to search for suckers. These are shoots which come up from the roots or the base of the stem of the raspberry plant. If you find a sucker, you can cut it off, but you need to make sure that it has some roots already attached to it. If you transplant that sucker somewhere else, it will almost surely grow and develop into a new plant.

A second way is to take the tip of a raspberry branch and bury it in the ground while keeping it attached to the main plant. You need to secure it in the ground by placing a stone or something heavy on it. After a while, roots should begin to grow from the tip. When this happens, you can cut the tip off, and then you will have a brand-new raspberry plant. You can either let it remain in the ground, or you can dig it up and transplant it in a new location.

해석

W Professor: 저를 라즈베리를 너무나 좋아하는데, 라즈베리는 제가 가장 좋아하는 과일이에요. 사실 저희 집 뒷마당에 라즈베리 나무가 몇 그루 심어져 있습니다. 흥미롭게도 라즈베리는 씨앗에서 자라나는 경우가 극히 드물어요. 실제로 그러한 시도를 해서 성공한 사람이 거의 없습니다. 그 대신, 라즈베리는 보통 무성 생식으로 번식을 해요.

원예가들이 새로운 라즈베리 식물을 얻는 한 가지 일반적인 방법은 흡지를 찾는 것입니다. 이는 라즈베리 식물의 뿌리나 줄기 아랫부분에서 자라나는 눈이에요. 흡지를 발견하면 이를 잘라내면 되는데, 거기에 붙어 있던 뿌리가 계속 붙어있도록 해야합니다. 그 흡지를 다른 곳에 이식하면 거의 틀림없이 이들이 자라서 새로운 식물로 성장하게 됩니다.

두 번째 방법은 라즈베리 가지의 끝을, 식물에 계속 붙어 있는 상태로, 땅에 묻는 것이에요. 돌이나 무거운 것을 그 위에 올려 놓음으로써 땅속에 고정되어 있

도록 해야 합니다. 얼마 후 가지 끝에서 뿌리가 자라날 거예요. 그런 일이 일어나면 가지 끝을 잘라낼 수 있는데, 그 후 새로운 라즈베리 식물을 얻게 됩니다. 그대로 땅에 놔두어도 되고 혹은 캐내서 다른 곳에 옮겨 심어도 되죠.

Organization

1 Raspberries are extremely difficult to grow from seeds, so they typically reproduce through asexual methods.

2 A sucker is a shoot which comes up from the roots or the base of the stem of a plant.

3 A person can cut off a sucker with roots already attached to it. Then, the person can transplant that sucker somewhere else, and it will almost surely grow and develop into a new plant.

4 A person can take the tip of a raspberry branch and bury it in the ground while keeping it attached to the main plant. After a while, roots should begin to grow from the tip.

5 The person can either let it remain in the ground or can dig it up and transplant it in a new location.

Comparing

Sample Response

Script 🎧 03-16

The professor tells the class that raspberry plants are difficult to grow from seeds, so they typically produce asexually. She gives two examples of raspberry reproduction. The first method is to find a sucker, a shoot that comes from the roots or the base of the plant. A person can cut off a sucker with roots growing and plant it in the ground, which should result in a new plant. The second method is to bury the tip of a branch in the ground and to keep it secure by putting a rock on top. Over time, the tip will grow roots. A person can cut off the tip and dig up the new plant to transplant. Both methods utilize vegetative propagation. This refers to the variety of ways plants can reproduce through methods not using seeds.

해석

교수는 학생들에게 라즈베리 식물이 씨앗에서 자라나는 경우가 드물며 보통 이들은 무성 생식을 한다고 말한다. 교수는 라즈베리의 번식에 관한 두 가지 예를 제시한다. 첫 번째 방법은 흡지를 찾는 것으로, 흡지는 식물의 뿌리나 아랫부분에서 자라는 눈이다. 뿌리가 자라나는 흡지를 잘라서 땅에 심으면 새로운 식물이 성장하게 될 것이다. 두 번째 방법은 나뭇가지의 끝을 땅에 묻고 그 위에 돌을 올려 놓아 이를 고정시키는 것이다. 시간이 지나면 가지 끝에서 뿌리가 자라날 것이다. 그리고 가지 끝을 잘라서 새로운 식물을 캐내면 된다. 두 가지 방법 모두 영양 번식을 활용하는 것이다. 이는 씨앗을 이용하지 않는 방법을 통해 여러 식물들이 번식을 하는 방법을 가리킨다.

Unit 38 Business II

Exercise p.98

Reading
해석

시장 점유율

하나의 업계에는 그 안에서 활동하는 다수의 기업들이 있을 수 있다. 각 기업은 해당 업계에서 일정한 퍼센트의 판매량을 나타낸다. 전체 판매량 중 하나의 기업이 차지하는 퍼센트를 시장 점유율이라고 부른다. 시장 점유율은 업체의 크기를 알아내는데 사용될 수 있다. 또한 시장 점유율이 크다는 것은 기업이 그 산업에서 지배적이라는 점을 나타낸다. 일반적으로 기업들은 경쟁자들보다 많은 이익을 내기 위해 업계에서 자신의 시장 점유율을 높이려고 한다. 이는 또 다시 기업들의 성장에 도움을 주며 수익을 증대시킨다.

Comprehension

1 It is the percentage of sales in an industry produced by one company.
2 It can be used to tell how large a company is.
3 It indicates that a company is dominant in its business.
4 Companies look to increase their market share in their industry to make gains over their competition.
5 It helps companies grow larger and increase their revenues.

Listening
Script 🎧 03-17

W Professor: It's important for businesses to increase their revenues as this helps them become bigger. But businesses are also competing against other companies in their own sectors. Let me tell you a bit about this.

Around a decade ago, I owned a small electronics firm. My company made high-end appliances for people's homes. At one point, my company recorded sales of around ten million dollars a year. That's pretty good, isn't it? Well, yes and no. I mean, uh, ten million dollars is a lot of money. However, in comparison to the other companies in the same industry, it was a very small amount.

You see, uh, my company's market share in that particular industry was less than one percent. So despite having nice sales and making a good profit, my company was not very influential in the industry. We just couldn't compete with the other companies that were much bigger. As a result, I eventually sold my company to a large conglomerate. It was really the only thing I could do since my company was too small to be competitive.

해석

W Professor: 기업들이 수익을 증대시키는 것은 중요한데, 그 이유는 그렇게 함으로써 기업이 더 커질 수 있기 때문입니다. 하지만 기업들은 또한 자신들의 분야에서 다른 기업들과 경쟁을 하고 있어요. 이에 대해 약간 말씀을 드릴게요.

약 10년 전 저는 작은 전자 제품 회사를 소유하고 있었습니다. 저희 회사는 고급 가전 제품을 만들었어요. 어느 시기에 이르자 저희 회사는 1천만 달러라는 연 매출을 기록하게 되었습니다. 상당히 괜찮은 편이었죠, 그렇지 않나요? 음, 그렇기도 하고 아니기도 했습니다. 제 말은, 어, 1천만 달러는 큰 돈이에요. 하지만 동종 업계의 다른 기업들과 비교를 하면 매우 적은 편이었죠.

아시다시피, 어, 그러한 특정 업계에서 저희 회사의 시장 점유율은 1%도 되지 않았습니다. 그래서 매출이 높고 상당한 이익이 났지만 저희 회사는 업계에서 그다지 영향력이 크지 않았어요. 저희는 훨씬 더 큰 다른 기업들과 경쟁할 수가 없었습니다. 그 결과 저는 결국 제 회사를 대기업에 매각했어요. 회사가 경쟁력을 갖추기에는 너무 작았기 때문에 그것이 제가 할 수 있는 유일한 일이었죠.

Organization

1 She owned a company that made high-end appliances.
2 It had sales of around ten million dollars a year.
3 Its market share was less than one percent of the market, so it was not very influential.
4 She sold the company to a large conglomerate because it could not compete with other firms.

Comparing
Sample Response
Script 🎧 03-18

The professor starts her lecture by telling the students that she once owned a company that made high-end appliances. According to her, it had sales of around ten million dollars a year. The professor notes that ten million dollars is a lot of money; however, she points out that her company had a very small market share. In fact, its market share was less than one percent. As a result, her company was not influential because there were other much larger companies. The professor wound up selling the company because it was not competitive against the bigger firms in the industry. This relates to market share, which is the percentage of sales a company records in a certain industry. A company with a large market share is dominant and influential, two things that the professor's company was not.

해석

교수는 학생들에게 자신이 한때 고급 가전 제품을 생산하는 기업을 소유했다고 말하면서 강의를 시작한다. 그녀에 의하면 회사의 연 매출은 약 1천만 달러였다. 교수는 1천만 달러가 큰 금액이라고 말하지만 자신의 회사의 시장 점유율은 매우 낮았다는 점을 지적한다. 실제로 시장 점유율이 1%가 되지 않았다. 그 결과 훨씬 더 규모가 큰 기업들이 많았기 때문에 그녀의 회사의 영향력은 크지 않았다. 업계 내 더 큰 업체들을 상대로 경쟁을 할 수 없었기 때문에 교수는 결국 자신의 회사를 매각했다. 이는 시장 점유율과 관련이 있는데, 시장 점유율은 특정 업계에서 한 기업이 기록하는 판매량이다. 시장 점유율이 높은 기업은 지배력과 영향력이 큰 편으로, 교수의 회사는 이 두 가지를 가지고 있지 못했다.

Unit 39 Environmental Science

Exercise p.100

Reading

해석

사막화

사막화는 비옥한 토지의 토질이 낮아지는 것을 가리킨다. 한때 식물과 곡식이 자랄 수 있었던 토지가 말라 버린다. 그 결과 그곳은 불모의 사막으로 변하게 된다. 이러한 일은 여러 가지 이유 때문에 일어날 수 있다. 가장 주요한 자연적인 이유는 장기간의 가뭄이다. 또한 인간도 원인이 된다. 과도한 산업화로 인해 토질이 크게 낮아질 수 있다. 또한 대규모 농업 및 산림 전용, 즉 일정 지역에서 나무를 베어 내는 활동으로 그렇게 될 수도 있다. 마지막으로 인간이 일정 지역 내의 수원을 고갈시킬 수도 있는데, 그렇게 되면 해당 지역이 사막으로 변하게 된다.

Comprehension

1 It is the decline in quality of fertile land.
2 It transforms into infertile desert.
3 It is an extended period of drought.
4 It is excessive industrialization.
5 Some other human causes are extensive farming, deforestation, and the depletion of groundwater supplies in an area.

Listening

Script 🎧 03-19

M Professor: Sixty years ago, the Aral Sea was the world's fourth largest lake. This saltwater lake was located in the former Soviet Union. Today, what remains of it lies on the border between Uzbekistan and Kazakhstan. What happened is a sad story involving human actions.

There were two major rivers that emptied into the Aral Sea. However, the flows of both rivers were diverted by the Soviets to provide water to irrigate crops growing on farms. As a result, less water flowed into the Aral Sea.

This started a change that began around 1960. Slowly, the Aral Sea started to shrink. The area around the Aral Sea only averaged around ten centimeters of precipitation a year. This meant that rainfall alone could

not replenish the sea. Today, the Aral Sea is a fraction of the size it was once. The surrounding area has also suffered from desertification. Millions of people lost their livelihoods due to the Aral Sea becoming a desert. And the lack of water has caused summers in the region to be hotter and drier and winters to be colder than before.

해석

M Professor: 60년 전 아랄해는 세계에서 네 번째로 큰 호수였습니다. 이 해수 호수는 구 소련에 위치해 있었어요. 오늘날에는 우즈베키스탄과 카자흐스탄 간의 국경 지대에 그 일부가 남아 있습니다. 그곳에서 안타까운 일이 일어났는데, 이는 인간의 활동과 관련된 것이었죠.

아랄해로 흘러 들어오는 두 개의 큰 강이 있었습니다. 하지만 농장에서 기르는 작물에 물을 공급하기 위해 소련 사람들이 두 강의 물길을 바꾸어 놓았습니다. 그 결과 아랄해로 유입되는 물의 양이 줄어들었죠.

이로 인해 1960년 무렵에 변화가 일어나기 시작했어요. 서서히 아랄해가 작아지기 시작했습니다. 아랄해 주변 지역의 연 평균 강수량은 약 10센티미터밖에 되지 않았습니다. 이는 강수량만으로 그곳 바다에 물이 채워질 수 없다는 점을 의미했어요. 오늘날 아랄해는 한때 차지하고 있던 면적의 매우 적은 부분만을 차지하고 있습니다. 그 주변 지역 또한 사막화를 겪고 있습니다. 아랄해가 사막이 되면서 수백만 명의 사람들이 생업을 잃었어요. 그리고 물이 부족해져서 해당 지역의 여름은 더 덥고 건조해졌고 겨울은 이전보다 더 추워졌습니다.

Organization

1 It is on the border between Uzbekistan and Kazakhstan.
2 The Soviets diverted the flows of two rivers to irrigate crops, so less water flowed into the Aral Sea.
3 It started to shrink around 1960.
4 The area around it has suffered from desertification. In addition, summers are hotter and drier than before, and winters are colder than before.

Comparing

Sample Response
Script 🎧 03-20

The professor lectures to the class about the Aral Sea. He remarks that it was once the fourth largest lake in the world, but nowadays it is much smaller. The professor states that the Soviet Union divert the flows of two rivers so that water could be provided to farmers. The rivers flowed into the Aral Sea, but after they were diverted, the Aral Sea began to shrink since less water flowed into it. Starting around 1960, the Aral Sea became smaller and smaller. Today, it is much smaller than it used to be. In addition, the surrounding area suffers from desertification. This refers to the changing of fertile land into infertile land. One reason for this is human actions, which is clearly what happened to the Aral Sea and the area around it.

해석

교수는 아랄해에 대해 강의를 하고 있다. 그는 그곳이 세계에서 네 번째로 큰 호수였지만 현재 그 크기가 많이 줄어들었다고 말한다. 교수는 소련이 농부들에게 물을 공급하기 위해 두 강의 물길을 바꾸어 놓았다고 언급한다. 강물이 아랄해로 흘러 들었지만 물길이 바뀐 이후에는 그곳으로 유입되는 수량이 줄어들어서 아랄해의 크기가 줄어들기 시작했다. 약 1960년부터 아랄해는 점점 더 작아졌다. 오늘날 그 크기는 예전보다 훨씬 더 작은 것이다. 또한 그 주변 지역은 사막화를 겪고 있다. 이는 비옥한 토지가 불모지로 바뀌는 것을 가리킨다. 사막화의 한 가지 원인은 인간의 활동인데, 아랄해 및 그 주변 지역에서 일어났던 일도 분명 그 때문이었다.

Unit 40 Business III

Exercise p.102

Reading

해석

내부 경쟁

많은 기업들이 직원들 사이의 경쟁을 장려한다. 그들은 그러한 결과로서 직원들의 효율성과 생산성이 증대될 수 있다고 믿는다. 직원들에게 상과 보너스를 주고 승진을 시켜 줌으로써 내부 경쟁을 자극할 수 있다. 일부 대기업들은 심지어 두 개 이상의 팀을 동일한 프로젝트에 참여시킴으로써 각각의 팀이 더 열심히 그리고 더 빠르게 일을 하도록 만들 수도 있다. 하지만 이러한 방식이 항상 효과적인 것은 아니다. 일부 직원들은 내부 경쟁 때문에 자신의 업무에 대해 두려움과 불안감을 느낄 수도 있다. 그리고 동료들과 경쟁하기 위해 부적절하거나 불법적인 행동을 하는 직원들도 있을 수 있다.

Comprehension

1 They believe it can result in employees being more efficient and productive.

2 They can receive awards, bonuses, and promotions.

3 Some large companies may have two or more teams working on the same project to get each team to work harder and faster.

4 They can suffer from anxiety and fear for their jobs.

5 They may engage in improper or illegal behavior to compete against their colleagues.

Listening

Script 🎧 03-21

W Professor: It's natural for humans to compete against others. Students compete for higher grades, athletes compete to win contests, and workers compete to get promotions and other benefits. However, these competitions aren't always positive.

Did you read the story about the local bank a few days ago? Apparently, the manager wanted his employees to work harder, so he offered bonuses for various activities. For instance, employees who opened the most accounts and signed up the most people for credit cards would receive bonuses each month. It sounds like a wonderful idea, doesn't it?

Well, maybe not . . . You see, uh, a couple of employees weren't doing well. They felt like they were in danger of getting fired. So here's what they did . . . They opened unauthorized bank accounts for existing customers. By that, I mean the customers never requested new accounts. But the bank employees opened them anyway. One employee even issued unrequested credit cards to customers. So what happened? Well, those employees are going to prison, and the bank is likely to get shut down for illegal activities.

해석

W Professor: 인간이 다른 이들을 상대로 경쟁을 하는 것은 자연스러운 일이에요. 학생들은 더 높은 점수를 받기 위해 경쟁을 하고, 운동선수는 경기에서 승리하기 위해 경쟁을 하며, 직원들은 승진 및 기타 혜택을 위해 경쟁을 하죠. 하지만 이러한 경쟁이 항상 긍정적인 것은 아닙니다.

며칠 전에 있었던 지역 은행에 관한 이야기를 읽어 보셨나요? 듣자 하니 그곳 매니저는 직원들이 더 열심히 일하기를 바라는 마음에서 여러 실적에 대한 보너스를 지급했어요. 예를 들면 가장 많은 계좌를 신설하고 가장 많은 사람들에게 서명을 받아 신용카드를 발급한 직원들은 매달 보너스를 받게 되었죠. 멋진 아이디어처럼 들립니다, 그렇지 않나요?

음, 아닐 수도 있는데… 아시다시피, 어, 두어 명의 직원은 그다지 성과가 좋지 못했어요. 그들은 자신이 해고될 위험에 처해 있다고 생각했죠. 그래서 그들이 어떻게 했는지 말씀을 드리면… 기존 고객들에게 무단으로 은행 계좌를 개설해 주었습니다. 제 말은 고객들이 새로운 계좌를 요청하지 않았다는 뜻이에요. 하지만 은행 직원들이 개설을 했던 것이죠. 한 직원은 심지어 요청을 받지도 않았는데 고객들에게 신용카드를 발급해 주었어요. 어떤 일이 일어났을까요? 음, 그 직원들은 수감될 예정이고 해당 은행은 불법적인 행위를 했다는 점 때문에 문을 닫을 가능성이 큽니다.

Organization

1 He offered employees bonuses to make them work harder.

2 They were encouraged to open bank accounts and to sign up people for credit cards.

3 They opened unauthorized bank accounts and approved unrequested credit cards.

4 The employees will go to prison, and the bank may be shut down.

Comparing

Sample Response

Script 🎧 03-22

The professor talks to the class about a news event concerning a local bank. She states that a manager at the bank wanted to have some internal competition between his employees. This happens when companies encourage their employees to compete against one another for various rewards such as bonuses, awards, and promotions. The bank employees could get paid bonuses for opening the most bank accounts and for signing up the most people for credit cards. Unfortunately, internal competition sometimes has negative results. This happened at the bank. What happened is that some employees opened unauthorized bank accounts and approved unrequested credit cards. As a result, those employees will go to prison, and there is a chance that the bank will get closed down. In this case, the internal competition at the bank had negative results.

해석

교수는 수업에서 지역 은행과 관련된 뉴스에 대해 이야기한다. 그는 은행 매니저가 직원들 간에 내부 경쟁이 일어나는 것을 바랐다고 말한다. 이는 기업들이 보너스, 상, 그리고 승진과 같은 보상을 얻기 위해 직원들이 서로 경쟁하도록 만들 때 이루어진다. 은행 직원들은 가장 많은 은행 계좌를 신설하고 가장 많은 사람들에게서 서명을 받아 신용카드를 발급하면 보너스를 받을 수 있었다. 안타깝게도 내부 경쟁은 때때로 부정적인 결과를 가져다 준다. 은행에서도 그런 일이 발생했다. 일부 직원들이 무단으로 은행 계좌를 개설하고 요청을 받지도 않고서 신용카드를 발급했다. 그 결과 이 직원들은 수감될 예정이며 은행이 문을 닫게 될 가능성도 있다. 이 경우 은행에서의 내부 경쟁이 부정적인 결과를 초래했다.

Unit 41 Psychology II

Exercise p.104

Reading

해석

역사의 종말 환상

많은 사람들은 자신의 과거, 현재, 그리고 미래의 삶에 대한 특정한 믿음을 가지고 있다. 예를 들어 대다수의 사람들은 과거의 자아와 현재의 자아가 매우 다르다고 생각한다. 실제로 이러한 사람들은 자신이 몇 년에 걸쳐 크게 변했다고 주장한다. 하지만 종종 같은 사람들이 현재의 자아가 미래에는 바뀌지 않을 것이라고 생각한다. 미래에 자신들이 어떻게 변할 것인지 질문을 받으면 대부분의 사람들은 자신이 전혀 바뀌지 않거나 거의 바뀌지 않을 것이라고 말한다. 이는 역사의 종말 환상으로 알려져 있다.

Comprehension

1 They think that their past selves and their present selves are very different.
2 They claim that they have changed a great deal from the past.
3 They think that they will not change in the future.
4 It can be inferred that they think they will remain the same for the rest of their lives.
5 It is called the end-of-history illusion.

Listening

Script 🎧 03-23

M Professor: I'd like to tell you about an experiment I conducted a couple of years ago. I think you'll find it fairly interesting regarding the way that people think.

I conducted a survey of more than 1,000 people. They ranged in age from eighteen to sixty-five. I asked these people about their tastes in music in the past, the present, and the future. Interestingly, many people responded that their musical tastes had changed very much in the past ten years. In other words, the music they preferred in the past decade ago was very different from the music they like today.

However, most of these people believed that in the future, their tastes in music would remain the same. Nearly everyone claimed that ten years in the future, they would like the same type of music. They believed that their current selves were basically the final versions and that nothing more would change in their lives. Even though they could clearly see that their musical preferences had changed a tremendous amount in one decade, they refused to believe that their preferences would continue to evolve. Interesting, isn't it?

해석

M Professor: 2년 전에 제가 진행했던 한 가지 실험에 대해 말씀을 드리고자 합니다. 사람들이 생각하는 방식과 관련해서 매우 흥미로운 점을 알게 되실 거예요.

저는 1,000명 이상의 사람들을 대상으로 설문 조사를 실시했어요. 18세에서 65세까지가 그 대상이었죠. 저는 사람들에게 과거, 현재, 그리고 미래의 음악적인 성향에 대해 물었습니다. 흥미롭게도 많은 사람들은 자신의 음악적인 성향이 지난 10년 동안 크게 바뀌었다고 응답했어요. 즉 10년 전에 좋아했던 음악과 현재 좋아하는 음악이 매우 달랐던 것이었죠.

하지만 이들 대부분은 자신들의 음악적인 성향이 미래에도 똑같을 것이라고 믿었습니다. 거의 모두가 10년 후에도 자신들이 똑같은 종류의 음악을 좋아할 것이라고 말을 했어요. 현재의 자아가 기본적으로 마지막 버전이며, 삶에서 더 이상의 변화는 없을 것이라고 믿었습니다. 10년 동안 자신들의 음악적 취향이 크게 바뀌었다는 점은 알면서도 미래의 취향이 계속 바뀔 것이라는 점은 믿지 않았어요. 흥미롭지 않나요?

Organization

1 He conducted a survey of more than 1,000 people.

2 He asked them about their tastes in music in the past, the present, and the future.

3 They believed that their tastes in music from the past to the present had changed very much.

4 They believed that their tastes in music would not change from the present to the future.

Comparing

Sample Response

Script 🎧 03-24

The professor discusses a survey he conducted. He asked more than 1,000 people between the ages of eighteen and sixty-five about their musical tastes in the past, the present, and the future. He learned that almost everyone thought they liked different music in the past than they did today. In fact, he discovered that their tastes differed greatly. However, when he asked about the future, their answers were different. Most of the respondents thought they would not change their tastes in music in the future. This is an example of the end-of-history illusion. It happens when people believe they have changed a lot from the past to the present. However, the same people also think they won't change in the future. So the current version of themselves is the one that will always exist.

해석

교수는 자신이 실행했던 설문 조사에 대해 논의한다. 그는 18세에서 65세 사이의 1,000명이 넘는 사람들에게 과거, 현재, 그리고 미래의 음악적 취향에 대해 물었다. 그는 거의 모든 사람이 과거에 좋아했던 음악과 현재 좋아했던 음악이 다르다고 생각한다는 점을 알게 되었다. 실제로 그는 그들의 취향이 크게 변했다는 점을 밝혀냈다. 하지만 그가 미래에 대해 물었을 때 이들의 답변은 달랐다. 대부분의 응답자들이 미래에는 자신의 음악적인 취향이 변하지 않을 것이라고 생각했다. 이는 역사의 종말 환상의 한 가지 예이다. 이는 사람들이 과거에서 현재에 걸쳐 자신이 변했다고 믿을 때 일어난다. 하지만 같은 사람들이 미래에는 자신이 바뀌지 않을 것이라고 생각한다. 따라서 현재 버전의 자아가 계속 존재하게 될 것이다.

Unit 42 Botany

Exercise p.106

Reading

해석

혼식

일부 농부들 및 정원사들은 혼식을 한다. 이는 두 종류 혹은 세 종류의 식물을 서로 가까운 곳에, 혹은 함께 심음으로써 여러 가지 혜택을 얻으려는 것이다. 장

점으로는 식물에 피해를 주는 해충의 수가 줄어든다는 점과 유익한 곤충들이 유입된다는 점을 들 수 있다. 한편 자라나는 잡초의 수를 줄이고 식물의 성장을 촉진시키기 위해서 혼식이 사용될 수도 있다. 이러한 방식은 또한 이용 가능한 모든 부지를 활용하기 위해, 특히 규모가 다소 한정된 정원에서 사용될 수도 있다.

Comprehension

1 Some farmers and gardeners engage in companion planting.

2 It involves planting two or three plants close to one another to obtain various benefits.

3 It can reduce the number of pests that harm the plants and attract beneficial insects.

4 People do it to decrease the number of weeds that grow and to boost the growth of the plants.

5 They do it to utilize all of the space available, especially in small gardens.

Listening

Script 🎧 03-25

W Professor: I've been a gardener for thirty years. Gardening is a relaxing hobby and provides me with nutritious food. Over the years, I have also discovered that it can be really educational. For instance, I've learned that it's helpful to grow some plants together.

I love corn, so I always plant a lot of it annually. As you know, corn plants grow very high, and summers here can be quite hot. I therefore always plant lettuce around the corn plants. The corn provides shade for the lettuce, which can wilt in the summer heat. I also plant peas, which are a climbing plant. They climb up the corn as they grow. Peas additionally replenish the soil by adding nitrogen to it, so I don't have to add fertilizer. Great, isn't it?

Next, I plant tomatoes and parsley together. I love tomatoes, but they often get attacked by various insects. Well, parsley attracts other insects that eat the ones which attack my tomatoes. By engaging in companion planting, I can avoid using pesticides on my plants, so no harmful chemicals get on them.

해석

W Professor: 저는 30년 동안 텃밭을 가꾸어 왔습니다. 텃밭을 가꾸는 것은 마음을 느긋하게 만들어 주는 취미로서 영양분이 많은 음식도 제공해 주죠. 수년 동안 저는 그 일이 실제로 교육적일 수도 있다는 점을 깨달았어요. 예를 들어 저는 몇 가지 식물들을 함께 심는 것이 도움이 된다는 점을 알게 되었습니다.

저는 옥수수를 매우 좋아하기 때문에 해마다 항상 옥수수를 많이 심습니다. 아시다시피 옥수수는 매우 높은 높이로 자라며, 이곳 여름은 상당히 더울 수 있어요. 그래서 저는 항상 옥수수 주변에 상추를 심습니다. 옥수수는 여름 더위에 시들기 쉬운 상추에게 그늘을 제공해 주죠. 저는 또한 덩굴 식물인 콩도 심습니다. 이들은 자라면서 옥수수를 타고 올라가요. 게다가 콩은 토양에 질소를 공급

해 줌으로써 토양에 영양분을 보충해 주기 때문에 저는 따로 비료를 쓸 필요가 없습니다. 괜찮지 않습니까?

다음으로 저는 토마토와 파슬리를 함께 심습니다. 저는 토마토를 매우 좋아하지만 이들은 종종 다양한 곤충들의 공격을 받아요. 음, 파슬리는 토마토를 공격하는 곤충들을 잡아먹는 또 다른 곤충들을 유인합니다. 혼식을 함으로써 저는 제 식물에 살충제를 쓰지 않아도 되기 때문에 해로운 화학 물질이 식물에 묻을 일이 전혀 없습니다.

Organization

1 Her hobby is gardening.

2 The corn provides shade for the lettuce during summer, so it doesn't wilt.

3 The peas grow up on the corn plants, and they also return nitrogen to the soil.

4 Parsley attracts insects that eat bugs that attack her tomatoes.

Comparing

Sample Response

Script 🎧 03-26

The professor's lecture is about her gardening hobby. She mentions that she has learned to have some plants grow together in her garden, and then she explains why. She first remarks that she plants corn, lettuce, and peas together in her garden. The corn grows tall and provides shade for the lettuce, which could wilt during summer. The peas grow up the corn plants and also provide the soil with nitrogen. Next, she states that she plants tomatoes and parsley together. According to the professor, parsley attracts some insects that are known to eat the bugs that attack tomato plants. The professor therefore doesn't have to use pesticides. The professor's actions are examples of companion planting. This is the act of planting two or more plants together to obtain various benefits from doing that.

해석

교수의 강의는 텃밭을 가꾸는 그녀의 취미에 관한 것이다. 교수는 자신이 텃밭에서 몇 가지 식물들을 함께 기르는 법을 알게 되었다고 말한 후 그 이유에 대해 설명한다. 먼저 그녀는 옥수수, 상추, 그리고 콩을 함께 텃밭에 심는다고 말한다. 옥수수는 높은 높이로 자라서 상추에게 그늘을 제공해 주는데, 상추는 여름에 시들기가 쉽다. 콩은 자라면서 옥수수를 타고 올라가며 또한 토양에 질소를 공급해 준다. 다음으로 교수는 자신이 토마토와 파슬리를 함께 심는다고 말한다. 교수에 의하면 파슬리는 토마토를 공격하는 벌레를 잡아먹는 것으로 알려진 곤충들을 유인한다. 따라서 교수는 살충제를 사용할 필요가 없다. 교수의 행동은 혼식의 예에 해당된다. 이는 두 가지 이상의 식물을 함께 심음으로써 그에 따른 다양한 혜택을 얻으려는 행위이다.

Exercise ⋯⋯⋯⋯⋯⋯⋯⋯⋯⋯⋯⋯⋯⋯⋯⋯⋯⋯⋯⋯⋯⋯ p.108

Reading

해석

동물들의 사회적 촉진

때때로 동물들은 특정한 행동을 한다. 털 고르기, 사냥, 먹이 찾기, 혹은 기타 다양한 행동을 할 수 있다. 일부 경우, 첫 번째 동물이 그러한 행동을 할 때, 같은 종에 속한 다른 동물들이 그 동물을 지켜볼 수 있다. 이를 지켜본 동물들은 때때로 똑같은 행동을 할 수도 있고, 혹은 첫 번째 동물이 자신이 하는 행동의 강도를 높일 수도 있다. 이는 동물들의 사회적 촉진이라고 불린다. 사회적 촉진은 지난 수십 년 동안 학자들에 의해 관찰되고 연구되어 왔다.

Comprehension

1 They may do grooming, hunting, or foraging.

2 The animals may observe the first animal as it does that activity.

3 They may begin to do the same behavior.

4 It may do the action more intensely.

5 They have observed this behavior in animals for decades.

Listening

Script 🎧 03-27

M Professor: Now, uh, we've studied social facilitation in humans, but let me tell you that animals also do this type of behavior. In many cases, whenever animals engage in social facilitation, it has a beneficial effect on them. However, that is not always true.

Here's an example of when social facilitation has a detrimental effect. I have a couple of dogs. Sometimes at night, another dog in the neighborhood begins howling. What happens next . . . ? That's right. My dogs start howling, too. They usually howl much louder than the original dog. Other neighborhood dogs howl as well, and it takes a while before they all cease being noisy.

What about beneficial effects of social facilitation? Chimpanzees are social animals that live together in big troops. At times, one chimp might start grooming another. Grooming involves a chimp manipulating the hair and skin of another. It can be soothing, and it removes bugs from the chimp being groomed. Well, when one chimp starts grooming another, other chimps may do the same thing. In this way, many of the chimps in the troop benefit by getting groomed.

M Professor: 자, 어, 우리는 인간의 사회적 촉진에 대해 공부를 했는데, 동물들도 이러한 행동을 한다는 점을 말씀드리죠. 많은 경우, 동물들이 사회적 촉진과 관련된 행동을 할 때마다 이로운 효과가 나타납니다. 하지만 항상 그런 것은 아니에요.

사회적 촉진이 해로운 결과를 가져 오는 경우에 대한 예를 알려 드릴게요. 제게는 두 마리의 개가 있습니다. 때때로 밤에 이웃집의 다른 개가 울부짖기 시작하는 경우가 있어요. 그 다음에 어떤 일이 일어날까요…? 맞습니다. 제 개들도 울부짖기 시작해요. 원래 개보다 더 큰 소리로 울부짖습니다. 다른 이웃집 개들 또한 울부짖는데, 어느 정도 시간이 지나야 모두가 잠잠해 집니다.

사회적 촉진의 이로운 효과는 무엇일까요? 침팬지는 커다란 무리를 지어 함께 사는 사회적 동물입니다. 때때로 한 마리의 침팬지가 다른 침팬지의 털을 골라 주기 시작할 수 있어요. 털을 골라 주는 행동을 하면서 침팬지는 다른 침팬지의 털과 피부를 만져 줍니다. 이는 마음을 진정시켜 줄 수 있고, 상대 침팬지의 몸에서 벌레를 제거해 줍니다. 음, 한 침팬지가 다른 침팬지의 털을 골라 주는 경우, 다른 침팬지들 또한 같은 행동을 할 수가 있어요. 이렇게 함으로써 무리 내의 많은 침팬지들이 털을 골라 주는 행위를 통해 혜택을 받습니다.

Organization

1 It can have both positive and negative effects.
2 They sometimes howl whenever a neighborhood dog starts to howl.
3 It might start grooming another chimp.
4 Many other chimps begin to groom one another.

Comparing

Sample Response

Script 🎧 03-28

The professor says that animals can engage in social facilitation like humans and gives two examples. The first example concerns his dogs. He mentions that whenever a neighborhood dog starts to howl, his dogs and others howl, too. They don't quiet down for a while. This is an example of how social facilitation can be negative. However, he then provides a positive example. He notes that a single chimpanzee may start to groom another. When other chimpanzees witness this activity, they begin grooming others as well. In this way, many chimps benefit. These activities are examples of social facilitation. This happens when one animal does a certain behavior and others of the same species witness it. The result may be that others do the same activity or that the original animal does the activity more intensely.

해석

교수는 인간과 마찬가지로 동물들에게도 사회적 촉진이 일어날 수 있다고 말하면서 두 가지 예를 제시한다. 첫 번째 예는 그의 개와 관련이 있다. 교수는 이웃집 개가 울부짖기 시작할 때마다 자신의 개와 다른 개들도 울부짖는다고 말한다. 이들은 한동안 소리를 지른다. 이는 사회적 촉진이 부정적인 것일 수 있다는 예가

된다. 하지만 교수는 그 다음으로 긍정적인 사례를 제시한다. 그는 한 마리의 침팬지가 다른 침팬지의 털을 골라 줄 수 있다고 말한다. 다른 침팬지들이 이러한 행동을 목격하면 그들도 다른 침팬지들의 털을 골라 주기 시작한다. 이런 식으로 많은 침팬지들이 혜택을 보게 된다. 이러한 활동은 사회적 촉진의 예이다. 이는 한 동물이 특정한 행동을 하고, 같은 종의 다른 동물들이 이를 목격하는 경우에 일어난다. 그 결과로서 다른 동물들이 동일한 행동을 할 수도 있고, 최초의 동물이 자신의 행동을 보다 격렬하게 할 수도 있다.

Unit 44 Psychology III

Exercise p.110

Reading

해석

위험 과대 평가

사람들이 다양한 활동을 고려하는 경우 특정한 행동이 얼마나 위험한 것인지에 대해 생각할 수 있다. 스쿠버 다이빙과 등산같이 힘든 활동뿐만 아니라 계단 오르기 및 자동차 타기와 같은 일상적인 활동에 대해서도 그럴 수 있다. 이러한 모든 활동에는 약간의 위험성이 수반될 수 있지만 좋지 않은 일이 일어날 가능성은 적다. 그럼에도 불구하고 사람들은 종종 이러한 활동과 관련된 위험의 크기를 과대 평가한다. 특정한 행동이 너무 위험하다는 이러한 생각은 불안, 혹은 특정 행동에 대한 기피 현상과 같은 부정적인 효과를 야기할 수 있다.

Comprehension

1 They think about how dangerous certain ones are.
2 The activities are scuba diving, mountain climbing, climbing stairs, and riding in a car.
3 They could all involve some danger.
4 They often overestimate the amount of risk involved in some activities.
5 They include anxiety and people being unwilling to do certain actions.

Listening

Script 🎧 03-29

W Professor: I do a lot of cycling. In fact, I cycle from my home to school every day. Sadly, over the past few years, the number of cyclists in this city has greatly decreased. Let me tell you why.

About five years ago, the city government eagerly promoted cycling. It constructed bicycle lanes for cyclists to use, and there were numerous promotions encouraging people to cycle. They were effective. A large number of people bought bicycles and began riding around the city.

Well, unfortunately, several months after the promotions started, a few cyclists were involved in accidents. There were, I believe, five accidents. Four involved cars hitting bicycles while a cyclist hit a pedestrian another time. They were all minor accidents. Nobody even had to visit the hospital. But there were many news reports about these accidents, and they started to frighten people. This caused many people to think cycling was too dangerous even though the chance of being in an accident was tiny. Most of the cyclists got rid of their bikes and refused to cycle anymore.

해석

W Professor: 저는 사이클을 자주 탑니다. 실제로 매일 집에서 학교까지 사이클을 타고 다니죠. 안타깝게도 지난 몇 년에 걸쳐 이곳 시내에서 사이클을 타는 사람들의 수가 크게 줄어들었어요. 그 이유를 알려 드리죠.

약 5년 전에 시 정부는 사이클 타기를 적극적으로 장려했습니다. 사이클을 타는 사람들이 이용할 수 있는 전용 도로가 만들어졌고, 사이클 타기를 장려하는 프로모션들도 많이 진행되었어요. 이는 효과가 있었습니다. 꽤 많은 사람들이 자전거를 구입해서 자전거를 타고 시내를 돌아다니기 시작했죠.

음, 안타깝지만, 프로모션이 시작되고 몇 달 후에 몇 명의 사람들이 자전거를 타다가 사고를 당했습니다. 제 생각에 다섯 건 정도 있었던 것 같아요. 네 명은 자동차가 자전거를 치는 사고를 당했고, 그와 별개로 한 명은 자전거로 보행자를 치는 사고를 냈죠. 모두 경미한 사고였습니다. 아무도 병원에 갈 필요가 없었어요. 하지만 이러한 사건에 관한 뉴스가 많이 보도되자 사람들은 겁을 먹기 시작했습니다. 이로써 많은 사람들이, 사고를 당할 확률이 매우 낮음에도 불구하고, 사이클은 위험한 것이라고 생각하게 되었어요. 사이클을 타던 대부분의 사람들은 자전거를 처분하고 더 이상 사이클을 타지 않게 되었죠.

Organization

1 It constructed bicycle lanes and had promotions encouraging people to cycle.
2 Many people bought bikes and began to cycle.
3 There were around five accidents involving bicycles.
4 They thought cycling was too dangerous, so they got rid of their bikes and stopped cycling.

Comparing

Sample Response

Script 🎧 03-30

The professor lectures about cycling in the city. She points out that a few years ago, the city encouraged people to cycle. It made bicycle lanes and had promotions to get more people to cycle. This resulted in many people buying bicycles and riding them. Then, there were five minor accidents involving bicycles. Even though nobody was severely hurt, news reports

publicized these accidents and made people scared. People began to think that cycling was dangerous, so they got rid of their bicycles. This is an example of risk overestimation. This happens when people believe certain activities are dangerous even though that is not the case. In most situations, the chance of a real problem is tiny. When risk overestimation happens, people can suffer from anxiety and also refuse to take part in an activity.

해석

교수는 시내에서 사이클을 타는 것에 관한 강의를 하고 있다. 그녀는 몇 년 전 시가 사람들에게 사이클을 타는 것을 장려했다고 말한다. 자전거 전용 도로가 만들어졌고, 보다 많은 사람들이 사이클을 타도록 프로모션이 진행되었다. 그 결과 많은 사람들이 자전거를 구입해서 타고 다녔다. 이후 다섯 건의 미미한 자전거 사고가 발생했다. 아무도 심하게 다치지 않았지만 뉴스 보도로 이러한 사건이 알려지자 사람들은 겁을 먹게 되었다. 사람들은 사이클을 타는 것이 위험한 것이라고 생각했기 때문에 자전거를 처분했다. 이는 위험 과대 평가의 예이다. 이는 사람들이, 위험한 것이 아닐 지라도, 특정 행동이 위험한 것이라고 생각할 때 발생한다. 대부분의 경우 실제로 문제가 발생할 가능성은 매우 낮다. 위험 과대 평가가 이루어지면 사람들은 불안을 느낄 수도 있고 어떤 행동에 참여하는 것을 거부할 수도 있다.

Unit 45 Zoology II

Exercise p.112

Reading

해석

중간 기착지

매년 수많은 종의 새들이 가을과 겨울에 보다 날씨가 따뜻한 곳으로 이동을 한다. 이들은 이듬해 봄이 되어 원래 살던 곳의 날씨가 따뜻해지면 다시 그곳으로 돌아간다. 이러한 새들 중 일부는 수백 킬로미터 혹은 심지어 수천 킬로미터에 이르는 거리를 이동해야 한다. 이러한 새들은 무착륙으로 이동을 할 수가 없다. 따라서 중간 기착지를 이용해야만 하는데, 이는 먹이와 안식처를 구할 수 있고 포식자들로부터 안전할 수 있는 이동 경로 상의 장소이다. 새들은 중간 기착지에서 몇 시간 정도 머물 수도 있고, 혹은 며칠 동안이나 머무를 수도 있다. 중간 기착지가 존재하기 때문에 새들은 안전하게 목적지에 도달할 수 있다.

Comprehension

1 They go to warmer climates in fall and winter and return to their homes in spring.
2 Some birds migrate hundreds or even thousands of kilometers.
3 They use stopover habitats because they cannot make their journeys nonstop.
4 They can find food, shelter, and safety from predators.

5 They may stay at stopover habitats for a few hours or even several days.

4 They get shelter from storms, they can sleep in tree branches, and they can find food.

Listening

Script 🎧 03-31

W Professor: Have you ever wondered how birds manage to migrate such long distances? For instance, the Canadian warbler lives in Canada and northern parts of the United States. Each fall, it migrates south. It flies to forests in the mountains of South American countries. That journey takes several weeks and requires the birds to fly thousands of kilometers.

The birds cannot fly continually. They need to stop at places on the way. And let's remember that there's lots of water, including the Gulf of Mexico, that the birds must fly over. Obviously, it's faster for the birds to fly straight over the water. But what happens when there's a storm?

When stormy weather hits, the Canadian warbler heads for the Texas coast. That's a stopover habitat which billions of migrating birds use. The warblers look for forests and large groves of trees on the coast. The trees provide shelter from storms. The birds can sleep on tree branches and avoid predators, too. Finally, there's enough food in these areas for the birds to restore their energy when they continue migrating.

해석

W Professor: 새들이 어떻게 그처럼 먼 거리를 이동하는지에 대해 궁금했던 적이 있나요? 예를 들어 캐나다솔새는 캐나다와 미국의 북쪽에서 서식합니다. 매년 가을이 되면 남쪽으로 이동을 하죠. 남미 국가들의 숲으로 날아갑니다. 그러한 여정에는 몇 주가 걸리며, 이때 새들은 수천 킬로미터를 날아가야 해요.

이 새는 계속해서 날 수가 없습니다. 도중에 멈춰야만 하죠. 그리고 이 새들은 멕시코만을 포함하여 넓은 수역 위로 날아가야 한다는 점을 기억해 주세요. 분명 새가 그러한 수역을 곧장 지나가는 것이 더 빠를 것입니다. 하지만 폭풍이 발생하면 어떻게 될까요?

폭풍이 치는 경우 캐나다솔새는 텍사스의 해변으로 향합니다. 이곳은 수십억 마리의 철새들이 이용하는 중간 기착지이죠. 솔새들은 해안가에서 숲과 거대한 수풀을 찾습니다. 나무들이 비바람을 피할 수 있는 피난처를 제공해 주어요. 또한 새들은 나뭇가지에서 잠을 자고 포식자들도 피할 수가 있죠. 마지막으로 이러한 지역에는 충분한 양의 먹이가 있어서 새들이 에너지를 비축하고 계속해서 이동을 할 수가 있습니다.

Organization

1 It flies from Canada and the northern United States to forests in mountains in parts of South America.

2 It takes several weeks and is thousands of kilometers long.

3 They fly to the coast of Texas and look for forests or groves of trees.

Comparing

Sample Response
Script 🎧 03-32

The professor discusses the Canadian warbler in her lecture. She remarks that each year, it migrates from Canada and places in the northern United States to mountainous areas in South America. This journey of several thousand kilometers takes them a few weeks. The birds cannot fly nonstop and often fly over the Gulf of Mexico. When there are dangerous storms, the birds fly to the coast of Texas. There, they can find forests and groves of trees which provide food and shelter for the birds. They also keep the birds safe from predators. These places in Texas are stopover habitats. These are defined as places where migrating birds can stay for a few hours or days during their journeys. The birds are safe in these places and can get food in them, too.

해석

교수는 강의에서 캐나다솔새에 대해 이야기한다. 그녀는 매년 캐나다솔새가 캐나다 및 미국 북부 지역에서 남미의 산악 지역으로 이동을 한다고 언급한다. 길이가 수천 킬로미터에 이르는 이러한 여정에는 몇 주의 시간이 걸린다. 이 새는 무착륙으로 비행을 하지 못하며 종종 멕시코만 위를 날아간다. 위험한 폭풍이 발생하면 이 새들은 텍사스의 해안가로 날아간다. 그곳에서 새들에게 먹이와 피난처를 제공해 주는 숲과 수풀을 찾을 수 있다. 또한 이러한 곳에서는 새들이 포식자들로부터 안전할 수 있다. 텍사스의 이러한 장소들은 중간 기착지이다. 이는 철새들이 이동 중에 몇 시간 혹은 며칠 동안 머물 수 있는 장소로서 정의된다. 이러한 장소에서 새들은 안전하게 지내며 또한 먹이를 먹을 수 있다.

Unit 46 Writing

Exercise ·· p.120

Listening

Script 🎧 04-03

W Professor: Before we get started on today's writing assignment, I want to go over a couple of literary conventions I believe you'll find to be rather effective in enhancing the overall, uh, quality of your work when writing both short stories and novels. Ironically, these two literary conventions are opposites. I'm referring, of course, to exaggeration and its opposite, understatement.

Let's look at exaggeration first. It's something we've all used. Exaggeration is, simply, overstating something. It's saying that something is greater than what it is in reality. Why don't I give you some examples? Have you ever been really hungry? Sure, everyone has. Well, one exaggeration would be to say, "I'm so hungry I could eat a horse." Of course, you couldn't really do that, but you're exaggerating to get your point across. You might also say, "That was the greatest play I've ever seen," to compliment your actor friend. It probably wasn't . . . You're just, well, overstating. But he'll appreciate the compliment.

Now for understatement. What's that? Well, it's merely saying that something is less than what it is in reality. Often, in fact, your understatement may appear to be negative when you're actually praising or complimenting someone. Here's an example. Have you ever tasted something that was quite delicious, but when the person asked how it was, you said, "Not bad?" This would typically indicate that the quality is low, but in this case, you're using understatement, so you really mean, "It's delicious." Additionally, after getting an A on a test, you might understate your performance and merely say, "Okay," when someone asks how you did. All right, now let's see if we can use them in our writing.

해석

W Professor: 오늘의 작문 수업을 시작하기에 앞서, 어, 단편 및 장편 소설을 쓰는 경우, 어, 작품의 전반적인 질을 향상시키는데 도움이 되리라고 생각되는 두 가지 문학적 관습을 살펴보고자 해요. 아이러니컬하게도 이 두 가지 문학적 관습은 상반되는 것입니다. 당연하게도 과장과 그것의 반대에 해당되는 축소를 말씀드리는 것입니다.

우선 과장에 대해 살펴보죠. 과장은 우리 모두 사용하는 것입니다. 과장이란 간단히 말해서 무엇인가를 부풀려 말하는 것이죠. 어떤 것이 실제보다 더 크다고 말하는 것이에요. 예를 들어 볼까요? 정말로 배가 고파 본 적이 있으세요?

물론 모두 있으실 것입니다. 음, 하나의 과장은 "배가 고파서 말 한마리도 먹을 수 있겠어."라고 말하는 것이 될 거예요. 물론 실제로는 그럴 수가 없지만 자신의 의도를 전하기 위해 과장을 하는 것이죠. 또한 배우인 친구를 칭찬해 주기 위해 "내가 이제까지 본 연극 가운데 최고였어."라고 말할 수도 있습니다. 아마 그렇지 않았을 텐데… 여러분은, 음, 과장을 한 것뿐이에요. 하지만 친구는 그러한 칭찬에 고마워 할 것입니다.

이제 축소를 살펴보죠. 축소란 무엇일까요? 음, 어떤 것을 실제보다 깎아내려서 말하는 것입니다. 사실 축소는, 여러분이 실제로 누군가를 칭찬하거나 칭송하는 하는 경우, 종종 부정적으로 보일 수도 있어요. 한 가지 예를 들어 드리죠. 꽤 맛있는 음식을 먹었지만 상대방이 음식이 어땠냐고 물었을 때 "나쁘지 않은데?"라고 대답해 본 적이 있나요? 이는 일반적으로 음식의 질이 낮다는 점을 뜻하지만 이 경우 축소를 사용하고 있기 때문에 실제로는 "맛있어."라는 의미를 나타냅니다. 또한 시험에서 A를 받았는데도 누군가 시험이 어땠냐고 물으면 성적을 축소해 "그저 그랬어."라고 말할 수도 있습니다. 좋아요, 이제 작문에서 이 두 가지 요소를 사용할 수 있는지 알아 봅시다.

Organization

1 The lecture is about some literary conventions writers can use in both short stories and novels.

2 Exaggeration is saying that something is greater than it actually is.

3 People use exaggeration to get their points across to other people.

4 Understatement is saying that something is less than it actually is.

5 People use understatement to give compliments or to praise to a person while giving the appearance of saying something negative.

Comparing

Sample Response

Script 🎧 04-04

During the lecture, the professor tells the students about a couple of literary conventions that they can use to improve their creative writing ability. These two conventions are exaggeration and understatement. The professor mentions that they are opposites. First, exaggeration is saying that something is greater than it really is. Some people might say they could eat a horse when they are hungry or that something was the greatest thing they have ever seen. In both cases, they are overstating how they feel. Understatement, on the other hand, is saying that something is less than it is in reality. Two examples of this are saying that something is not bad when it is really delicious and saying that a grade of A on a test or paper is just okay.

해석

강의에서 교수는 학생들에게 창의적인 글쓰기 실력을 향상시키는데 필요한 두 가지 문학적 관습에 대해서 이야기한다. 이 두 가지 문학적 관습은 과장과 축소이다. 교수는 이 두 가지가 서로 반대되는 것이라고 말한다. 우선 과장은 실제보다 부풀려서 말하는 것이다. 어떤 사람들은 배가 고플 때 말도 먹을 수 있겠다고 말할 수도 있고, 혹은 어떤 것이 자신이 본 것 중 최고라고 말할 수도 있다. 이 두 가지 경우 모두 사람들은 자신이 느낀 바를 과장하고 있다. 반면에 축소는 실제보다 깎아내려서 이야기하는 것이다. 이에 대한 두 가지 예는 음식이 정말 맛있는데 나쁘지 않다고 이야기하는 것과 시험이나 보고서 점수로 A를 받고도 그저 그렇다고 이야기하는 것이다.

Unit 47 Botany

Exercise ··· p.121

Listening

Script 🎧 04-05

M Professor: Let's move on to something different. As you are no doubt aware, nature strives to keep everything in balance. This includes both plants and animals. By keeping a perfect balance, no single species can take over and upset the stability of an environment. However, there are some invasive species that do exactly this. The acacia is one such invader.

Acacias are a family of trees and shrubs, most of which are native to Australia. However, some of them have found their way to other countries, where they often dramatically upset the balance of nature. How? Well, there are, uh, two separate ways. First is the fact that acacias' roots are not only strong but also extensive. So they dig deep into the soil and stretch in all directions. Imagine hundreds of hands stretching in every possible direction. Interesting, huh? What this does is it lets the acacia's roots absorb all of the soil's nutrients. This, in turn, starves the other trees nearby, causing them to die from a lack of nutrients.

I can explain the second way acacias harm other species by telling you about the tree called the Australian blackwood, which is a typical member of the acacia family. It can grow to be almost 150 feet in height. Why, you may ask, is this important? Well, the leaves of the acacia help prevent sunlight from ever reaching the ground. This, in turn, causes many smaller plants and trees to die because they don't get exposed to enough sunlight. Unsurprisingly, much effort is currently being put into keeping the acacia out of forests where it is not native.

해석

M Professor: 다른 이야기로 넘어 갑시다. 여러분도 분명히 아시다시피 자연은 모든 것을 균형 상태로 유지시키려 합니다. 여기에는 식물과 동물이 모두 다 해당되죠. 완벽한 균형을 유지함으로써 어느 종도 환경의 안정성을 해치거나 무

너뜨릴 수가 없습니다. 하지만 정확히 그런 일을 해내는 침입종들이 있습니다. 아카시아도 그러한 침입종 중 하나이죠.

아카시아는 교목 및 관목에 해당되며 대부분 호주가 원산지입니다. 하지만 일부가 다른 나라로 옮겨져서 종종 자연의 균형을 크게 훼손시키고 있습니다. 어떻게 그럴까요? 음, 각각, 어, 두 가지, 어, 각각 다른 방법이 있습니다. 첫째, 아카시아의 뿌리는 강할 뿐만 아니라 넓게 퍼지는 편이에요. 그래서 토양 깊숙이 파고 들어가 사방으로 뿌리를 뻗치죠. 수백 개나 되는 뿌리가 사방으로 퍼져 있는 모습을 상상해 보세요. 흥미롭습니다, 그렇죠? 이렇게 되면 아카시아의 뿌리가 토양에 있는 양분을 전부 흡수해 버립니다. 이로 인해 근처의 다른 나무들이 양분을 흡수하지 못해서 영양 부족으로 죽게 됩니다.

아카시아가 다른 종에 해를 미치는 두 번째 방법은 아카시아과에 속하는 전형적인 나무인 호주흑목에 대해 이야기함으로써 설명해 드릴 수 있어요. 호주흑목은 거의 150피트 높이까지 자랄 수 있습니다. 이러한 점이, 만약 질문을 하신다면, 왜 중요할까요? 음, 이 아카시아 나무의 잎 때문에 햇빛이 지면에 닿지 못합니다. 이로써 작은 식물들과 나무들이 충분한 햇빛을 받지 못해서 죽게 되죠. 당연히 아카시아의 자생지가 아닌 곳에서는 현재 아카시아를 제거하기 위한 많은 노력들이 진행되고 있습니다.

Organization

1 The professor discusses how various invasive species like the acacia can disrupt the balance of nature that exists in most environments.

2 The professor mentions that the acacia has an extensive root system that stretches very far.

3 Because the roots absorb so many nutrients from the ground, the other plants and trees cannot get enough of them and therefore die.

4 The professor states that some acacias, like the Australian blackwood, can grow to be very high.

5 The leaves of the high acacia trees prevent sunlight from reaching the ground, so many trees do not get exposed to enough light and then die.

Comparing

Sample Response
Script 🎧 04-06

The professor's lecture mentions that invasive species often disrupt the balance of nature by changing the environment. He cites the acacia family of trees as one example. To begin with, the professor mentions the extensive root system of these trees. He states that they are very far reaching and that they tend to absorb a lot of nutrients from the ground. In fact, they absorb so many nutrients that other plants and trees nearby don't get enough, which causes them to die. He also describes the Australian blackwood, a member of the acacia family. It can be over 150 feet high. Because of this, it has a lot of leaves, which block sunlight from reaching shorter trees and plants near the ground. Since they don't receive any sunlight, they eventually wind up dying.

해석

교수는 강의에서 종종 침입종이 환경을 변화시켜 자연의 균형을 훼손시킨다고 말한다. 그는 한 가지 예로 아카시아과의 나무를 든다. 우선, 교수는 넓게 뻗어가는 아카시아의 뿌리를 언급한다. 그는 아카시아의 뿌리가 상당히 멀리까지 뻗어가기 때문에 토양에서 많은 양분을 흡수하는 경향이 있다고 말한다. 실제로 아카시아가 너무 많은 양분을 흡수하기 때문에 근처의 나무와 식물들이 충분한 양분을 흡수하지 못해서 죽게 된다. 그는 또한 아카시아과에 속하는 호주흑목에 대해 설명한다. 이는 150피트 이상의 높이까지 자랄 수 있다. 이러한 점 때문에 많은 잎을 갖게 되는데, 그로 인해 햇빛이 지면 가까이에 있는 키 작은 나무나 식물에게 닿지 못하게 된다. 이러한 식물들은 햇빛을 받지 못해 결국 죽게 된다.

Unit 48 Education I

Exercise p.122

Listening

Script 🎧 04-07

M Professor: Parents often have to resort to giving rewards to their children to entice them to do various actions. We've already discussed the psychological reasoning behind this. However, strangely enough, there are actually a couple of different reactions by children when they are rewarded. It basically depends upon the child's attitude toward the action for which he is being rewarded. The results may actually, uh, surprise you.

For example, let's consider a young girl who really hates cleaning her room. Out of all of her chores, that's the one she dislikes the most and often refuses to do. As a result of this, her parents finally tell her that they'll give her a reward like, uh, maybe, take her out to her favorite pizza restaurant. The little girl, excited by the prospect of having pizza for dinner, reacts positively and immediately heads to her room to clean it up. That's an example of how rewards can work, you know, positively.

However, let's imagine another little girl the same age as the first one. She is learning the piano and, in fact, absolutely adores playing it. Her parents are really excited about her positive attitude, so they decide to reward her by taking her out to her favorite restaurant. Unfortunately, since they only go there after piano practice, the little girl begins to feel that playing the piano is an obligation and not something fun to do. Over time, she becomes less enamored of playing and eventually quits. In this case, we can quite clearly see how her

being rewarded for something she already enjoyed had a negative effect on her.

해석

M Professor: 부모들은 자녀들로부터 다양한 행동을 유도하기 위해 종종 보상을 주는 방법을 이용합니다. 그 이면에 존재하는 심리적 이유에 대해서는 이미 살펴보았어요. 하지만 이상하게도 보상을 받은 아이들이 각기 다른 두 가지 반응을 나타내기도 합니다. 이는 기본적으로 보상을 받는 행동에 대한 자녀의 태도에 달려 있습니다. 결과를 들으면, 어, 놀라실 수도 있을 거예요.

예를 들어 방 정리를 정말로 싫어하는 여자 아이가 있다고 가정해 보죠. 여러 가지 해야 할 일 가운데 방 정리를 가장 싫어하며 종종 이를 거부하는 경우도 있습니다. 그 결과 부모는 결국 아이에게 아이가 가장 좋아하는, 어, 피자 레스토랑에 데려가겠다는 것과 같은 보상을 해 주겠다고 말을 합니다. 아이는 저녁으로 피자를 먹을 생각에 들떠 긍정적인 반응을 보이고 곧바로 방으로 가서 정리를 하죠. 이는 아시다시피 보상이 긍정적으로 작용하는 사례입니다.

하지만 첫 번째 아이와 똑같은 나이의 또 다른 여자 아이를 가정해 보죠. 아이는 피아노를 배우고 있는데, 실제로 피아노를 치는 것을 너무나 좋아합니다. 부모는 그녀의 긍정적인 태도에 정말로 기분이 좋아서 그녀가 가장 좋아하는 식당으로 데려감으로써 아이에게 보상을 해 주겠다고 결심을 해요. 안타깝게도 피아노 연습이 끝난 후에야 그곳에 갈 수 있기 때문에 아이는 피아노 연습이 의무적인 것이며 즐길 수 있는 것이 아니라고 생각하기 시작합니다. 시간이 지나면서 소녀는 피아노 치기를 점점 싫어하게 되고 결국 그만두게 되죠. 이러한 경우를 통해 이미 아이가 좋아하던 것에 보상이 주어지는 경우 아이에게 어떻게 부정적인 효과가 일어나는지 확실히 알 수가 있습니다.

Organization

1 The professor focuses on how children react differently to rewards depending upon the situation.
2 The parents offer to take their daughter to her favorite pizza restaurant if she cleans her room.
3 The daughter becomes excited about going out for pizza, so she immediately goes to clean her room.
4 Every time the girl finishes piano practice, her parents reward her by taking her out to her favorite restaurant.
5 Even though she enjoys the piano, she feels playing it is an obligation; otherwise, she will never get to go out to her favorite restaurant.

Comparing

Sample Response
Script 🎧 04-08

The professor says that children react differently to rewards depending upon the reason they are getting them. In his first example, he mentions a little girl who hates cleaning her room. Her parents convince her to do so by offering her a reward. They will take her out to her favorite pizza restaurant. The girl reacts positively and goes to clean her room in anticipation of getting to eat pizza. The second example is about a girl who enjoys playing the piano. However, her parents mistakenly start rewarding her after piano practice by taking her to her favorite restaurant. Because that's the only time she ever goes there, playing the piano becomes a burden, so she starts to dislike playing it and eventually quits. This is an example of a reward with a negative result.

해석

교수는 아이들이 보상을 받는 이유에 따라 보상에 대해 다르게 반응한다고 말한다. 첫 번째 예에서 그는 방 정리를 싫어하는 여자 아이를 언급한다. 아이의 부모는 아이에게 보상을 제안함으로써 방 정리를 하도록 설득한다. 그들은 아이가 가장 좋아하는 피자 가게에 아이를 데리고 갈 것이다. 아이는 긍정적으로 반응해서 피자를 먹을 기대감으로 방 정리를 한다. 두 번째 예는 피아노 치기를 좋아하는 여자 아이에 관한 것이다. 하지만 부모는 잘못 생각하고 아이에게 피아노 연습 후 아이가 가장 좋아하는 식당에 데려가겠다는 보상을 제안한다. 아이가 그곳에 갈 수 있는 유일한 시간이 그때뿐이기 때문에 피아노 연습은 의무적인 것이 되어서 아이는 피아노를 싫어하게 되고 결국 그만두게 된다. 이는 부정적인 결과를 가져오는 보상의 예이다.

Unit 49 Earth Science

Exercise ·· p.123

Listening

Script 🎧 04-09

W Professor: Okay, so that concludes my lecture on dinosaurs and their natural habitats. Now, let's move to one of the Earth's greatest mysteries. It is, of course, what caused the dinosaurs to go extinct. After all, these were enormous creatures, much larger than anything living now. They were so strong and lived everywhere. So . . . what made them suddenly die? There are a couple of major theories on dinosaur extinction. Let me expand upon them for you.

The first is that there was a large meteor or asteroid that hit the Earth. Some scientists have even, in their opinions, pinpointed the exact places where these celestial objects struck the planet. Anyway, what happened, they say, is that after the strike, lots of dirt and debris were thrown into the atmosphere. There was so much dust that it actually blocked the sun. This cooled the planet, and with a lack of sunlight, caused most plant life to die. The herbivorous dinosaurs, unable to eat, first died, and then the carnivorous ones followed them down the path to extinction.

The second theory is that a supervolcano, that is, one hundreds of times more powerful than the Krakatoa

explosion, erupted and filled the atmosphere with carbon dioxide. This caused a rapid onset of the greenhouse effect. Why would this kill the dinosaurs, which were essentially giant reptiles and should like hot weather? Well, reptile eggs are very vulnerable and sensitive to heat. One thing that often happens in extreme heat is that the sex of the unborn reptile changes from female to male. Thus, there was a proliferation of males, who couldn't reproduce. Over time, the dinosaurs all quickly died out because of this.

해석

W Professor: 좋아요, 이것으로 공룡과 공룡의 자연 서식지에 대한 강의를 마무리하죠. 이제 지구의 가장 큰 미스터리 중 하나에 대한 이야기로 넘어갑시다. 바로, 당연하게도, 공룡이 멸종한 이유입니다. 어찌되었든 이들은 크기가 엄청난 생물이며 현존하는 어떤 동물보다도 훨씬 더 크기가 컸어요. 매우 강했고 어디에서나 살고 있었고요. 그런데… 왜 갑자기 소멸했을까요? 공룡의 멸종에 관한 두 가지 주요 이론이 존재합니다. 이에 관해 자세히 살펴보도록 하죠.

첫 번째는 커다란 운석이나 소행성이 지구와 충돌했다는 것입니다. 일부 과학자들은, 그들 생각에, 이러한 천체들이 지구와 충돌한 정확한 지점을 찾아내기도 했습니다. 어쨌든 그들의 설명에 따르면 충돌 후 엄청난 양의 먼지 및 잔해가 대기에 유입되었어요. 먼지가 너무 많아서 실제로 햇빛이 차단되었죠. 이로 인해 지구가 차가워졌고, 햇빛이 부족해지자 대부분의 식물들이 죽었습니다. 먹이를 먹을 수 없었던 초식 공룡들이 먼저 죽었고, 이후 육식 공룡이 그 뒤를 이어 멸종했습니다.

두 번째 이론은 크라카토아 화산 폭발보다 백배나 강력한 초화산이 분출해서 대기가 이산화탄소로 가득찼다는 것이에요. 이로 인해 급속한 온실 효과가 진행되었습니다. 본질적으로 공룡은 거대 파충류로서 따뜻한 날씨를 좋아할 텐데 왜 그러한 점 때문에 공룡이 죽게 되었을까요? 음, 파충류의 알은 열에 매우 취약하고 민감합니다. 무더운 날씨에서는 아직 태어나지 않은 파충류의 성이 암컷에서 수컷으로 종종 바뀌어요. 따라서 수컷의 수가 많아졌는데, 수컷은 번식을 할 수가 없었죠. 시간이 지나면서 이러한 점 때문에 공룡은 빠르게 소멸했습니다.

Organization

1 The professor describes two of the more popular theories on why the dinosaurs became extinct.

2 After an object from space hit the Earth, lots of dirt and debris were thrown into the air, which decreased the amount of sunlight getting through to the Earth.

3 Because there was less sunlight, plants died, so herbivorous dinosaurs no longer had a food source and died, and then the carnivores died soon afterward.

4 After a supervolcano erupted, it spewed carbon dioxide into the atmosphere, which caused global warming to occur rapidly.

5 The dinosaur eggs reacted badly to the heat, so more males were born, which meant that the dinosaurs could not reproduce.

Sample Response

Script 🎧 04-10

The professor states that dinosaurs once ruled the Earth but suddenly became extinct. She gives two different theories to explain their disappearance. The first is that a meteor or asteroid struck the Earth. She even says that some scientists know where it hit. The strike sent dirt up into the atmosphere, which hid the planet from the sun. It got colder, and there was no sunlight, so all the plants died. Without food sources, the dinosaurs all died. The second theory is that there was an eruption of a supervolcano. This filled the air with carbon dioxide, which caused the greenhouse effect to start on the Earth. When subjected to heat, lizard and dinosaur eggs change. Females in eggs become males. So there were no more females being born, which meant that the dinosaurs couldn't reproduce.

해석

교수는 공룡들이 한때 지구를 지배했지만 갑자기 멸종했다고 말한다. 그녀는 공룡의 소멸에 관한 두 가지 이론을 소개한다. 첫 번째는 운석 또는 소행성이 지구와 충돌했다는 것이다. 그녀는 일부 과학자들이 충돌 위치까지 알고 있다고 말한다. 충돌로 인해 대기에 먼지가 퍼져나갔고 이로 인해 지구가 햇빛을 받지 못하게 되었다. 기온이 내려갔으며 햇빛이 사라지자 모든 식물이 죽었다. 먹이가 없어진 공룡들도 모두 사라졌다. 두 번째 이론은 초화산 폭발이 일어났다는 것이다. 이로 인해 대기가 이산화탄소로 가득 차게 되었고 지구에서 온실 효과가 나타나기 시작했다. 열에 취약한 도마뱀과 공룡의 알에 변화가 일어났다. 알 속에 있던 암컷이 수컷으로 바뀌었다. 따라서 더 이상 암컷이 태어나지 않았고 공룡은 번식을 할 수 없었다.

Unit 50 Ecology

Exercise p.124

Listening

Script 🎧 04-11

M Professor: You all saw the news about that huge forest fire out in the national park, didn't you? Yeah, it looks like hundreds of acres have burned to the ground. It's too bad, isn't it? Actually, it's not. No, I'm not kidding. I'm one-hundred-percent serious. Contrary to common belief, fires can be very helpful to forests. There are several reasons why, so let me cover a few.

First, some trees cannot spread their seeds without heat. For example, the pine cones, which are where the seeds are, of some pine trees will simply not open unless they are subjected to extreme heat. In addition,

redwoods, you know, those giants in California, spread their seeds after forest fires, too. Some trees need fire to enable their seeds to spread. Without the spreading of their seeds, there is no way for these trees to increase in numbers. So one tree may die, but many more are born from its sacrifice.

A second example is that forest fires actually help rejuvenate forests. When they burn trees and bushes to the ground, the fires often get rid of old, weak trees. Additionally, by burning trees, the fires are providing the ground with nutrients. What then happens is that, a couple of years later, the places which the fire passed through are already full of new, young, strong plant life. Not only that but the diversity of the forest also becomes greater immediately after a fire, as every tree and plant have an equal opportunity to thrive since one species hasn't had enough time yet to crowd out the others.

해석

M Professor: 여러분 모두 국립 공원에서 발생한 대규모 산불의 소식을 접했을 거예요, 그렇죠? 네, 수백 에이커의 면적이 잿더미로 변한 것으로 보입니다. 매우 안타까운 일이죠, 그렇지 않나요? 실제로는 그렇지가 않습니다. 아니에요, 농담이 아닙니다. 정말 진심으로 하는 말이에요. 일반적인 생각과 반대로 산불은 숲에 매우 유익할 수 있어요. 여러 가지 이유가 있는데, 몇 가지만 살펴보도록 하죠.

우선, 일부 나무들은 열기가 없으면 씨를 퍼뜨릴 수가 없습니다. 예를 들어 소나무의 씨앗이 들어있는 솔방울은 극심한 열기에 노출되지 않는 경우 벌어지지 않아요. 또한 캘리포니아에 존재하는 커다란 나무인 삼나무 역시 산불이 발생한 후 씨를 퍼뜨리죠. 몇몇 나무들은 씨를 퍼뜨리기 위해 불을 필요로 합니다. 씨를 퍼뜨리지 않고서는 이러한 나무들이 개체수를 증가시킬 수 있는 방법이 없어요. 따라서 한 그루의 나무는 죽을 수도 있지만 그러한 희생으로 훨씬 더 많은 나무들이 자라나게 됩니다.

두 번째 예는 산불이 실제로 숲을 회복시킨다는 점입니다. 산불로 수목과 관목들이 타 버리면 종종 오래되거나 약한 나무들이 사라집니다. 또한 산불은 나무를 태워 토양에 양분을 공급해 주어요. 그렇게 되면 몇 년 후 산불이 훑고 간 자리에 새로 자라난, 어리고 튼튼한 식물들이 가득하게 됩니다. 뿐만 아니라 산불이 난 직후에는 한 종이 다른 종을 압도할 수 있을 정도의 충분한 시간이 없기 때문에 모든 나무와 식물들에게 번성할 수 있는 동일한 기회가 주어져서 숲의 다양성이 증대됩니다.

Organization

1 The professor is explaining the reasons why forest fires are actually beneficial to some forests.

2 The professor says that without forest fires, some pine cones would never open to spread their seeds, which enables new pine trees to grow.

3 Many trees need forest fires for their seeds to spread, so even though the fires kill some trees, more can grow after the fire.

4 According to the professor, forest fires kill many old and weak trees and help rejuvenate forests by providing nutrients for the soil.

5 After forest fires, there are many strong, young trees, and the forests are more diverse because one species has not yet taken over.

Sample Response

Script 🎧 04-12

The professor claims that, opposite what most people believe, forest fires are not totally bad. He gives two reasons for this. The first one he mentions is that many trees—pine trees, for instance—cannot spread their seeds without very high heat. The reason is that their pine cones won't open until they're subjected to something extremely hot. So while the forest fire may kill the tree, it can still spread countless seeds to allow new pine trees to grow. The second example cited is that forest fires help reinvigorate forests by burning down old, weak trees. After the fire ends, new, young, strong trees start growing. In addition, since all the trees have an equal chance to grow afterward, the forest is more diverse, which the professor feels is positive.

해석

교수는 대부분의 사람들이 생각하는 것과 반대로 산불이 완전히 해로운 것은 아니라고 주장한다. 이에 대해 그는 두 가지 이유를 제시한다. 그가 언급한 첫 번째 이유는, 예컨대 소나무와 같은 많은 나무들은 고열 없이 씨앗을 퍼뜨릴 수 없다는 점에 있다. 그 이유는 솔방울들이 고온에 노출되지 않는 이상 벌어지지 않기 때문이다. 따라서 산불로 인해 나무는 죽을 수 있지만 수많은 씨앗이 퍼져서 새로운 소나무들이 자라날 수 있다. 두 번째 예는 산불이 오래 되고 약한 나무를 태워 버림으로써 숲의 회복을 돕는다는 것이다. 산불이 꺼진 후에는 어리고 튼튼한 나무들이 새로 자라나기 시작한다. 또한 산불이 난 후에는 모든 나무들이 성장할 수 있는 동일한 기회를 갖기 때문에 숲의 다양성이 증가하는데, 교수는 이를 긍정적인 것으로 생각한다.

Unit 51 Geography

Exercise p.125

Listening

Script 🎧 04-13

W Professor: One of the most important aspects of geography is the ability to read a map and then to apply that knowledge to a practical purpose. While most people think it's rather simple, on the contrary, it's not. As an example, think about the distance between two points on a globe or map as compared to the distance between the same two points in reality. They are, in most cases, quite different.

Take a look at this globe . . . Let's say that you wanted to go from New York City to London. If I measure the distance with this string here . . . That's the distance, right? But what route do airplanes follow? The straight one? Not at all. They follow the curvature of the Earth, like this . . . so that they can take a much shorter trip in reality. You can see clearly that the straight-line distance between two places on a globe doesn't always equal that in reality.

Okay, now let's look at this map at the distance between this point . . . here and this point over . . . here. Can everyone see? Good. If I measure the distance according to the map's scale, it's about 150 miles as the crow flies. Not too far, right? But we're talking about actual distance. Let's consider the geographical features involved. Here's a big lake. Oops. We can't drive through it. We'll have to drive around it. And these mountains aren't flat of course. Driving up and down them on a winding road adds even more distance. So . . . The distances on a map and in reality are clearly different with actual distances always being longer than ones shown on maps.

해석

W Professor: 지리학에서 가장 중요한 것 중 하나는 지도를 읽고 그러한 지식을 실용적인 목적으로 사용하는 능력입니다. 대부분의 사람들은 이를 비교적 간단한 것으로 생각하지만 사실 그렇지가 않죠. 예를 들어 지구의나 지도상의 두 점 사이의 거리를 실제의 두 점 간의 거리와 비교해 보세요. 대부분의 경우 상당한 차이가 납니다.

이 지구의를 보시면⋯ 여러분이 뉴욕에서 런던으로 가려고 한다고 해 보죠. 이 줄로 거리를 재어 보면⋯ 거리가 나옵니다, 그렇죠? 하지만 비행기가 어떤 경로를 따르나요? 직선 경로인가요? 전혀 그렇지 않습니다. 비행기는 이렇게 지구의 만곡을 따라 움직이는데⋯ 실제로 훨씬 더 짧은 경로를 택하기 위해서죠. 지구의의 두 점 사이의 직선 거리가 항상 실제와 동일한 것은 아니라는 점을 분명히 알 수가 있습니다.

좋아요, 그럼 이제 지도상에서⋯ 여기 이 점과⋯ 여기 이 점 사이의 거리를 살펴볼게요. 다들 보이죠? 좋아요. 지도의 축적에 따라 이 거리를 측정해 보면 최단 거리로 약 150마일 정도 됩니다. 그리 멀지 않은 거리입니다, 그렇죠? 하지만 우리는 실제 거리에 대해 말하고 있어요. 이제 그와 관련된 지형적 특성들을 살펴봅시다. 여기에 커다란 호수가 있어요. 이런. 차를 몰고 호수를 지나갈 수는 없죠. 호수를 돌아가야 할 거예요. 그리고 이 산들도 물론 평평하지 않습니다. 구불구불한 길을 오르고 내려가며 운전을 하면 거리는 훨씬 더 늘어나죠. 따라서⋯ 지도상의 거리와 실제 거리는 분명한 차이를 나타내며 실제 거리는 지도상의 거리보다 항상 더 깁니다.

Organization

1 The professor emphasizes that the distances measured on globes and maps are always different from reality.

2 The professor shows the class the distance between New York City and London.

3 She concludes that distances as measured on globes and in reality are different.

4 The professor measures the distance on a map between two points but then shows how the geographical features involved will make it a longer trip.

5 The professor states that actual distances are always longer than those listed on maps.

Comparing

Sample Response

Script 🎧 04-14

The professor tells the class that measuring distances is not always accurate because distances measured on globes and maps are different from reality. She first discusses distances on a globe. She uses a string to measure the distance from New York City to London. She says that it is the straight-line distance. But she says that airplanes take different routes, ones which follow the curvature of the Earth, so the trip will actually wind up being shorter in reality. She then tells the class to observe a map. She measures the distance between two points at 150 miles. However, she then points out the geography and mentions that a straight trip is impossible. Instead, they have to go around a lake and up and down mountains, which will make their trip longer.

해석

교수는 학생들에게 지구의 및 지도상에서 측정되는 거리가 실제와는 다르기 때문에 거리 측정이 언제나 정확한 것은 아니라고 말한다. 그녀는 먼저 지구의의 거리에 대해 말한다. 그녀는 실을 사용해 뉴욕에서 런던까지의 거리를 잰다. 그녀는 이것이 직선거리라고 말한다. 하지만 비행기는 지구의 만곡을 따르는 다른 경로를 택하기 때문에 실제로는 경로가 더 짧을 것이라고 말한다. 그런 다음 그녀는 학생들에게 지도를 보라고 말한다. 그녀는 150마일 떨어진 두 지점 사이의 거리를 잰다. 하지만 그녀는 지형을 지적하며 직선 코스가 불가능하다고 말한다. 대신 호수를 돌아가야 하고 산을 오르내려야 하는데, 이로써 실제 코스는 더 길어지게 된다.

Unit 52 Marketing I

Exercise p.126

Listening

Script 🎧 04-15

M Professor: Have you ever considered how much thought goes into the item display process at various stores? Quite a lot, to tell the truth. Stores are always interested in the impressions they make on their customers, so they try to display all of their products according to what various research and studies tell them.

One such example of this is the fact that many stores display their most expensive items in the front. They either do that, or they display their expensive items more prominently on shelves. What is the purpose of this? It's simple really. Many people associate high costs with quality. So when they look into a store and notice the high prices of its products, they immediately associate that store with quality products. This, in turn, helps bolster the company's image with its customers. Pretty ingenious, huh?

Then what about cheaper products? Stores typically put them in harder-to-find places for a couple of reasons. The first is that they don't, as a general rule, want to be associated with low prices. These symbolize low quality to many shoppers. The second reason is actually somewhat more interesting. Many people love shopping for bargains. So when a shopper has to look around a bit to find a cheaper product, he feels more of a sense of achievement than he would have had the item been right in front of him. In his mind, he worked hard to find that lower-priced item. And according to studies, he's more likely to purchase the product that he looked so hard for.

해석

M Professor: 여러 매장에서 상품 진열 과정에 얼마나 많은 숙고가 이루어지는지 생각해 본 적이 있나요? 사실대로 말하면 엄청난 숙고가 이루어집니다. 매장들은 항상 고객들에게 주는 인상에 관심을 기울이기 때문에 다양한 연구 및 조사 결과에 따라 모든 제품들을 진열하려고 하죠.

이에 대한 한 가지 예는 많은 매장들이 가장 비싼 제품을 앞쪽에 진열한다는 것이에요. 매장들은 이렇게 하거나, 아니면 가장 고가의 제품들을 진열대에서 가장 잘 보이도록 진열합니다. 그 목적이 무엇일까요? 사실 간단합니다. 많은 사람들이 높은 가격을 품질과 연관시켜요. 그래서 매장 안을 들여다보고 제품의 높은 가격을 보게 되면 곧바로 해당 매장과 고품질 제품을 연관시키게 됩니다. 이는 또 다시 소비자들에게 해당 업체의 이미지를 좋게 만듭니다. 상당히 기발하죠?

그러면 보다 저렴한 제품들은 어떨까요? 매장들은 보통 이러한 제품들을 두 가지 이유에서 찾기 힘든 곳에 둡니다. 첫 번째 이유는 대체적으로 자신과 낮은 가격이 연관되는 것을 원하지 않기 때문이에요. 이는 많은 쇼핑객들에게 종종 낮은 품질을 상징하죠. 두 번째 이유가 사실 더 흥미롭습니다. 많은 사람들이 값싼 물건을 사는 것을 좋아합니다. 그래서 한 쇼핑객이 약간 둘러보고 보다 싼 제품을 찾는 경우 바로 눈앞에 제품이 있는 경우보다 더 큰 성취감을 느끼게 되죠. 자신이 열심히 노력해서 보다 저렴한 제품을 찾았다고 생각하는 것이에요. 그리고 연구에 따르면 열심히 노력해 찾아낸 제품을 구매할 가능성이 더 높습니다.

Organization

1 The professor's main point is that there are psychological reasons behind the locations that stores put their expensive and cheap products.

2 Stores typically put their expensive items at the front or display them prominently on shelves.

3 According to the professor, people associate price with quality, so they will think a store sells quality items if its products are expensive.

4 Stores often put their cheaper-priced items in harder-to-find places.

5 Stores hide their cheaper products to keep people from thinking that they sell low-quality products and to give people a feeling of accomplishment when, after looking around, they find a low-priced object.

Comparing

Sample Response

Script 🎧 04-16

During his lecture, the professor emphasizes that stores put expensive and inexpensive products in different places for psychological reasons. First, he discusses expensive products. Stores usually put them in the front or make sure they are displayed very obviously so that people can see them clearly. The reason is that people believe expensive items are higher in quality, so they will have a positive image of a store selling expensive products. The second explanation deals with cheaper products. Stores usually make them harder to find. First, they don't wish to be associated with low-quality products since those are what people often think of as inexpensive goods. Second, if a person looks hard for something and then finds it, he is more likely not to waste his effort and will therefore probably purchase that object.

해석

교수는 강의에서 매장들이 심리적인 이유로 고가의 제품과 저가의 제품을 서로 다른 위치에 놓는다는 점을 강조한다. 우선 그는 고가의 제품들에 대해 논의한다. 매장들은 보통 고가의 제품들을 앞쪽에 진열하거나 또는 사람들이 잘 볼 수 있는 곳에 진열한다. 그 이유는 사람들이 고가의 제품의 품질이 더 좋다고 생각해서 고가의 제품을 파는 매장에 대해 긍정적인 이미지를 갖게 되기 때문이다. 두 번째 설명은 보다 저렴한 제품들에 관한 것이다. 매장들은 보통 저가의 제품을 찾기 힘든 곳에 진열한다. 첫째, 사람들은 저렴한 제품을 품질이 낮은 제품으로 생각하기 때문에 매장들은 품질이 낮은 제품과 자신이 연관되는 것을 원하지 않는다. 둘째, 어떤 사람이 열심히 노력해서 무언가를 찾게 되면 가급적 자신의 노력을 헛되이 만들지 않으려고 하지 않을 것이기 때문에 해당 물건을 구매하게 될 것이다.

Unit 53 Zoology I

Exercise ·· p.127

Listening

Script 🎧 04-17

W Professor: We got rain for more than a week recently, and it resulted in flooding. Several streams and a river overflowed their banks. I'm sure some of you wondered what happened to all of the fish caught in the flood. Well, some certainly got displaced from where they live. But most of them will find their way home again. Interestingly, contrary to what most people think, fish often benefit from flooding.

One major benefit concerns food. Insects such as mayflies and dragonflies live in water during their larva stages. Well, the larvae get displaced from their hiding places during floods, so fish can easily find and eat them. In addition, when rising water gets on land, lots of insects get cast into the water. This includes beetles and ants. So too do spiders and worms get swept into the water. As a result, fish can gorge themselves on food during floods. Many fish actually become larger during floods since they eat so well then.

A second benefit of floods concerns fish habitats. Fast-moving water can deepen holes in streams that fish like to hide in, which gives them bigger habitats. It can widen parts of streams and rivers as well. Large rocks can be dislodged and washed into the water. Fish often hide or seek shelter from the sun beneath these rocks. Finally, biological matter, such as trees, branches, and small plants, gets washed into the water. They provide more places for fish to hide and to lay their eggs. So as you can see, floods aren't too much of a problem for fish. In fact, they provide advantages to fish.

해석

W Professor: 최근 일주일 넘게 비가 내려서 그 결과로 홍수가 발생했어요. 몇몇 시내와 강에서 물이 둑을 넘쳐 흘렀죠. 틀림없이 여러분 중 일부는 홍수가 발생하면 물고기들에게 어떤 일이 일어나는지 궁금해 할 것 같군요. 음, 분명 일부는 자신이 사는 곳을 벗어나기도 합니다. 하지만 대부분은 다시 살던 곳으로 돌아올 거예요. 흥미롭게도, 대부분의 사람들이 생각하는 것과 반대로, 물고기들은 종종 홍수로 이득을 얻습니다.

한 가지 주요한 혜택은 먹이와 관련이 있어요. 하루살이 및 잠자리와 같은 곤충들은 유충일 때 물속에서 삽니다. 음, 홍수 기간에는 유충들이 은신처에서 나오게 되는데, 그러면 물고기들이 이들을 쉽게 발견해서 먹을 수가 있어요. 게다가 수위가 올라가 물이 육지에 닿으면 많은 곤충들이 물에 쓸려서 물속으로 들어옵니다. 여기에는 무당벌레와 개미가 포함되죠. 거미와 지렁이도 마찬가지로 물속으로 쓸려 들어옵니다. 그 결과 물고기들은 홍수 기간 동안 포식을 할 수가 있어요. 많은 물고기들이 실제로 홍수 시기에 잘 먹어서 몸집이 커집니다.

홍수의 두 번째 혜택은 물고기의 서식지와 관련이 있어요. 유속이 빠른 물 때문에 시내에서 물고기가 숨기 좋아하는 구멍이 깊어질 수 있는데, 이로써 서식지가 더 커집니다. 또한 시내와 강의 일부가 넓어질 수도 있어요. 커다란 바위가 제자리를 벗어나 물에 떠내려갈 갈 수도 있습니다. 물고기들은 종종 햇빛을 피해 이러한 바위 밑에 숨거나 피신을 하죠. 마지막으로 생물학적인 물질들이, 예컨대 나무, 나뭇가지, 그리고 작은 식물들이 물에 떠내려갑니다. 이로써 물고기가 몸을 숨기고 알을 낳을 수 있는 장소가 더 많아져요. 따라서 아시다시피 홍수는 물고기들에게 그다지 큰 문제가 되지 않습니다. 실제로는 물고기들에게 이점을 제공해 주죠.

Organization

1 The lecture is about two benefits to fish that happen during floods.
2 They eat insect larvae as well as land animals such as beetles, ants, spiders, and worms.
3 Fish can gorge themselves on food during floods.
4 Some fish habitats become deeper and bigger, which benefits fish.
5 They can hide in them and lay their eggs in them.

Comparing

Sample Response
Script 🎧 04-18

The professor lectures to the students about what happens to fish during floods. The professor remarks that most people don't realize that fish can benefit during floods. According to the professor, the first benefit concerns food. She states that fish can eat a lot during floods. The reason is that insect larvae that hide in water are washed away, so fish can eat them. In addition, animals that live on land such as spiders, ants, worms, and beetles get swept into the water. There, fish can find and eat them. The second benefit the professor mentions concerns habitats. Floodwaters make holes that fish hide in deeper and bigger. They also put material such as trees, branches, and plants in the water. Fish can hide in this material and lay their eggs in it.

해석
교수는 학생들에게 홍수 발생시 물고기들에게 일어나는 일에 대해 강의를 한다. 교수는 물고기가 홍수 기간에 이득을 볼 수 있다는 점을 대부분의 사람들이 모른다고 언급한다. 교수에 의하면 첫 번째 혜택은 먹이와 관련된 것이다. 그녀는 물고기들이 홍수 기간 동안 먹이를 많이 먹을 수 있다고 말한다. 그 이유는 물속에서 몸을 숨기고 있던 유충들이 물에 쓸려 나와서 물고기들이 이들을 잡아먹기 때문이다. 또한 거미, 개미, 지렁이, 그리고 무당벌레와 같이 지상에서 사는 동물들이 물에 떠내려간다. 이때 물고기들이 이들을 발견해서 잡아먹을 수 있다. 교수가 언급한 두 번째 혜택은 서식지와 관련된 것이다. 홍수의 물로 물고기들이 몸을 숨기는 구멍이 더 깊어지고 커진다. 또한 나무, 나뭇가지, 그리고 식물 같은 물체들이 물속으로 들어오게 된다. 물고기들은 이러한 물체들 안에 몸을 숨기고 그곳에서 알을 낳을 수도 있다.

Unit 54 Advertising

Exercise p.128

Listening

Script 🎧 04-19

M Professor: There are a wide variety of advertisements that businesses use to reach their customers. One of them is broadcast advertisements. These are essentially ads placed on television or on the radio. Many people claim that the Internet and print media are better uses of financial resources. I, however, disagree with these individuals. If you ask me, broadcast advertisements offer some powerful advantages. Let me tell you a couple of them right now.

I'll start by talking about radio advertisements. These days, the majority of people listen to the radio when they are doing other activities. For instance, they might be driving their cars or riding in them as they go to work. They might also be doing chores around the house. These are not the most stimulating activities. Therefore, people listening to the radio are more receptive to advertisements. Because radio ads are generally not expensive, advertisers can ensure that the same people hear their ads multiple times. This enables people to become familiar with, uh, and more interested in, the products that are being advertised.

What about television advertisements? Well, an important advantage of TV ads is that they have the potential to reach millions of potential customers at the same time. Sure, uh, TV is declining in popularity. But there are still some TV shows and special events, especially sports and entertainment programs, that millions of people watch at the same time. As a result, companies try to create visually and auditorily stimulating ads that attract the attention of people. In some cases, successful TV ads have helped companies attract large numbers of new customers. And that is exactly what advertisers are hoping for.

해석
M Professor: 기업체가 고객에게 다가가기 위해 사용할 수 있는 매우 다양한 광고들이 존재합니다. 그중 하나가 방송 광고이죠. 이는 기본적으로 텔레비전이나 라디오에서 이루어지는 광고입니다. 많은 사람들은 인터넷 및 인쇄물 광고가 자금을 더 잘 활용하는 방법이라고 주장합니다. 하지만 저는 그러한 사람들의 말에 동의하지 않아요. 제게 물으신다면 방송 광고는 몇 가지 강력한 이점을 제공해 줍니다. 이제 그러한 이점 중 두 가지를 알려 드리죠.

라디오 광고에 대한 이야기로 시작해 보겠습니다. 요즘 대다수의 사람들이 다른 일을 하면서 라디오를 듣습니다. 예를 들어 운전을 하고 있을 수도 있고, 차를 타고 출근 중일 수도 있습니다. 또한 집에서 집안일을 하고 있을 수도 있죠. 이러한 일들은 크게 자극적인 활동이 아니에요. 따라서 라디오를 듣는 사람들은 광고를 보다 잘 받아드립니다. 라디오 광고는 일반적으로 비싸지 않기 때문에 광고주들은 동일한 사람들이 자신의 광고를 여러 차례 들을 수 있도록 할 수가 있어요. 이로써 사람들은 광고의 제품에 친숙해지고, 어, 더 많은 관심을 갖게 됩니다.

텔레비전 광고는 어떨까요? 음, TV 광고의 중요한 이점은 동시에 수백만 명의 잠재 고객들에게 다가갈 수 있는 잠재력이 존재한다는 점입니다. 그래요, 어, TV의 인기는 줄어들고 있어요. 하지만 여전히 수백만 명의 사람들이 동시에 시청하는 TV 프로그램과 특별 이벤트 방송, 특히 스포츠 및 연예 오락 프로그램이 존재합니다. 그 결과 기업들은 사람들의 주의를 끌어 모으는, 시각적으로 그리고 청각적으로 자극적인 광고를 만들려고 노력합니다. 일부 경우, 성공적인 TV 광고로 인해 기업들이 다수의 신규 고객들을 유치하고 있습니다. 이는 정확히 광고주들이 바라는 것이죠.

Organization

1 The lecture is about two advantages of broadcast advertisements.
2 They listen to the radio when they are doing other activities, such as driving or doing household chores.
3 They are receptive to these advertisements.
4 They can reach millions of people at the same time.
5 They try to create visually and auditorily stimulating ads that attract the attention of people.

Comparing

Sample Response

Script 🎧 04-20

In his lecture, the professor talks about advertisements. He says he believes broadcast advertisements, which air on television and the radio, have many advantages. He then proceeds to describe two of them. The first type he discusses is radio advertisements. The professor points out that people often listen to the radio when doing other activities, including driving, riding in cars, and doing chores. As a result, they are receptive to information broadcast on advertisements. They also hear these ads many times, so they can become familiar with some products. Next, the professor discusses television advertisements. He notes that sometimes millions of people watch the same show, so some ads can reach those people simultaneously. That is why companies try to make ads that appeal to people's senses of sight and hearing.

해석

강의에서 교수는 광고에 대해 이야기한다. 그는 텔레비전과 라디오에서 나오는 방송 광고에 많은 장점이 있다고 생각한다고 말한다. 그 후 두 가지 장점을 설명하기 시작한다. 그가 언급하는 첫 번째 유형은 라디오 광고이다. 교수는 사람들이 운전을 하고, 차량에 탑승하고, 집안일을 하는 등의 기타 활동을 할 때 종종 라디오를 듣는다고 주장한다. 따라서 그들은 광고에서 나오는 정보를 잘 받아드린다. 또한 이러한 광고를 여러 번 듣기 때문에 제품에 친숙해질 수 있다. 다음으로

교수는 텔레비전 광고를 언급한다. 그는 때때로 수백만 명의 사람들이 동일한 프로그램을 시청하기 때문에 광고가 그러한 사람들에게 동시에 다가갈 수 있다고 주장한다. 이는 기업들이 사람들의 시각과 청각에 호소하는 광고를 만들려고 노력하는 이유가 된다.

Unit 55 Geology

Exercise ······· p.129

Listening

Script 🎧 04-21

M Professor: Take a look at this picture . . . and this one . . . and this one . . . These pictures show cliffs. What is a cliff? Hmm . . . It's basically a vertical or nearly vertical expanse of rock. Cliffs can be tens or even hundreds of meters high. They also usually have scree at their bottoms. In case you don't know, scree is an accumulation of stones at the bottom of a cliff. It forms from the cliff itself as the cliff is created. Cliffs can be found near water, in mountainous areas, by rivers, and even underwater. I'd like to discuss two ways they can be formed now.

The first is through the action of water and erosion. Most cliffs formed this way are along the shore of an ocean or a sea. Remember that not all shorelines are beaches. In many cases, mountains, hills, or just rocks go all the way to the sea. In these cases, waves constantly beat against them. Over time, this continuous exposure to water breaks down the rock. It washes away the softer rock, leaving only the hardest rock. This typically results in sheer vertical cliffs being formed.

A second way that cliffs form is due to the movement of glaciers. Recall that glaciers are enormous sheets of snow and ice packed together. Glaciers can move both forward and backward. As they do so, their massive weight tends to destroy anything in their paths. This includes the sides of mountains. Go to places such as the Alps in Europe, and you'll see extremely high cliffs. These were formed when glaciers moved and simply broke away the parts of the mountains that were in their way.

해석

M Professor: 이 사진을 보시면… 그리고 이것도… 그리고 이것도요… 이 사진들은 절벽을 보여 줍니다. 절벽이 무엇일까요? 흠… 기본적으로 암석이 수직으로, 혹은 거의 수직으로 펼쳐져 있는 곳입니다. 절벽의 높이는 수십 미터 혹은 심지어 수백 미터에 이를 수도 있어요. 또한 아랫부분에는 보통 애추가 있습니다. 모르시는 경우를 위해 말씀을 드리면, 애추는 절벽 아래쪽에 쌓여 있는 돌들

이에요. 절벽이 만들어졌을 때 절벽 자체에서 만들어지는 것이죠. 절벽은 물가, 산, 강가, 그리고 심지어 수중에서도 발견될 수 있어요. 이제 이들이 형성되는 두 가지 방식에 대해 논의하고자 합니다.

첫 번째는 물과 침식 작용에 의한 것이에요. 이러한 방식으로 형성된 절벽은 대부분 해안가를 따라 존재합니다. 모든 해안선이 해변은 아니라는 점을 기억해 주세요. 많은 경우에 산, 언덕, 혹은 암석이 바다까지 이어져 있습니다. 이러한 경우 파도가 항상 이들을 치게 됩니다. 시간이 지남에 따라 이처럼 지속적으로 물에 노출이 되면 바위가 부서집니다. 보다 무른 바위들은 조금씩 쓸려 내려가고 가장 단단한 바위들만 남게 되죠. 그 결과 전형적으로는 완전히 수직인 절벽이 형성됩니다.

절벽이 형성되는 두 번째 방식은 빙하의 이동 때문이에요. 빙하는 눈과 얼음이 쌓여 이루어진 거대한 층이라는 점을 기억하세요. 빙하는 앞으로도, 뒤로도 움직일 수 있습니다. 그렇게 하는 동안 거대한 무게에 의해 이동 경로에 있는 모든 것이 파괴되는 경향이 있습니다. 여기에는 산의 경사면도 포함되어요. 유럽의 알프스 산맥과 같은 곳에 가시면 극도로 높은 절벽을 보실 수 있습니다. 이들은 빙하가 이동하면서 그 경로에 있는 산의 일부 지역을 부숴 놓았을 때 형성되었습니다.

해석
강의에서 교수는 절벽이 형성되는 두 가지 방식에 대해 이야기한다. 첫째, 그는 절벽이 암석으로 이루어진 수직이거나 거의 수직인 벽이며, 그 높이가 수백 미터에 이를 수 있다고 이야기한다. 교수에 의하면 절벽이 형성되는 한 가지 방식은 물과 침식 작용에 의한 것이다. 때때로 암석 지대가 바다까지 뻗어 있을 수 있다. 그러면 파도가 끊임없이 바위에 부딪쳐서 무른 바위가 닳게 된다. 이로써 단단한 암석만 남으면 절벽이 형성된다. 절벽이 형성되는 두 번째 방법은 빙하의 이동에 따른 것이다. 눈과 얼음으로 이루어진 거대한 층인 빙하는 매우 무겁다. 따라서 이들이 이동을 하면 그 경로에 있는 모든 것이 파괴된다. 빙하가 산을 통과할 때 산비탈을 깎아내릴 수 있는데, 그렇게 되면 절벽이 형성된다.

Unit 56 Zoology II

Exercise p.130

Organization

1 The lecture is about two ways that cliffs are formed.
2 The first way that cliffs are formed is through the action of water and erosion.
3 Waves beat against rocks by the shore, and over time, they wear away soft rock, leaving cliffs made of harder rock.
4 The second way that cliffs are formed is through the movement of glaciers.
5 When glaciers move forward or backward, they destroy everything in their paths. This includes the sides of mountains, which are worn away to become cliffs when glaciers move past them.

Comparing

Sample Response
Script 🎧 04-22

In his lecture, the professor talks about two ways that cliffs are formed. First, he tells the class that cliffs are vertical or nearly vertical walls of rock which can be hundreds of meters high. According to the professor, one way cliffs form is through the action of water and erosion. Sometimes rocky areas extend to oceans and seas. Then, waves continually beat against the rock, which causes the soft rocks to be worn away. This leaves hard rock, which forms cliffs. The second way that cliffs form is through glacier movements. Glaciers, which are massive sheets of snow and ice, are very heavy. As a result, when they move, they destroy anything in their way. When glaciers run into mountains, they can wear away the mountainsides, which then forms cliffs.

Listening
Script 🎧 04-23

M Professor: Zoos have improved in quality in the past few decades. They no longer confine animals to small cages but instead attempt to create living spaces for animals that resemble their actual habitats. While this is highly admirable, animals that live in zoos still have very different lives than animals that live in the wild. Let me give you a couple of examples.

First of all, in the wild, animals are constantly on the lookout for food. Let's think about zebras as an example. Zebras frequently graze as they need to eat a large amount of vegetation each day. In parts of Africa, they engage in long migrations at different times of the year. The reason they do that is that they are in search of food. Zebras are always wary of predators such as lions, leopards, and hyenas. So they spend a great amount of time and energy searching for food, avoiding predators, and just trying to survive. In zoos, however, zebras receive a continual supply of food each and every day. There are also no predators for them to be concerned about.

Another thing to consider is environmental factors. In the wild, the seasons change. As I just mentioned, zebras have to migrate to different places in order to find a sufficient amount of food. Basically, whenever a place is going through its dry season, the zebras move elsewhere. There are also storms, droughts, fires, and other environmental factors that affect them. But there are no problems like this in zoos. The environments in zoos are controlled well. As a result, zebras behave differently in captivity than they do in the wild.

M Professor: 지난 수십 년 동안 동물원은 질적으로 크게 발전했습니다. 더 이상 작은 우리에 동물들을 가두지 않으며, 대신 실제 서식지와 비슷한 생활 공간을 동물에게 만들어 주려고 하죠. 이는 매우 높이 평가할 만하지만, 동물원에서 지내는 동물들은 여전히 야생에서 지내는 동물과는 매우 다른 삶을 살고 있습니다. 두 가지 예를 들어 드리죠.

먼저 야생에서는 동물들이 항상 먹이를 찾아 다닙니다. 한 가지 예로서 얼룩말에 대해 생각해 봅시다. 얼룩말은 매일 많은 양의 식물을 먹어야 하기 때문에 자주 풀을 뜯어 먹어요. 아프리카의 몇몇 지역에서 이들은 연중 다양한 시기에 긴 이동을 하게 됩니다. 그렇게 하는 이유는 먹이를 찾고 있기 때문이에요. 얼룩말은 항상 사자, 표범, 그리고 하이에나와 같은 포식자들을 경계합니다. 그래서 많은 시간과 에너지를 써서 음식을 찾고, 포식자를 피하고, 그리고 생존하려고 노력을 하죠. 하지만 동물원에서 얼룩말은 매일 지속적으로 먹이를 공급받습니다. 또한 그들이 걱정해야 할 포식자도 존재하지 않아요.

고려해야 할 또 다른 점은 환경적인 요인입니다. 야생에서는 계절이 변합니다. 제가 방금 언급했듯이 얼룩말은 충분한 양의 먹이를 찾기 위해 다양한 곳으로 이동을 해야 해요. 기본적으로 어떤 장소가 건기를 겪을 때마다 얼룩말은 다른 곳으로 이동을 합니다. 또한 폭풍, 가뭄, 화재, 그리고 이들에게 영향을 미치는 기타 환경적인 요인들도 존재하죠. 하지만 동물원에는 그와 같은 문제들이 존재하지 않습니다. 동물원의 환경은 잘 관리됩니다. 따라서 포획된 상태에 있는 얼룩말은 야생에 있을 때와 다르게 행동을 합니다.

Organization

1 The lecture is about how zebras in zoos and in the wild have different lives.
2 They migrate because they need to find food.
3 They receive a continual supply of food.
4 Storms, droughts, and fires are some of the environmental factors that affect zebras in the wild.
5 They live in environments that are controlled well.

Comparing

Sample Response
Script 🎧 04-24

The professor tells the students that animals in the wild and in zoos have different lives. He uses zebras in the wild and in captivity as examples. First, he notes that zebras in the wild have to graze all the time and search for food. They sometimes even have to migrate to other places to get food. They also have to watch out for predators such as lions and leopards. On the contrary, zebras in zoos are provided with food and do not have to worry about any predators at all. The second example is environmental factors. The professor remarks that zebras must migrate when the seasons change and also may be affected by droughts, fires, and storms. However, zebras in zoos live in controlled environments, so those factors do not bother them.

교수는 학생들에게 야생에 있는 동물들과 동물원에 있는 동물들이 서로 다른 삶을 살아간다고 말한다. 교수는 야생에 사는 얼룩말과 포획된 상태로 살아가는 얼룩말을 예로 든다. 먼저 그는 야생에서 지내는 얼룩말들은 항상 풀을 뜯어 먹어야 하고 먹이를 찾아야 한다고 말한다. 이들은 먹이를 찾기 위해 때로 다른 곳으로 이동을 해야할 수도 있다. 또한 사자와 표범과 같은 포식자들도 경계해야 한다. 그와 반대로 동물원에서 지내는 얼룩말은 먹이를 공급받으며, 포식자에 대해 전혀 걱정할 필요가 없다. 두 번째 예는 환경적인 요인이다. 교수는 계절이 변하면 얼룩말들이 이동을 해야 하고, 또한 이들이 가뭄, 화재, 그리고 폭풍에 의해 영향을 받을 수 있다고 언급한다. 하지만 동물원의 얼룩말들은 통제된 환경에서 살기 때문에 그러한 요인들이 이들에게 영향을 끼치지 못한다.

Unit 57 Education II

Exercise p.131

Listening
Script 🎧 04-25

W Professor: I'd like to talk to you for a bit about cooperative learning. This basically involves students in a classroom environment working together in order to learn. They may engage in cooperative learning in a single class or during an entire semester. They do this because they share the same learning goals, so they can learn more efficiently by working together, such as by jointly completing various tasks. Let me give you a couple of examples of cooperative learning to help you understand it better.

One such method is called jigsaw reading. A teacher first divides a class into small groups and then gives the group a paper to read. Each member of the group reads only a section of the paper. The members read their section again and again until they are completely familiar with it. Then, each member talks about his or her individual sections with the rest of the group. The other members may ask questions in order to become more familiar with that specific information. When each person finishes describing his or her section, all of the members should be familiar with the entire paper.

A second way that students can engage in cooperative learning is to use peer tutoring. Teachers may put students into pairs and provides some material for the pairs to learn. The two students paired up then take turns teaching the material to each other. Since students have different learning methods, the student doing the teaching must often adapt by using the teaching method most likely to get the other student to learn well. In addition, the student doing the teaching learns the information better by talking about it.

W Professor: 협동 학습에 대해 잠깐 이야기를 하고 싶군요. 이는 기본적으로 배우기 위해 교실 환경에서 협동을 하는 학생들과 관련이 있습니다. 하나의 수업에서, 혹은 한 한기 전체에 걸쳐 협동 학습을 할 수도 있어요. 동일한 학습 목표를 가지고 있기 때문에 그렇게 하는 것인데, 이로써 그들은, 예컨대 다양한 과제를 공동으로 완수하는 것과 같이, 협동을 함으로써 보다 효과적으로 배울 수가 있습니다. 여러분의 이해를 돕기 위해 협동 학습의 두 가지 예를 알려 드리죠.

그러한 한 가지 방법은 직소 읽기라는 것이에요. 교사가 먼저 학급을 소규모 그룹으로 나눈 다음 그룹에게 읽을 종이를 한 장 줍니다. 그룹의 멤버들은 종이의 한 부분만 읽게 되어요. 멤버들은 그에 대해 완전히 친숙해질 때까지 자신들의 섹션을 계속해서 읽습니다. 그런 다음 각 멤버들은 같은 그룹의 나머지 멤버들과 자신의 영역에 대해 이야기를 해요. 그러한 특정 정보에 더 많이 익숙해지기 위해 다른 멤버들이 질문을 할 수도 있습니다. 각자가 자신의 섹션에 대한 설명을 마치면 모든 멤버들이 전체 종이의 내용에 대해 친숙해질 것입니다.

학생들이 협동 학습을 할 수 있는 두 번째 방법은 또래 교수를 활용하는 것이에요. 교사가 학생들의 짝을 지어 주고 이들에게 학습할 내용을 제공해 줍니다. 두 명의 학생들은 짝을 이룬 후 번갈아 가면서 상대방에게 학습 내용을 가르쳐 주죠. 학생마다 학습 방법이 다르기 때문에 가르치는 학생은 상대 학생에게 보다 효과적인 학습이 가능한 학습 방법을 사용함으로써 적응해야 하는 경우가 종종 있습니다. 또한 가르치는 학생은 말을 함으로써 관련 내용을 더 잘 익히게 됩니다.

Organization

1 The lecture is about two different ways students can engage in cooperative learning.
2 Group members learn different sections of a paper and then teach one another the information in their sections.
3 They can ask one another questions to learn the material better.
4 They put students into pairs and have them work together.
5 The student may have to adjust his or her teaching method to fit the other student's style.

Comparing

Sample Response
Script 🎧 04-26

In her lecture, the professor talks about cooperative learning. She states that this kind of learning involves students working together because they share the same learning goals. She then describes two ways to do cooperative learning. The first method is jigsaw learning. First, the teacher divides students into groups and then gives each group a paper. Group members individually learn one section of the paper well and then teach it to the others. When every member is done, all of them have an understanding of the paper. The second method is peer tutoring. This requires a teacher to put students into pairs. Then, the students take turns teaching material to

each other. Sometimes the teaching student may have to use the teaching method that is best for the other student to learn.

강의에서 교수는 협동 학습에 대해 이야기한다. 그녀는 이러한 유형의 학습이 협력을 하는 학생과 관련이 있는데, 그 이유는 그들이 동일한 학습 목표를 가지고 있기 때문이라고 설명한다. 그리고 나서 교수는 협동 학습을 할 수 있는 두 가지 방법을 설명한다. 첫 번째 방법은 직소 학습이다. 먼저 교사가 학생들을 그룹으로 나눈 뒤 각 그룹에 종이를 준다. 그룹 멤버들은 종이의 한 부분을 각자 익힌 후 이를 다른 멤버들에게 가르친다. 모든 멤버가 일을 마치면 모두가 종이의 내용을 이해하게 된다. 두 번째 방법은 또래 교수이다. 이 경우 교사가 학생들의 짝을 지어 준다. 그런 다음에 학생들은 번갈아 가면서 학습 내용을 서로에게 가르친다. 때때로 가르치는 학생은 다른 학생에게 최적인 학습 방법을 사용해야 할 수도 있다.

Unit 58 Psychology

Exercise ·· p.132

Listening
Script 🎧 04-27

M Professor: When making plans for the future, one of the best ways to do that is to set goals. Goals are essentially objectives people set for themselves. They can help people improve their skills and abilities and also improve various aspects of themselves. Now, let me tell you a couple of aspects of goals that are absolutely necessary when you're setting them.

The first one is that you must be as specific as possible when setting a goal. What I mean by that is that setting vague goals such as saying, "I want to lose some weight," is not actually beneficial. Instead, when you decide you want to lose weight, determine an actual number. Set a goal that is something like, "I want to lose five kilograms," or, "I want to get my weight down to fifty-five kilograms." By establishing a concrete goal—you know, one that's very specific—you'll work harder and be more motivated to complete your goal successfully.

A second thing you ought to remember is to set realistic goals. For example, when I was younger, I decided that I wanted to read more books. I loved reading, but I didn't always have time for it. So I told myself I would read 100 pages a day. Do you know what? I failed miserably. I was just too busy and didn't have enough time to read that many pages. My goal was simply unrealistic. So what I did was make a better, more realistic goal. I told myself that I needed to read 100 pages a week. That was an attainable goal, and it helped me start to read much more than I had been doing.

해석

M Professor: 미래에 대한 계획을 세울 때 가장 좋은 방법 중 하나는 목표를 설정하는 것입니다. 목표는 기본적으로 사람들이 스스로 설정하는 지향점입니다. 이로써 사람들은 자신의 기술과 능력을 향상시킬 수 있고, 또한 자기 자신의 다양한 측면들을 발전시킬 수 있죠. 자, 목표를 설정할 때 꼭 필요한 목표의 두 가지 측면에 대해 이야기를 하겠습니다.

첫 번째는 여러분들이 목표를 설정할 때 최대한 구체적이어야 한다는 점이에요. 무슨 말인지 알려 드리면, "나는 살을 약간 빼고 싶다"는 말과 같은 모호한 목표를 세우는 것은 사실상 도움이 되지 않습니다. 대신 살을 빼겠다고 결심하는 경우 실체적인 수치를 정하도록 하세요. "나는 5킬로그램을 빼고 싶다" 혹은 "나는 55칼로그램까지 몸무게를 낮추고 싶다"는 식의 목표를 세우세요. 특정한 목표를 세움으로써, 아시다시피 매우 구체적인 목표를 세움으로써, 목표를 성공적으로 달성하기 위해 더 열심히, 보다 적극적으로 행동하게 될 것입니다.

기억해야 할 두 번째 측면은 현실적인 목표를 세우는 것이에요. 예를 들어 저는 젊었을 때 책을 더 많이 읽겠다고 결심했습니다. 저는 독서를 좋아했지만 독서를 할 수 있는 시간이 항상 있었던 것은 아니었어요. 그래서 저는 하루에 100페이지를 읽겠다고 다짐했습니다. 어떻게 되었는지 아시나요? 저는 처참히 실패했어요. 너무 바빠서 그처럼 많은 페이지를 읽을 수 있는 시간이 없었죠. 제 목표는 비현실적인 것이었어요. 그래서 저는 보다 적절하고 보다 현실적인 목표를 세웠습니다. 일주일에 100페이지를 읽겠다고 다짐을 했죠. 이는 실현 가능한 목표였으며, 그로 인해 저는 전보다 더 많은 양을 읽을 수 있게 되었습니다.

Organization

1 The lecture is about how people can set goals for themselves.
2 A person must be as specific as possible when setting a goal.
3 A person will work harder and be more motivated to be successful.
4 A person should set realistic goals.
5 The professor set a goal of reading 100 pages a day, but that was unrealistic. So he changed it to reading 100 pages a week.

Comparing

Sample Response

Script 🎧 04-28

The professor lectures about setting goals. He calls it a great way to make future plans. He says there are a couple of important things to remember when setting goals. First, a person must be specific. For instance, instead of stating a desire to lose weight, a person should instead set a specific goal, such as losing five kilograms or getting down to a certain weight. That will make the person work harder and be more motivated to

succeed. The second important thing is to be realistic when setting a goal. The professor provides a personal example. Once, he set a goal of reading 100 pages a day. That was unrealistic, and he couldn't do it. So he set a realistic goal of reading 100 pages a week, which he did.

해석

교수는 목표 설정에 관한 강의를 하고 있다. 그는 목표 설정이 향후 계획을 세울 수 있는 좋은 방법이 된다고 말한다. 교수는 목표를 설정할 때 기억해야 할 두 가지 중요한 점이 있다고 이야기한다. 첫째, 구체적이어야 한다. 예를 들어 살을 빼겠다는 바람을 이야기하는 대신에 구체적인 목표, 예컨대 5킬로그램 감량 혹은 특정 몸무게로의 감량과 같은 구체적인 목표를 세워야 한다. 이로써 목표 달성을 위해 더 열심히, 더 적극적으로 행동할 수 있게 될 것이다. 두 번째 중요한 점은 목표를 세울 때 현실적이어야 한다는 것이다. 교수는 개인적인 사례를 이야기한다. 한때 그는 하루에 100페이지의 글을 읽겠다는 목표를 세웠다. 이는 비현실적이었고 그는 그렇게 할 수 없었다. 그래서 일주일에 100페이지를 읽겠다는 현실적인 목표를 세웠는데, 이러한 목표는 달성되었다.

Unit 59 Zoology III

Exercise ··· p.133

Listening

Script 🎧 04-29

W Professor: Nowadays, in some places, it's nearly as bright during the night as it is during the day. This is due to artificial lighting. You can find it everywhere. There are lights in people's houses, streetlights, spotlights, signs, and many others. Unfortunately, artificial light has negative effects on many animals.

Birds are some of the animals greatly harmed by artificial light. This is especially true in large cities. Birds often collide with buildings that are illuminated at night. This almost always results in the birds dying. When migrating birds fly near big cities, they can become confused by all of the artificial lights. This can cause them to get lost and to fly off course. Some never make it to their final destinations. Others depart too early or too late, which can have negative effects on their food acquisition and reproduction.

Many animals are also active at night. This is when they often search for food. However, due to artificial lighting, a lot of animals are unable to get enough food to eat. Let's take rats and mice as examples. They are nocturnal animals that are awake mostly at night. They thrive on moving around in the dark. But when there is too much light, they spend less time searching for food. They are also easier for predators to see, so a lot of them get killed and eaten by predators since they cannot hide in darkness. Nocturnal predators also have problems hunting. Cougars, for example, have outstanding night vision and like to hunt in the dark. However, artificial lighting affects their sight, so they can not hunt as effectively as they can in total darkness.

해석

W Professor: 오늘날 일부 지역에서는 밤에도 낮처럼 밝습니다. 바로 인공 조명 때문이에요. 어디에서나 인공 조명을 찾아볼 수 있습니다. 사람들의 집에서, 가로등에서, 스포트라이트에서, 간판에서, 그리고 기타 여러 곳에서 찾아볼 수가 있죠. 안타깝게도 인공 조명은 많은 동물들에게 부정적인 영향을 미칩니다.

인공 조명으로 큰 피해를 받는 동물들 중 하나가 새들이에요. 대도시의 경우에 특히 그렇습니다. 밤에 새들이 빛이 나는 건물과 충돌하는 경우가 많습니다. 그 결과 새들은 거의 죽게 되죠. 철새들도 대도시 주변을 지나가는 경우 온갖 인공 조명 때문에 혼란을 겪을 수 있습니다. 그로 인해 길을 잃고 경로를 이탈할 수도 있어요. 최종 목적지에 도달하지 못하는 새들도 있죠. 너무 일찍, 혹은 너무 늦게 출발을 하는 새들도 있는데, 이들은 먹이 획득과 번식에 있어서 부정적인 영향을 받게 됩니다.

또한 많은 동물들이 밤에 활동을 해요. 밤에 종종 먹이를 구하러 다닙니다. 하지만 인공 조명 때문에 많은 동물들이 충분한 양의 먹이를 구할 수가 없어요. 들쥐와 생쥐를 예로 들어 볼게요. 이들은 야행성 동물로서 밤에 주로 깨어 있습니다. 이들은 어둠 속에서 잘 돌아다니죠. 하지만 지나치게 밝으면 먹이를 찾으러 다니는 시간이 줄어듭니다. 또한 포식자들의 눈에 띄기가 쉽기 때문에 어둠 속에 몸을 숨기지 못하는 많은 쥐들은 포식자에 잡혀서 먹히게 되죠. 야행성 포식자들 또한 사냥에 문제를 겪습니다. 예를 들어 퓨마는 야간 시력이 뛰어나며 어두울 때 사냥하는 것을 좋아해요. 하지만 인공 조명이 이들의 시력에 영향을 미치기 때문에 퓨마는 완전히 어두울 때만큼 효과적으로 사냥을 할 수가 없습니다.

Organization

1 The lecture is about how artificial light harms animals.
2 Birds often collide with buildings that are illuminated at night, so they frequently die.
3 Artificial light can confuse them, so they may wander off course and get lost.
4 They have a hard time getting enough food, and predators can find them more easily.
5 It affects their sight, so they cannot hunt as well as normal.

Comparing

Sample Response

Script 🎧 04-30

The professor talks about the harm artificial light can cause for animals. She mentions its effects on a few animals. The first animals she discusses are birds. She comments that birds flying near buildings lit up at night often hit them, which kills the birds. Other times, when birds migrate near cities, the light makes them get lost. Birds may also get confused and migrate too early or too late because of artificial light. She then covers nocturnal animals, such as rats, mice, and cougars. Rats and mice have a difficult time finding food when there's too much light. Predators can also find them more easily since there's no darkness to hide in. As for cougars, they can't see well because of artificial light, so they do not hunt as well as possible.

해석

교수는 인공 조명이 동물들에게 미칠 수 있는 피해에 대해 이야기한다. 교수는 몇몇 동물들에 대한 인공 조명의 영향을 언급한다. 첫 번째 동물은 새이다. 그녀는 새들이 밤에도 밝게 빛나는 건물 근처를 날아가다가 종종 건물에 부딪혀 죽는다고 설명한다. 새들이 도시 근처를 지나가다가 조명에 의해 길을 잃는 경우도 있다. 또한 새들은 인공 조명 때문에 혼란을 겪어서 너무 일찍, 혹은 너무 늦게 이동을 할 수도 있다. 그런 다음 교수는 들쥐, 생쥐, 그리고 퓨마와 같은 야행성 동물에 대해 이야기한다. 들쥐와 생쥐는 너무 밝은 경우 먹이를 구하는데 어려움을 겪는다. 또한 어둠 속에 몸을 숨길 수가 없기 때문에 포식자들이 이들을 보다 쉽게 찾아낼 수 있다. 퓨마의 경우, 이들은 인공 조명 때문에 잘 볼 수가 없어서 사냥 능력을 온전히 발휘하지 못한다.

Unit 60 Marketing II

Exercise p.134

Listening

Script 🎧 04-31

W Professor: Many companies have logos. These are various symbols or designs which represent companies or the products they manufacture. Some logos are highly recognizable, which helps the companies that use them. However, it's possible for companies to have poor logos that actually harm sales rather than improve them. Let me tell you about a couple of failed logos from the past.

A few years ago, a company that makes toothpaste came up with a new logo for its brand. Unfortunately, the designers chose poorly when creating the logo. Let me ask a question . . . What color do you think of when you think of teeth . . . ? White, right? Everyone wants shiny white teeth. However, the logo for this brand of toothpaste used black. When I think of black and teeth, nothing positive comes to mind. I think of cavities and decayed teeth, which are gross. Sales of the toothpaste fell quickly since nobody liked the logo. After a while, the logo was replaced by a better one.

Here's another example. This one involves the actual design of the logo, not the color. There are all kinds of companies that provide Internet service for their customers. I'm sure you've seen plenty of their logos. Well, a decade or so ago, one Internet provider had an old rotary phone on its logo. What does that make you think of . . . ? It makes me think of the old days when Internet connections were incredibly slow because people went online by using their phones. It didn't take a marketing genius to figure out that the telephone on the logo was sending the wrong message and that it was turning off customers.

해석

W Professor: 많은 기업들이 로고를 가지고 있습니다. 로고는 기업이나 기업에서 제조하는 제품을 나타내는 다양한 상징이나 디자인이에요. 몇몇 로고는 매우 알아보기가 쉬운데, 이는 해당 로고를 사용하는 기업에게 도움이 됩니다. 하지만 매출을 증가시키지 않고 오히려 매출에 실제로 피해를 가져다 주는 좋지 못한 로고가 있는 경우도 있어요. 과거에 있었던, 실패한 로고에 관한 두 가지 사례를 알려 드리죠.

몇 년 전에 치약을 생산하는 한 기업이 새로운 브랜드 로고를 생각해 냈습니다. 안타깝게도 디자이너들은 로고를 만들 때 잘못된 선택을 했어요. 질문을 하나 드리면… 치아를 생각할 때 어떤 색깔이 떠오르시나요…? 흰색이죠, 그렇죠? 모두가 하얗게 빛나는 치아를 원합니다. 하지만 이 치약 브랜드의 로고에서는 검은색이 사용되었어요. 저는 검정색과 치아를 생각하면 긍정적인 것이 전혀 머리에 떠오르지 않습니다. 충치와 썩은 이빨이 생각나는데, 이는 역겨운 것이죠. 아무도 그 로고를 좋아하지 않았기 때문에 치약의 매출은 급감했습니다. 얼마 후 이 로고는 보다 나은 로고에 의해 대체되었어요.

또 다른 예를 알려 드리죠. 색깔이 아니라 로고의 실제 디자인과 관련된 것입니다. 고객들에게 인터넷 서비스를 제공하는 회사들은 매우 많아요. 여러분들도 이들의 로고를 많이 보셨을 것이라고 확신합니다. 음, 10년 전쯤에 한 인터넷 서비스 기업이 로고에 오래된 다이얼 전화기를 사용했어요. 여러분은 무엇이 생각나시나요…? 저는 사람들이 전화를 사용해서 온라인에 접속을 했기 때문에 인터넷 연결이 엄청나게 느렸던 과거가 생각납니다. 마케팅 천재가 아니더라도 로고의 전화기가 잘못된 메시지를 전달하고 있으며 그로 인해 고객들이 떨어져 나가고 있다는 점을 알아차릴 수 있었어요.

Comparing

Sample Response

Script 🎧 04-32

The professor's lecture is about how some logos can cause harm to companies instead of improving their sales. The first example the professor provides is the logo for a toothpaste brand. The logo included the color black. The professor notes that people want shiny white teeth. When they associate the color black with teeth, they think of cavities and decayed teeth. This logo resulted in sales of the toothpaste declining. The second example the professor gives the students is the logo for an Internet provider. She mentions that the logo featured a rotary phone. This reminded people of the times in the past when they connected to the Internet over the phone. They received slow service then, so people didn't like the logo. According to the professor, it sent the wrong message to customers.

해석

교수의 강의는 일부 로고들이 매출을 증가시키는 대신 기업에 피해를 주는 경우를 다루고 있다. 교수가 제시한 첫 번째 사례는 한 치약 브랜드의 로고이다. 이 로고에는 검정색이 사용되었다. 교수는 사람들이 하얗게 빛나는 치아를 원한다고 말한다. 검정색과 치아를 연관시키는 경우, 사람들은 충치와 썩은 이빨을 떠올린다. 이 로고는 결국 치약 매출의 감소를 가져 왔다. 교수가 학생들에게 제시한 두 번째 사례는 한 인터넷 서비스 기업의 로고이다. 그녀는 이 로고에 다이얼 전화기가 포함되었다고 말한다. 이는 사람들이게 전화로 인터넷에 접속했던 예전 시절을 떠올리게 만들었다. 당시 서비스는 속도가 느렸기 때문에 사람들은 이 로고를 좋아하지 않았다. 교수에 의하면 이는 고객들에게 잘못된 메시지를 보내고 있었다.

Organization

1 The lecture is about poor logos used by companies in the past.

2 The professor mentions a toothpaste brand that had a logo that used the color black.

3 Black makes people think of cavities and decayed teeth.

4 The professor discusses an Internet provider that had a rotary phone in its logo.

5 The phone made people think of the slow Internet service they used to receive when they connected to the Internet with their phones.

Actual Test

Task 1

Sample Response 🎧 05-03

I prefer to buy books from bookstores rather than borrow them from libraries. Firstly, unlike libraries, bookstores always have the newest books by the best authors, so I can find many great books there. I like reading books right when they come out, and bookstores are the only places I can read newly released books. Second of all, I prefer bookstores because I like to own the books I read. That way, I can read them anytime that I want. I often read books more than once, so I don't want to have to bother checking out a book from the library again and again. Instead, I can have it sitting right on my bookshelf.

해석

나는 도서관에서 책을 빌리는 것보다 서점에서 책을 구입하는 것을 선호한다. 첫째, 도서관과 달리 서점에는 항상 최고의 작가가 쓴 신작 서적들이 있기 때문에 그곳에서 좋은 책들을 많이 찾아볼 수 있다. 나는 책이 출간되면 곧바로 읽는 것을 좋아하며, 서점은 신간 서적을 읽어볼 수 있는 유일한 장소이다. 둘째, 나는 내가 읽은 책을 소장하고 싶기 때문에 서점을 선호한다. 그렇게 함으로써 언제라도 내가 원하는 때에 책을 읽을 수 있다. 나는 종종 책을 두 번 이상 읽기 때문에 도서관에서 계속해서 책을 대출해야 하는 수고를 감수하고 싶지 않다. 그 대신 책장에 책을 꽂아두면 된다.

Task 2

Reading

해석

조각 수업 축소

미술학과에서 다음 학기부터 조각 수업의 수를 30개에서 15개로 축소하기로 결정했음을 알려 드리게 되어 유감스럽게 생각합니다. 해당 학과로서는 조각 수업을 50%까지 축소한 것이 안타까운 일이지만, 두 가지 이유에서 그러한 선택을 하게 되었습니다. 우선, 미술 학과 내 조각 교수님의 인원이 한정되어 있기 때문에 교수님들께서 매 학기마다 너무나 많은 수업을 담당하셨습니다. 이로 인해 학생에게 양질의 개인 지도가 제공되지 못했습니다. 뿐만 아니라 미술학과의 예산이 삭감되어 그처럼 많은 수의 수업에 제공할 수 있는 물품들이 충분하지가 않습니다.

Listening

Script 🎧 05-04

M Student: Well, this isn't very good news.

W Student: Are you talking about the cut in the number of sculpture classes?

M: Yeah, I'm not too pleased about it. After all, sculpture is a required class here at the school, so how are all of the students going to be able to take it now? What about all of the seniors like me who've waited until our last semester to sign up for it? Now we might not get in.

W: Well, that's your fault for waiting so long. You should have gotten rid of your required classes earlier.

M: Okay, well, forget about seniors then. The announcement said that the professors have too many classes to give the students personal attention.

W: What's your point?

M: Well, I think it's more important to have the classes than to get personal attention. I mean, I rarely talk to the professors in my other classes. They don't give me any personal attention. Why should sculpture be different?

W: Okay, you've actually got a point on that one.

해석

M Student: 음, 이러한 결정은 그다지 좋은 소식이 아니군.

W Student: 조각 수업의 수가 축소된 것을 말하는 거니?

M: 그래, 난 그다지 마음에 들지 않아. 어찌되었든 조각은 이곳 학교에서 필수 과목인데, 이제 모든 학생들이 어떻게 들어야 할까? 마지막 학기까지 기다렸다가 그 수업을 들으려 했던 나같은 4학년생들은 모두 어떻게 하고? 이제 듣지 못하게 될 수도 있어.

W: 음, 그렇게 오래 기다린 건 네 잘못이지. 필수 과목들은 더 일찍 끝냈어야 해.

M: 좋아, 음, 그럼 4학년생 얘기는 빼자고. 공지에는 교수님들의 수업이 너무 많아서 학생들에게 개별적인 주의를 기울일 수가 없다고 나와 있었어.

W: 요점이 뭐니?

M: 음, 나는 개별적인 주의보다 수업을 듣는 것이 더 중요하다고 생각해. 내 말은, 다른 강의에서도 교수님과 이야기를 나누는 일은 거의 없어. 나한테 개별적인 주의를 주시지는 않지. 왜 조각 수업은 달라야 할까?

W: 그래, 실제로 그 점에 대해서는 네 말에 일리가 있네.

Sample Response 🎧 05-05

According to the notice, the number of sculpture classes the university's Fine Arts Department will offer the next semester will decrease by fifty percent. The man opposes this decision for a couple of reasons. One reason he gives is that sculpture is a required course that students need to graduate. He mentions that he is a senior and has not yet taken the class. With fewer classes available, he might not be able to get into the class, which would cause him problems when he tries to graduate. Furthermore, the man doesn't really feel that getting personal attention in a class is that important. He claims that he never gets personal instruction in his other classes, so he asks why the sculpture classes should be different and require personal attention by the professors.

공지에 따르면 다음 학기부터 대학의 미술학과에서 제공하는 조각 수업의 수가 절반으로 줄어들 예정이다. 남자는 두 가지 이유에서 그러한 결정을 반대한다. 그가 제시하는 첫 번째 이유는 조각 수업이 학생들이 졸업을 하기 위해 들어야 하는 필수 과목이기 때문이다. 그는 자신이 4학년인데 아직 그 수업을 듣지 못했다고 언급한다. 강의의 수가 줄면 그는 수업을 듣지 못해서 졸업에 문제를 겪을 수도 있다. 뿐만 아니라 남자는 수업에서 개별적인 주의를 받는 것이 사실 그다지 중요하지 않다고 생각한다. 그는 자신이 다른 수업에서 개인적인 지도를 받아 본 적이 없다고 말하면서 왜 조각 수업에서는 다른 수업과 달리 교수의 개별적인 주의가 필요한 것인지 묻는다.

Task 3

Reading

해석

양의 외부 효과

비즈니스에 있어서 대부분의 기업들은 최대한 많은 수익을 얻기를 갈망한다. 하지만 일부 경우 기업 활동의 사회적인 효과가 실제로 금전적인 이익을 뛰어넘기도 한다. 이러한 현상이 일어나면 이를 양의 외부 효과라고 부른다. 양의 외부 효과는 교육, 환경, 보건, 그리고 기술을 포함하여 여러가지 다양한 모습의 이익으로 나타날 수 있다. 일반적으로는 기업들이 이러한 이익을 특별히 추구하는 것은 아니지만 이들의 존재는 환영한다.

Listening

Script 🎧 05-06

W Professor: It is unfortunate that companies do not always consider, uh, the negative ramifications of their actions. For example, sometimes they pollute the environment or inadvertently harm the health of their, uh, employees.

This is where, fortunately, the government often steps in to help. Did you read in the newspaper that the city government is going to provide the Metro Bus Company with a low-interest loan? Anyone? Well, the government is providing a million-dollar loan that will, uh, help the company change some of its buses from gas guzzlers to users of electricity. Yeah, that's pretty cool. What benefit will that have? Well, there really isn't much of a financial benefit for the company. That's why the government loaned the firm the money. However, there will be other positive benefits.

For one, the buses will be more environmentally friendly. They won't be spewing any more nasty fumes into the atmosphere. That means that we can all breathe much cleaner air. Second of all, the buses are no longer going to rely upon gasoline, which, as we all know, the Earth is running out of. So while the company itself will see no improvement in its bottom line, you know, its profits, its new buses will benefit everyone in the city by helping clean up the environment we all live in.

해석

W Professor: 기업들이 자신의 행동에 따른, 어, 부정적인 효과를 항상 고려하지는 않는다는 점은 안타까운 일이에요. 예를 들어 기업이 때로는 환경을 오염시키기도 하고, 혹은 의도치 않게, 어, 직원들의 건강에 해를 끼치기도 하죠.

다행히도 이때 정부가 종종 도움을 주기 위해 개입을 합니다. 신문에서 시 정부가 Metro 버스 회사에 저리로 융자를 제공할 것이라는 기사를 읽으셨나요? 읽어보신 분? 음, 정부가 백만 달러 규모의 융자를 제공함으로써, 어, 버스 회사는 연료 소비가 많은 버스들을 전기 버스로 전환할 예정이에요. 그래요, 잘 된 일이죠. 그러면 어떠한 혜택이 생길까요? 음, 사실 버스 회사가 금전적으로 큰 이익을 보지는 않습니다. 그 때문에 정부가 버스 회사에 융자를 해 준 것이죠. 하지만 다른 긍정적인 이익이 발생할 것입니다.

우선 버스들이 보다 환경 친화적으로 바뀔 거예요. 더 이상 대기 속으로 매연을 뿜어내지 않을 것입니다. 다시 말해 우리가 숨 쉬는 공기가 훨씬 깨끗해질 수 있다는 얘기죠. 두 번째로 더 이상은 버스들이, 여러분도 아시는 것처럼 지구에서 고갈되고 있는 휘발유를, 사용하지 않게 될 것입니다. 따라서 회사의 이윤, 그러니까, 수익이 전혀 증가하지 않더라도 새로운 버스로 인해 우리 모두가 살고 있는 환경이 깨끗해짐으로써 시내의 모든 사람들이 혜택을 보게 될 것입니다.

Sample Response 🎧 05-07

In the lecture, the professor focuses on a loan the city will provide to a bus company so that it can change its buses into ones that are electric powered. She mentions that it will provide a couple of benefits. One thing she states is that the buses will become more environmentally friendly and won't pollute the air as much as gas-powered buses. She also claims that the buses won't use gasoline anymore, which is important because the Earth's gasoline supply is running out. These two points relate to positive externalities because they are social rather than financial benefits. The professor mentions that the bus company won't make extra profits from this move; however, society itself will improve because of its move to electric-powered buses. In this case, the positive externality created is a cleaner environment.

해석

강의에서 교수는 기존 버스를 전기 버스로 바꿀 수 있도록 시가 버스 회사에 제공할 융자에 초점을 맞춘다. 그녀는 이로 인해 두 가지 혜택이 생길 것이라고 언급한다. 그녀가 말하는 한 가지 혜택은 버스가 보다 환경친화적으로 됨으로써 휘발유 버스만큼 대기를 오염시키지 않을 것이라는 점이다. 또한 그녀는 버스가 더 이상 휘발유를 사용하지 않게 될 것이라고 주장하는데, 이러한 점은 지구의 휘발유가 소진될 것이라는 점에서 중요하다. 이러한 두 가지 혜택은 금전적인 이익보다 사회적인 이익이라고 할 수 있기 때문에 양적 외부 효과와 관련이 있다. 교수는 버스 회사가 이러한 조치로 특별한 이익을 얻는 것은 아니지만 전기 버스의 도입으로 사회 자체가 이익을 볼 것이라고 언급한다. 이 경우에 발생하는 외부 효과는 보다 깨끗한 환경이다.

Task 4

Listening

Script 🎧 05-08

M Professor: I imagine that, at some time in most of

your lives, you will consider opening your own business. It may be something small, like a convenience store, or it may be something much larger. Nevertheless, you'll most likely need to attract investors, especially if it's a large business. Unless you win the lottery of course. Anyway, in order to attract investors, you'll definitely need to prepare a couple of important documents for them.

One of the most important ones you'll need is a business plan. Please don't laugh. I know that it sounds obvious, but you actually have no idea how many people simply open a business without having a solid business plan. But trust me. Without one of these, the only investor you'll get is yourself. Or maybe a relative. So what is a business plan? Well, it's a comprehensive plan that includes specific content such as the product you intend to sell, the strategy you intend to employ, and various other details concerning how you plan to run your business. It's crucial. You'll need to have this one well thought out to get any kind of significant investment.

The second thing you'll definitely require is an executive summary. You should have heard of this one, too. It's merely a summary of the business plan, so it's obviously much shorter, yet it goes right to the point and explains your objectives. This is the first document you'll show any potential investors. You'll need to make it as attractive as possible because this will, hopefully, induce potential investors to read your detailed business plan and then put their own money into your project.

해석

M Professor: 여러분들도 살다가 어느 시점에 이르면 자신의 사업체를 시작하는 것을 고려하게 될 거예요. 편의점과 같은 작은 것일 수도 있고, 아니면 훨씬 더 큰 것일 수도 있죠. 어쨌거나 여러분은 아마도, 특히 사업체가 큰 경우, 투자자를 유치해야 할 것입니다. 복권에 당첨되지 않는 한 말이죠. 어쨌든 투자자를 유치하기 위해서는 반드시 두 가지 중요한 문서를 준비해야 합니다.

여러분에게 필요한 가장 중요한 문서 중 하나는 사업 계획서입니다. 웃지 기를 바랍니다. 당연하게 들리겠지만, 실제로 얼마나 많은 사람들이 구체적인 사업 계획 없이 그냥 사업을 시작하는지 모르실 거예요. 하지만 제 말을 믿어 주세요. 이러한 것이 없으면 여러분 자신 말고는 아무런 투자도 만나지 못할 것입니다. 어쩌면 친인척은 가능하겠군요. 그러면 사업 계획서란 무엇일까요? 음, 판매하려는 제품, 사용하려는 전략, 그리고 사업체 운영 방식과 관련된 기타 여러 가지 세부 사항과 같은 구체적인 내용이 담긴 포괄적인 계획서입니다. 정말 중요해요. 의미 있는 투자를 유치하기 위해서는 사업 계획서를 신중히 작성해야 할 것입니다.

두 번째로 꼭 필요한 문서는 사업 개요서입니다. 이에 대해서도 들어보신 적이 있을 거예요. 이는 사업 계획에 대한 개요이기 때문에 길이가 확실히 더 짧으며 바로 본론으로 들어가 사업 목표를 설명해 줍니다. 바로 이것이 잠재 투자자에게 보여 줄 첫 번째 문서이죠. 이는 최대한 매력적으로 만들어야 하는데, 그 이유는 그렇게 해야, 일이 잘되는 경우, 잠재 투자자가 상세한 사업 계획을 읽고 자신의 돈을 여러분의 프로젝트에 투자할 것이기 때문입니다.

Sample Response 🎧 05-09

The focus of the professor's lecture is the two most important documents people planning to open businesses need to attract investors. The first explanation concerns the business plan. According to the professor, without a business plan, a person will almost never find investors. He states that a business plan is a comprehensive explanation of what the person intends to do with his business. It includes explanations on the product, strategy, and other details that pertain to the potential business. The second document the professor discusses is the executive summary. According to him, this is just a summary of the business plan, which makes it a much shorter document. The point of an executive summary is to highlight a person's business objectives and to make them attractive enough to convince potential investors to read the complete business plan.

해석

교수의 강의의 초점은 사업을 시작하려는 사람들이 투자자를 유치하려고 할 때 필요한 가장 중요한 두 가지 문서에 맞추어져 있다. 첫 번째 설명은 사업 계획서와 관련된 것이다. 교수에 따르면 사업 계획서가 없는 경우 투자자를 거의 찾을 수 없을 것이다. 그는 사업 계획서가 자신의 사업을 어떻게 이끌어 나갈 것인지를 포괄적으로 설명해 주는 것이라고 말한다. 여기에는 제품, 전략, 그리고 잠재적인 사업과 관련된 기타 세부 사항들이 설명되어 있다. 교수가 말하는 두 번째 문서는 사업 개요서이다. 그에 따르면 사업 개요서는 사업 계획서의 요약문으로 길이가 훨씬 더 짧은 문서이다. 사업 개요서의 핵심은 사업 목표를 부각시키는 것과 잠재 투자자가 사업 계획서 전체를 읽고 싶어할 정도로 이를 매력적으로 만드는 것이다.

Actual Test 02
p.144

Task 1

Sample Response 🎧 05-12

I always prefer to take my lunch to school. Firstly, taking my own lunch is healthier than eating in the cafeteria. My mother always makes my lunch, so it's quite good. She gives me sandwiches, some fruit, and yogurt or a granola bar. The sandwiches are healthy and very filling. Overall, my lunch is much better than the junk food the cafeteria often serves. The second reason I prefer to take my lunch is that the price of the food in the cafeteria is too high. In fact, the price is almost the same as a meal at a regular restaurant. By bringing my own lunch, I can save a lot of money every day.

해석

나는 언제나 학교에 도시락을 가지고 가는 것을 좋아한다. 우선, 도시락을 싸서 다니는 것이 교내 식당에서 식사하는 것보다 건강에 더 좋다. 내 어머니는 항상 도시락을 싸 주시는데 꽤 알차다. 샌드위치, 약간의 과일, 그리고 요구르트나 그래놀라 바를 싸 주신다. 샌드위치는 건강에도 좋고 포만감도 크다. 전체적으로 도시락은 교내 식당에서 종종 제공되는 정크푸드보다 훨씬 더 좋다. 내가 도시락을 선호하는 두 번째 이유는 교내 식당의 음식 가격이 너무 높기 때문이다. 실제로 그곳 가격은 일반 식당의 음식 가격과 거의 동일하다. 나는 도시락을 가지고 다님으로써 매일 많은 돈을 아낄 수 있다.

Task 2

Reading

해석

Jonathan Davis의 졸업식 연설

Central 대학은 5월 15일에 열릴 예정인 졸업식에서 Jonathan Davis를 졸업식 연사로 모시게 된 점을 영광스럽게 생각합니다. Davis 씨는 사업 분야의 리더입니다. 자신의 회사인 DP Solutions를 파산 위기에서 구한 후 이를 세계에서 가장 유명한 금융 회사로 빠르게 바꾸어 놓았습니다. 그는 본교 졸업생들을 위해 분명 비즈니스에 관한 소중한 말씀을 들려 줄 것입니다. Davis 씨는 Central 대학의 졸업생으로, 학교측은 졸업생 중 한 명에게 경의를 표하고 그가 사회에 끼친 공헌을 기릴 수 있기를 고대합니다.

Listening

Script 🎧 05-13

M Student: Wow, I can't wait to hear from Jonathan Davis. I've read so much about him. It'll be great to see him in person.

W Student: I'm not so sure. I think the university made a poor decision.

M: Why do you feel that way?

W: First, the school should have invited someone different, like, say, a famous teacher or professor.

M: What makes you say that?

W: All Jonathan Davis has done is make money. Who cares about that? The purpose of a university is to educate people, so the school should invite a prominent educator to give the commencement address.

M: Uh, well, I don't think that's too important.

W: I'm not finished yet. The school missed a really great opportunity to support some of its education programs. We could have gotten someone else who would have talked about how important education is. I bet Jonathan Davis only talks about how he made a lot of money for his company.

M: Why don't we just wait until graduation and see what he talks about? Then, we can decide how his speech was.

해석

M Student: 와, Jonathan Davis의 연설을 빨리 듣고 싶은걸. 그에 대한 기사를 정말 많이 읽었거든. 직접 보게 된다면 정말 멋질 것 같아.

W Student: 난 그렇게 생각하지 않아. 나는 대학측이 잘못된 결정을 내렸다고 생각해.

M: 왜 그렇게 생각하는데?

W: 우선 학교는 다른 사람, 예컨대, 그러니까, 유명한 교사나 교수를 초빙했어야 해.

M: 어떤 이유에서 그렇지?

W: Jonathan Davis가 한 일은 그저 돈을 번 것이야. 누가 그런데 신경을 쓰니? 대학의 목적은 교육에 있으니까 유명한 교육자를 졸업식 연사로 초빙했어야 해.

M: 어, 음, 난 그러한 점이 그렇게 중요하다고는 생각하지는 않는데.

W: 그게 다가 아니야. 학교측은 몇몇 교육 프로그램을 뒷받침할 수 있는 정말 좋은 기회도 놓쳤어. 교육이 얼마나 중요한 것인지에 대해 연설할 수 있는 다른 누군가를 섭외할 수도 있었을 거야. 분명 Jonathan Davis는 자신이 회사에 얼마나 많은 돈을 벌어다 주었는지에 대해서만 말을 할 걸.

M: 졸업식까지 기다렸다가 그가 어떤 이야기를 하는지 들어보는 것이 어때? 그런 다음에 연설이 어땠는지 평가하면 되니까.

Sample Response 🎧 05-14

The students talk about the announcement that Jonathan Davis, a wealthy businessman, will be giving the school's commencement speech at graduation. In the woman's mind, the school has made a poor decision in its choice of speakers. First of all, the woman believes that universities only exist to teach people, so the school should not invite a businessman. She instead feels that the school should have asked a famous educator to speak to the students. The woman then continues by saying that the school should have shown some support for its education programs. By getting a speaker to talk about education, the school could have done this. She declares that it's better for a speaker to talk about the importance of education than to talk about how much money he has made.

해석

학생들은 부유한 사업가인 Jonathan Davis 대학 졸업식에서 연설을 할 예정이라는 공지에 대해 이야기한다. 여자는 학교측이 연설자를 잘못 선택했다고 생각한다. 우선 여자는 대학이 오직 사람들을 가르치기 위해 존재하는 것이기 때문에 학교측이 사업가를 초빙해서는 안 된다고 믿는다. 대신 그녀는 학교측이 유명한 교육자에게 연설을 요청해야 했다고 생각한다. 그런 다음 여자는 계속해서 학교측이 교육 프로그램에 대한 지지를 나타내야 한다고 말한다. 연설자로 하여금 교육에 대해 연설하게 함으로써 학교측은 그렇게 할 수 있을 것이다. 그녀는 연설자가 자신이 얼마나 많은 돈을 벌었는지보다 교육의 중요성에 대해 연설을 하는 것이 더 낫다고 주장한다.

Task 3

Reading

해석

장기 기억

인간의 뇌는 매일 엄청난 양의 정보를 처리한다. 그러한 정보 중 상당 부분은 폐기되지만 여전히 많은 정보가 남게 된다. 일부 정보는 즉각적인 회상을 위해 사용된다. 이는 단기 기억이라고 불린다. 때때로 수년 후의 회상될 순간을 기다리며 뇌 속에 남아 있는 정보들도 있다. 이는 장기 기억이다. 이를 위해 뇌는 정보를 분류해야 하는데, 이러한 일은 종종 감각 자극이나 연상 기법에 의해 이루어진다. 장기 기억 덕분에 사람들은 여러 가지 사실 뿐만 아니라 자전거를 타는 것과 같은 간단한 활동을 어떻게 하는지도 기억할 수 있다. 장기 기억이 없으면 인간은 제대로 기능할 수 없을 것이다.

Listening

Script 🎧 05-15

M Professor: Some of us have better memories than others, especially when considering long-term memory. But did you know that there are actually different types of memory? Sure there are. Right now, I want to talk about two types of memory: declarative memory and procedural memory.

Declarative memory comprises all of the facts that you learn, like in this class. Procedural memory constitutes the actions that you learn to do, like playing a musical instrument. Let me show you how these two go hand in hand and complement each other. I'm sure you all know how to ride a bicycle. At least, I hope you do. Now, actually remembering how to ride a bicycle—even if you haven't ridden one in years—is procedural memory. But remembering the names of the parts of the bike— the wheels, handle, brakes, and so on—is declarative memory.

Or how about this? I believe there's a football game tomorrow. Think about the players. All those plays that they have to remember are recalled through declarative memory. But actually running, throwing, tackling, and every other action associated with football rely upon procedural memory. And without both of these types of memory, you simply wouldn't be able to do much of anything except sit there and stare at me. Kind of like what you're doing now.

해석

M Professor: 우리 중 일부는 다른 사람들보다 뛰어난 기억력을 가지고 있는데, 특히 장기 기억을 고려하는 경우에 그러합니다. 하지만 실제로 여러 가지 종류의 기억이 존재한다는 것을 아셨나요? 분명 그렇습니다. 이제 서술 기억과 절차 기억이라는 두 가지 종류의 기억에 대해 이야기해 보겠습니다.

서술 기억은 이 수업에서와 같이 여러분들이 배우는 모든 사실들로 이루어집니다. 절차 기억은 악기 연주의 경우처럼 여러분이 배우는 행동들로 이루어지고요. 이 두 가지 기억이 어떻게 상호 협력하며 서로를 보완하는지 알려 드리죠. 여러분 모두 분명 자전거를 탈 줄 알고 있을 거예요. 적어도 그러기를 바랍니다. 자, 실제로 자전거 타는 법을 기억해 내는 일은, 여러 해 동안 타 본 적이 없을지라도, 절차 기억입니다. 하지만 자전거의 부속품, 즉 바퀴, 핸들, 브레이크, 기타 등등의 이름을 기억하는 것은 서술 기억이에요.

아니면 이런 건 어떨까요? 내일 축구 경기가 있는 것으로 알고 있습니다. 선수들을 생각해 보세요. 선수들이 기억해야 하는 모든 플레이는 서술 기억을 통해 기억됩니다. 하지만 실제로 달리고, 던지고, 태클을 걸고, 그리고 기타 축구와 관련된 모든 동작들은 절차 기억에 의존하죠. 그리고 이 두 가지 기억이 없다면 여러분은 그냥 자리에 앉아 멍하니 저만 쳐다보는 것 이외의 다른 일은 할 수 없을 거예요. 지금 여러분이 하고 있는 것처럼 말이죠.

Sample Response 🎧 05-16

During his lecture, the professor describes two different kinds of memory. The first is procedural memory. This is the process of remembering how to do a certain activity, even after several years of not doing it. The two examples the professor mentions are recalling how to ride a bicycle and knowing how to play football while remembering how to run, throw, and tackle. The second example of memory the professor gives is declarative memory, which is remembering various facts and other information. His two examples are remembering the different parts of a bicycle and remembering the plays to run in a football game. According to the professor, both of these are long-term memories, which is the brain's ability to catalog and store information that might need to be recalled months or even years after it is learned.

해석

강의에서 교수는 서로 다른 두 가지 종류의 기억에 대해 설명한다. 첫 번째는 절차 기억이다. 이것은 어떤 행동을 수년 동안 하지 않았더라도 특정한 행동을 하는 법을 기억하는 과정이다. 교수가 언급한 두 가지 예는 자전거 타는 법을 떠올리는 것과, 달리고, 던지고, 태클을 거는 방법을 기억하면서 어떻게 축구를 하는지 아는 것이다. 교수가 제시한 기억의 두 번째 예는 서술 기억으로, 이는 다양한 사실과 기타 정보를 기억하는 것이다. 교수가 든 두 가지 예는 자전거의 여러 부품을 기억하는 것과 축구 경기에서 이루어지는 플레이를 기억하는 것이다. 교수에 따르면 이 두 가지 모두 장기 기억에 속하는데, 이는 학습 후 수개월 혹은 수년이 지나서 회상될 수 있는 정보를 분류하고 저장하는 뇌의 능력이다.

Task 4

Listening

Script 🎧 05-17

M Professor: I believe everyone here has heard of Johannes Gutenberg, right? Of course you have. He's the man primarily responsible for the creation of the printing press in the West. Well, it was actually movable type that he created around 1450, but still we say that he invented the printing press. Anyway, his invention greatly changed people's reading habits in just a matter of decades.

Now, before Gutenberg's invention, all books were handwritten. This was a long, arduous process. It took a scribe around twenty years to write out the entire Bible. Yeah, that required a lot of dedication. And books were ridiculously expensive, too. So, obviously, there were not that many books in existence. In addition, few people could read. So how did people read books? I guess you could say that they listened to them instead. Oftentimes, many people would gather around one person—often the only literate individual in the group—who would then read aloud to everyone. Kind of like story time in elementary school.

However, once books were being, uh, mass-produced, unsurprisingly, people's reading habits began to change. First, with countless new books on the market, their prices plunged. They were still expensive, but they were affordable to the middle class. Soon, many families acquired Bibles as well as other books. This naturally led to an increase in the literacy rate since more people were reading now. And without a need to read books aloud, people began reading books quietly by themselves, which is probably the way that most of you read today, right?

해석

M Professor: 모두들 요하네스 구텐베르크에 대해 들어본 적이 있을 거예요, 그렇죠? 물론 그랬을 거예요. 그는 서양에서 인쇄기를 탄생시킨 일등 공신입니다. 음, 사실 1450년경에 그가 만든 것은 가동 활자였지만 우리는 여전히 그가 인쇄기를 발명했다고 말을 하죠. 어쨌든 그의 발명으로 인해 단 수십 년 만에 사람들의 독서 행태가 크게 바뀌었습니다.

자, 구텐베르크가 활자를 발명하기 전에는 모든 책을 손으로 썼습니다. 이는 길고도 힘든 과정이었어요. 필경사가 성경책 한 권을 전부 베끼는데 약 20년이 걸렸습니다. 그래요, 대단한 헌신이 요구되었습니다. 그리고 책값도 어마어마하게 비쌌어요. 그래서 확실히 책의 수량도 그다지 많지 않았습니다. 게다가 글을 읽을 수 있는 사람도 거의 없었죠. 그러면 사람들이 어떻게 책을 읽었을까요? 읽는 대신 읽는 걸 들었다고 말할 수도 있을 것 같군요. 종종 많은 사람들이 무리 중에 유일하게 글을 읽을 수 있었던 한 사람 주변에 모여 앉아 그가 큰 소리로 글을 읽어 주는 걸 듣곤 했습니다. 초등학교 때의 이야기 시간처럼 말이죠.

하지만 책이, 어, 대량으로 생산되자 놀랍게도 사람들의 독서 행태가 바뀌기 시작했습니다. 우선 수많은 새로운 책들이 시장에 쏟아져 나오면서 책값이 크게 내려갔어요. 여전히 비싼 편이긴 했지만 중산층이 구입할 수 있을 정도였습니다. 얼마 지나지 않아 많은 가정들이 성경뿐만 아니라 다른 책들도 구비하게 되었습니다. 이로 인해 당연하게도 문자 해독률이 올라갔는데, 그 이유는 보다 많은 사람들이 글을 읽게 되었기 때문이었죠. 그리고 책을 소리 내어 읽을 필요가 없어지자 사람들은 혼자서 조용히 책을 읽기 시작했는데, 아마 여러분도 대부분 이런 방식으로 책을 읽으실 거예요, 그렇죠?

Sample Response 🎧 05-18

The professor looks into the reading habits of people before and after Johannes Gutenberg's invention of movable type in the middle of the fifteenth century. First, he focuses on the time before Gutenberg. The professor stresses that books were handwritten and could take years to make. This meant that there were few books, so, naturally, few people could read. He states that the one literate person in a group would often read aloud to everyone. Instead of reading, therefore, most people listened. However, after Gutenberg created movable type, it became much faster and cheaper to produce books. Therefore, more middle-class people began buying books and reading them. The professor states that as more and more people became literate, they began to read silently instead of reading out loud to others.

해석

교수는 15세기 중반 요하네스 구텐베르크가 가동 활자를 발명하기 전과 그 이후의 사람들의 독서 행태를 살펴본다. 먼저 그는 구텐베르크 이전 시기에 초점을 맞춘다. 교수는 책이 손으로 쓰여졌으며 책이 만들어지기까지 여러 해가 걸릴 수 있었다는 점을 강조한다. 이는 책이 거의 없었고, 당연하게도 글을 읽을 수 있는 사람들도 거의 없었다는 점을 의미했다. 그는 무리 가운데 글을 읽을 수 있는 사람이 다른 사람들에게 큰 소리로 책을 읽어 주곤 했다고 말한다. 하지만 구텐베르크가 가동 활자를 발명한 후 책을 생산하는 일이 훨씬 빠르고 저렴해졌다. 따라서 보다 많은 중산층이 책을 구매해서 읽기 시작했다. 교수는 점점 더 많은 사람들이 글을 읽을 수 있게 되면서 사람들이 큰 소리로 다른 이들에게 책을 읽어 주는 대신 조용히 책을 읽게 되었다고 말한다.

MEMO